Bureaucrats and Leadership

Transforming Government

General Editor: **R. A. W. Rhodes**, Professor of Politics, University of Newcastle

This important and authoritative new series arises out of the seminal ESRC Whitehall Programme and seeks to fill the enormous gaps in our knowledge of the key actors and institutions of British government. It examines the many large changes during the postwar period and puts these into comparative context by analysing the experience of the advanced industrial democracies of Europe and the nations of the Commonwealth. The series reports the results of the Whitehall Programme, a four-year project into change in British government in the postwar period, mounted by the Economic and Social Research Council.

Titles include:

Nicholas Deakin and Richard Parry
THE TREASURY AND SOCIAL POLICY
The Contest for Control of Welfare Strategy

B. Guy Peters, R. A. W. Rhodes and Vincent Wright
ADMINISTERING THE SUMMIT
Administration of the Core Executive in Developed Countries

Martin J. Smith
THE CORE EXECUTIVE IN BRITAIN

Kevin Theakston
LEADERSHIP IN WHITEHALL

Kevin Theakston (*editor*)
BUREAUCRATS AND LEADERSHIP

Patrick Weller, Herman Bakvis and R. A. W. Rhodes (*editors*)
THE HOLLOW CROWN
Countervailing Trends in Core Executives

Transforming Government
Series Standing Order ISBN 0–333–71580–2
(*outside North America only*)

You can receive future titles in this series as they are published by placing a standing order. Please contact your bookseller or, in case of difficulty, write to us at the address below with your name and address, the title of the series and the ISBN quoted above.

Customer Services Department, Macmillan Distribution Ltd, Houndmills, Basingstoke, Hampshire RG21 6XS, England

Bureaucrats and Leadership

Edited by

Kevin Theakston
Professor of British Government
University of Leeds

First published in Great Britain 2000 by
MACMILLAN PRESS LTD
Houndmills, Basingstoke, Hampshire RG21 6XS and London
Companies and representatives throughout the world

A catalogue record for this book is available from the British Library.

ISBN 0–333–74968–5

First published in the United States of America 2000 by
ST. MARTIN'S PRESS, INC.,
Scholarly and Reference Division,
175 Fifth Avenue, New York, N.Y. 10010

ISBN 0–312–22658–6

Library of Congress Cataloging-in-Publication Data
Bureaucrats and leadership / edited by Kevin Theakston.
p.   cm. — (Transforming government)
Includes bibliographical references and index.
ISBN 0–312–22658–6 (cloth)
1. Bureaucracy.   2. Civil service.   3. Political leadership.
4. Government executives Biography.   I. Theakston, Kevin, 1958–   .
II. Series.
JF1501.B793   1999
351—dc21   99–33858
                                                            CIP

This book is printed on paper suitable for recycling and made from fully managed and sustained forest sources.

10   9   8   7   6   5   4   3   2   1
09   08   07   06   05   04   03   02   01   00

Printed and bound in Great Britain by
Antony Rowe Ltd, Chippenham, Wiltshire

Contents

List of Tables

Contributors

June Burnham is Senior Lecturer in European Government at Middlesex University and a research assistant at the London School of Economics. Recent publications include *The Politics of the Civil Service* (for the Politics Association), and (with J. M. Lee and G. W. Jones) *At the Centre of Whitehall*.

Geoffrey K. Fry is Professor of British Government and Administration at the University of Leeds. His recent books include *Reforming the Civil Service: the Fulton Committee and the British Home Civil Service 1966–68* and *Policy and Management in the British Civil Service*. He is currently writing a book on twentieth-century British political history.

Stephen Harrison is Professor of Health Policy and Politics at the University of Leeds Nuffield Institute for Health. His publications include *Managing the NHS in the 1980s, Controlling Health Professionals* (with Christopher Pollitt), *Just Managing: Power and Culture in the NHS* and *The Dynamics of British Health Policy* (both co-authored with David J. Hunter and Christopher Pollitt).

Kester Isaac-Henry is a Principal Lecturer in the Department of Public Policy at the University of Central England, Birmingham. Recent publications include *Appointed Agencies and Public Accountability* and *Changing Local Governance: Local Authorities and Non-elected Agencies* (both co-authored), and *Management in the Public Sector* (co-edited).

G. W. Jones is Professor of Government at the London School of Economics and Political Science. The biographer of Herbert Morrison, and a leading writer on the Prime Minister and the Cabinet system, as well as on local government, he is the co-author of *At the Centre of Whitehall: Advising the Prime Minister and the Cabinet*.

Christopher Lord is Jean Monnet Senior Lecturer in Politics at the University of Leeds. He is the author of *British Entry to the European Community under the Heath Government of 1970–4* and *Absent at the Creation: Why Britain did not join in the Beginnings of the European Community, 1950–2*.

Elizabeth Mellon is a Teaching Fellow in the Department of Organizational Behaviour and Director of the Senior Executive Programme and the Global Consortium at the London Business School. She is the author of journal articles and chapters on executive agencies.

Norma M. Riccucci is Professor of Public Administration and Policy at the Rockefeller College of the University at Albany, State University of New York. She has published extensively in the areas of public management and employment discrimination law, and is the author of *Unsung Heroes: Federal Execucrats Making a Difference*.

David Richards is Lecturer in Politics at the University of Liverpool. He is the author of *The Civil Service Under the Conservatives 1979–97: Whitehall's Political Poodles?*, and has been researching central government departments as part of the ESRC's Whitehall Programme.

Kevin Theakston is Professor of British Government at the University of Leeds and author of *Junior Ministers in British Government*, *The Labour Party and Whitehall*, *The Civil Service Since 1945*, and *Leadership in Whitehall*.

Gerald Wistow is Professor of Health and Social Care and Director of the Nuffield Institute for Health, University of Leeds. An adviser to the House of Commons Health Committee, his many publications include *Options for Long Term Care: Economic, Social and Ethical Choices*; *Social Care Markets: Progress and Prospects*; and *Developing Quality in Personal Social Services*.

Series Editor's Foreword: Transforming Government

There are enormous gaps in our knowledge of the key actors and institutions in British government. We cannot do simple things like describing the work of ministers of state, permanent secretaries, and their departments. Also, there have been large changes in British government during the post-war period, such as: the growth of the welfare state; the professionalization of government; the consequences of recession; the effects of New Right ideology; the impact of the European Union; the effects of new technology; the hollowing out of the state; and the new public management with its separation of policy and administration. We do not know how these changes affected British government. And we cannot understand the effects of these changes by focusing only on Britain. We must also analyse the experience of the advanced industrial democracies of Europe and the Commonwealth.

To repair these gaps in our knowledge and to explain how and why British government changed in the post-war period, the Eonomic and Social Research Council mounted the Whitehall Programme on 'The Changing Nature of Central Government in Britain'. This series on 'Transforming Government' reports the results of that four-year research programme. The series has five objectives:

- Develop theory – to develop new theoretical perspectives to explain why British government changed and why it differs from other countries.
- Understand change – to describe and explain what has changed in British government since 1945.
- Compare – to compare these changes with those in other EU member states and other states with a 'Westminister' system of government.
- Build bridges – to create a common understanding between academics and practitioners.
- Dissemination – to make academic research accessible to a varied audience covering sixth formers and senior policy-makers.

The books cover six broad themes:

- Developing theory about the new forms of governance.
- The hollowing out of the state in Britain, Europe and the Commonwealth.
- The fragmenting government framework.
- The changing roles of ministers and the senior civil service.
- Constitutional change.
- New ways of delivering services.

Kevin Theakston's edited collection on bureaucratic leadership is a distinctive addition to the series.[1] It develops the argument presented in his earlier volume, *Leadership in Whitehall*, that biography is an important tool in research on British government. It serves four objectives. It provides inspirational role models for practitioners; explores the impact of ideas on public policy; is an essential part of administrative history; and provides case studies for testing hypotheses and developing generalizations. Of course, the approach has its problems; for example, evidence such as diaries and other private papers is rarely available for civil servants and that evidence can be unreliable. None the less it is a valuable tool for studying administrative leadership, exploring such key topics as the role of senior bureaucrats in articulating core values, and providing an essential complement to institutional analysis and the conditions of effective administrative leadership.

This collection of essays illustrates the several functions of biography in the study of government. Thus, Norma Riccucci argues her six 'execucrats' exemplify such qualities as commitment to values, service to the public, empowering colleagues, and dedication to the public service. Stephen Harrison and Gerald Wistow show how Roy Griffiths' ideas on the public management of health shaped fundamental long-term change in the health service. June Burnham and George Jones show that biography is an essential part of the history of an institution, the Prime Minister's Office. They show how individuals helped to bureaucratize the Office. Finally, David Richards identifies five categories of civil servants (including, for example, the can-do civil servants, the traditionalists) to analyse the extent to which the UK civil service was politicized in the 1980s and 1990s. Of course, bureaucratic leadership exists beyond the UK higher civil service. Other chapters look at local government, agencies and the European Commission. Kevin Theakston and his colleagues make a strong case for theoretically informed biographical case studies. As ever, the ESRC looks for methodological innovation from its Programmes. Here we have such an innovation.

As Director of the ESRC Whitehall Programme, the workshop that piloted the book pleased me greatly, even though flu prevented me from attending. Political science was the largest single discipline represented on the Programme. This workshop brought together historians and political scientists with colleagues from the USA for fruitful exchanges. All too often interdisciplinary work is a pious aspiration. On this occasion, it was a concrete event which, to use a quaint sixties expression, generated 'good vibes' and lively discussion. And given the dread and boredom often induced by the mention of the word methodology, it does no harm to point out that the method is fun! These biographical studies not only expand the repertoire of skills we can draw on to study government but bring to life administrative history by producing portraits of individuals which flesh out the institutional concerns of students of public administration and British government.

R. A. W. Rhodes
Director, ESRC Whitehall Programme
and
Professor of Politics, University of Newcastle

Note

1. The ESRC Whitehall Programme had published eight books by December 1998:

Bradbury, J. and J. Mawson (eds), *British Regionalism and Devolution* (London, 1997).
Day, P. and Klein, R., *Steering but not Rowing? The Transformation of the Department of Health: a Case Study* (Bristol, 1997).
Rhodes, R. A. W., *Understanding Governance: Policy Networks, Governance, Reflexivity and Accountability* (Buckingham, 1997).
Rhodes, R. A. W. and P. Dunleavy (eds), *Prime Minister, Cabinet and Core Executive* (London, 1995).
Rhodes, R. A. W., P. Weller and H. Bakviss (eds), *The Hollow Crown* (London, 1997).
Seargeant, J. and J. Steele *Consulting the Public: Guidelines and Good Practice* (London, 1997).

Smith, M. J., *The Core Executive in Britain* (London, 1998).
Theakston, K., *Leadership in Whitehall* (London, 1999).

For further information about the Programme and its publications visit the Programme's website: http://www.ncl.ac.uk/~npol/whitehall/index/html or contact Professor R. A. W. Rhodes, Department of Politics, University of Newcastle, Newcastle-Tyne, NE1 7RU. E-mail address: r.a.w.rhodes@ncl.ac.uk

Acknowledgements

This book is the product of the Workshop on Comparative Biography and Administrative Leadership held at Fairbairn House, University of Leeds in February 1997, as part of the Economic and Social Research Council's Whitehall Programme. I am grateful to the ESRC, and particularly to the Director of the Whitehall Programme, Professor Rod Rhodes, for supporting the workshop, which brought together UK and US academics working in this field for what I believe we all felt were extremely interesting and enjoyable exchanges and discussions.

The authors of the individual chapters accept full responsibility for what they have written. But we all express thanks to the other writers whose work appears here and to the other workshop participants and discussants for their comments, advice and encouragement: Dr Peter Barberis (Manchester Metropolitan University), Dr Martin Burch (University of Manchester), Professor Kathy Burk (University College London), Dr Peter Catterall (Institute of Contemporary British History), Dr John Greenaway (University of East Anglia), Professor Erwin Hargrove (Vanderbilt University), Dr Owen Hartley (University of Leeds), Professor Michael Lee (University of Bristol), Professor Rodney Lowe (University of Bristol), Professor Edward Page (University of Hull).

Kevin Theakston

1

The Biographical Approach to Public Administration: Potential, Purpose and Problems

Kevin Theakston

What can biography add to our knowledge of public administration? What are or should be the aims or purpose of biographical research in this field? What are the uses and limits, the strengths and weaknesses of the biographical approach as applied to the study of who leading public administrators are, and what they do? This chapter, first, discusses the administrative biographer's possible aims and, second, examines the ways in which biographical research can connect to, and be used to explore, some specific issues on the agenda of leadership studies.

It was once claimed that there were only three motives for writing a biography: 'to erect a monument to a departed loved one, or to set an example for future generations, or to make money' (Garraty quoted in Peltason, 1964, p. 217). I identify and discuss here four possible functions or objectives: (1) an inspirational function; (2) connecting the study of ideas and the development of public policy; (3) underlining the importance of an historical perspective for the study of government; and (4) to furnish case studies as a basis on which to generalize, and to be used in exploring important issues in public administration and assessing relevant theories and models. These are not mutually exclusive categories: elements of more than one are usually combined in biographical accounts.

Role Models

The serving-up of examples to 'inspire, challenge and enlighten' (Peltason, 1964, p. 217) is, of course, one of the traditional aims of biography, going back to classical times and also seen in the Victorian tomes commemorating their subjects as models of public virtue. This moral and didactic purpose was seen both in the big, typically three-volume, 'Lives' entombing major public figures and also in the series of collective lives which appeared in the nineteenth century, with titles like *The Worthies of England, Heroes of Industry, Lives of Eminent Missionaries* and so on, even extending to a book entitled *Wrecked Lives; or, Men Who Have Failed*, planned as a sort of negative reinforcement to the popular Victorian success stories (Nadel, 1984, pp. 18–20). Post-Lytton Strachey, one would think that we would be distrustful of the idea of biography providing role models or illustrious examples to emulate. But, in fact, in a number of ways some contemporary biographical work in the field of public administration does – sometimes explicitly, sometimes implicitly – have that purpose.

Exploring ethical behaviour in government, Cooper and Wright (1992) openly acknowledge their aim, in their collection of case studies of *Exemplary Public Administrators*, of providing 'instructive and inspirational role models both for preservice students considering careers in public service and for working administrators in a field that often feels maligned and demeaned by the public and the media'; they hope to 'project . . . a more positive image of public service to the [American] citizenry' (pp. xii–xiii). Riccucci (1995) also celebrates 'unsung heroes': federal executives in US government who had made important contributions to society and promoted the public welfare. Though Lewis's (1980) book on US entrepreneurial 'rogue elephants' presents, in a sense, models to avoid, the idea of the 'public administrator as hero' (Bellavita, 1991) can perhaps be understood as a reaction against the pervasive 'bureaucrat-bashing' of American politics.

For a British case, we could look to the way in which the career and achievements of Sir Edward Bridges have often been interpreted in terms of him providing a powerful example of high standards and of 'rock-like integrity' (as one of his successors put it to me in an interview) to the civil service of which he was the official head from 1945 to 1956. We see clearly with him the role of a leader in articulating and embodying an organization's core values, in acting as a role model, and in setting a moral tone – something brought out in Winnifrith's (1970) tribute, published just a year after Bridges' death. On some occasions recent heads of the civil service have looked like apologists for dubious ministerial activities, and the fact that Chapman's (1988) full-length study of Bridges appeared just as Sir Robert Armstrong was embroiled in controversy because of his role in the Westland and *Spycatcher* affairs made him seem even more like a figure from some lost golden age of the civil service (though it must be said that Chapman's book is far from being a panegyric and provides material for a more critical view of Bridges).

Studies of women in senior administrative positions tend to have the same flavour, it could be argued, with the theme of the subjects providing role models or exemplars for women in public service more or less strongly emphasized, though the individuals concerned might be more anxious to be recognized for their accomplishments than for the fact of them being women (e.g. Stivers, 1992).

Ideas and Public Policy

Biography can, secondly, provide a useful framework, or at least a point of entry, for the exploration of the impact of ideas on the development of government thinking and public policy. To be sure, it is an exercise fraught with difficulties. Gillian Sutherland was writing about nineteenth-century government but her point had a wider relevance when she questioned whether it was right to assume that 'the majority of government servants were wholly pragmatic, tidy-minded men, pressing towards solutions inherent in . . . problems, as they arose', while at the other extreme noting that 'it is not too difficult to demonstrate that the views and attitudes of many government servants and, indeed, of many politicians, were neither consistent nor coherent enough to be dignified with the labels "idea" or "ideology"'. Often we are looking at a tangle of views and opinions: 'ideas keep merging into social attitudes, assumptions, rationalizations of vested interests, prejudices even' (Sutherland, 1972, pp. 3–4). However, through biography we may be able to consider the impact of, on the one hand, agenda-setting, innovative ideas on policy and decision-making and, on the other hand, the broader influence of the 'conventional wisdom' consensus thinking of a particular group or period.

Without entering into the details of the individual cases and debates, we can note a number of examples where the studies of public administration, biography and ideas intersect. Thus, an important theme in accounts of the stormy career of Edwin Chadwick, for instance, has to be the issue of the influence of Benthamism in the politics of government growth in the first half of the nineteenth century (Brundage, 1988). Through the example of someone like Hubert Llewellyn Smith at the Board of Trade we can get some insight into the influence of the Oxford idealists in shaping the reformist thinking of a new generation of public servants in the late nineteenth century (Davidson, 1972, pp. 239–41). In crucial areas of twentieth-century public policy, the examples of William Beveridge and welfare reform (Harris, 1977) and of advisers and officials such as James Meade and Sir Richard Hopkins (Peden, 1983) when analysing the introduction of Keynesian economic thinking into Whitehall in the 1940s also stand out. Lowe and Roberts' (1987) analysis of the career and influence of Horace Wilson in the 1920s and 1930s – a key official in the fields of unemployment and industrial relations policy, and the man 'always ready with a convincing "brief" as to why nothing could be done' – illustrates the conservatism of mainstream interwar political and economic thinking. The post-1945 confidence in government circles that the state should and could successfully control the economy, and also the technocratic views prevalent in the 1960s about the likely benefits of government reorganization, are seen in the career of a Whitehall official like Sir Richard ('Otto') Clarke (Hubback, 1988).

It is, of course, necessary to guard against simplistic claims and assumptions about the connections between ideas, individuals and policy impacts. The interplay of ideas, circumstances (favourable or unfavourable), interests and individuals is complex and variable (Seldon, 1996). The individuals identified as important in introducing new ideas have not necessarily been original thinkers: what has been crucial has been their institutional position (for example, Hopkins was head of the Treasury 1942–5) or, as seen with Beveridge, factors such as force of personality, personal drive and flair for publicity. Moreover, the need to consider the mechanisms by which ideas are transmitted or infiltrated into government, and the appraisal of their effective influence on administrative mentalities and policy-making, really calls for something like group biography rather than an individual case study. With all the problems and qualifications, the general point is that we can use biography as a way into learning about the intellectual history of government circles and/or a particular historical period, and about the influence of ideas on public policy.

Biography and Administrative History

A biographical approach can also be justified on the grounds that it is an essential part of a comprehensive historical understanding of government and public administration. Although biography (and autobiography and personal diaries more so) is sometimes criticized as a sort of gossip-sodden, unreliable form of history, there are advantages in getting the personal perspective and a better understanding of individual assumptions, motives and actions. It can take us beyond dry and anonymous 'institutional history' or historical accounts of policy-making narrated in terms of a succession of memoranda and official documents. It can show us something of the reality of 'life behind the scenes' in government, providing insights into how organizations work in practice, the informal aspects of decision-taking and policy-making, and variations in 'administrative style' (Spann and Curnow, 1975, p. 366). By putting the case for the public servant, biographical work on administrative leaders can also help to redress the balance and set the record straight against the sometimes skewed accounts presented by politicians' memoirs (or diaries) and outside critics (Chapman and O'Toole, 1994, p. 66). 'If you get in first, you create the myth', a critic of the *Crossman Diaries* once argued: it is helpful, for example, to have the account of Tony Benn's permanent secretary at the Industry Department in the 1970s to set against Benn's own version (Part, 1990; Benn, 1989).

That serious analytical and methodological problems are inherent in the biographical approach to history cannot be denied (Beattie, 1993). By focusing on one person, biography may give a distorted picture of both the historical record and the central figure itself (Batchelor, 1995, p. 46). It can lead to an exaggeration of the individual's role and influence; give a misleading notion of the degree of autonomy or discretion enjoyed; and neglect the conditioning limits within which people operate and the constraints of the wider environment and organizational context (Peltason, 1964, pp. 218–19). Public administrators tend to have highly institutionally-defined roles (with variable scope for individual interpretations and preferences); are subject to political direction and control; and are located in organizations with powerful ongoing procedures, conventions, norms, traditions and prejudices. And then policy-making and administration are typically collective and interactive processes: the focus may need to be on networks and committees, rather than individuals.

Assembling the evidence to measure or assess the individual's contribution can also be very difficult. In contrast to political leaders, there are usually no significant collections of private papers or diaries (civil servants in Whitehall are indeed officially discouraged from keeping diaries which might record details of their work). Officials may be 'tracked through the files', so to speak, at the Public Record Office or elsewhere, but the picture thus built up will necessarily be incomplete. We may get some idea of administrators' attitudes and views from comments and exchanges recorded in official files (for example, work on preliminary drafts of policy papers, records of minor decisions, or notes directed at other officials rather than political superiors) (Chapman, 1994, p. 9). But official memoranda are not 'the secret confessions of higher administrative officials' (Lowe and Roberts, 1987, p. 643): they contain advice tailored to fit the views and objectives of political or bureaucratic superiors or the needs of a particular political situation. And because of the telephone and private and informal talks, the files may anyway tell only part of the story. Interview research may fill some gaps but has its own well-known drawbacks and limitations.

Biography as Case Studies

To most practitioners of the form 'a biography is not so much a case study from which generalized knowledge can be developed or in which hypotheses can be tested, but a description of the life of a certain individual, an intellectual exercise carrying its own utility' (Peltason, 1964, p. 217). If political scientists are so often sceptical about how much biography can explain or illuminate it may be because whereas biographers tend to particularize, they by training and inclination want to generalize and to develop and test theories and models (Murphy, 1969, p. 728).

In addition to illuminating the history and the study of the contemporary practice of public administration in a narrative or 'story-telling' fashion, biographical research can be regarded or approached in terms of assembling case studies or profiles to explore important general issues in public administration theory and practice. The growing American literature in this field certainly has this character, using biographical case studies to probe leadership and innovation strategies (Doig and Hargrove, 1987), ethical behaviour in the public service (Cooper and Wright, 1992), the relationship between leadership and organizational culture (Hargrove, 1994), and the ingredients of effective performance in the Washington bureaucracy (Riccucci, 1995). The British literature is (so far) less developed in this sense. Jose Harris hints at what might be possible: while accepting that individual biography 'is an inadequate medium from which to generate general theories of administrative change, but ... may provide a miniature crucible in which such theories can be tested and tempered' (Harris, 1988, p. 224), she uses the career of William Beveridge as a case study from which to draw conclusions about the role of creative administrators in policy innovation, the administrative outlook of early twentieth-century Whitehall bureaucrats, and the applicability of the MacDonagh model of government growth (pp. 239–41).

Although case studies by definition focus on the exceptional, limiting the ability to make sweeping generalizations, their utility at all stages of the theory-building and -testing process has been acknowledged (Eckstein, 1975). Using the 'controlled comparison' research strategy, and focusing on a relatively small number of cases, may not provide fully satisfactory confirmation or invalidation of existing theories but is particularly suited for developing typological theory and contingent generalizations (George, 1979, pp. 58–9). (Doig and Hargrove, 1987, ch. 1, is a good example of this approach.) Spann and Curnow (1975, p. 366) argue strongly that biography has much to offer as a tool for the construction of administrative theory, and the case study method means that we can take biography beyond Disraeli's jibe about 'life without theory'. In a political science which seems increasingly to 'seek theoretical safety only in numbers' (Eckstein, 1975, p. 85), it may thus be possible to overcome biography's status as a 'disciplinary poor relation' (Pimlott, 1990, p. 224).

Comparative Biography and Administrative Leadership

James MacGregor Burns (1978, p. 28) has shown that the study of leadership is advanced by the study of particular leaders. The biographical approach is a particularly fruitful way in which to study administrative leadership: from each of the four 'angles' we have just reviewed we can set out to explore crucial issues about the meaning and nature of leadership in government bureaucracies. At this stage, I simply want to highlight some of the ways in which biographical research can connect to important issues and problems concerning the leadership of public bureaucracies, suggesting ways in which biographical research in this field could be framed and the agenda it could tackle.

The importance of senior officials being, and being *seen* to be, the key practitioners and upholders of what is permanently constructive and necessary in terms of the ethos, culture and standards of their profession as public servants cannot be doubted (Quinlan, 1995, p. 5). Senior officials do exert a powerful influence through the example they set – by setting and maintaining standards and by their personal conduct in office – and biography can alert us to the ways in which this important leadership role can be more or less successfully discharged, though it would be unwise to turn the study of bureaucratic leaders as role models and exemplars into a sort of administrative hagiography. Leaders send out signals through symbolic and ceremonial activities, either confirming a traditional order or trying to reinforce a new vision: Warren

Fisher's biographer, for example, shows how he went to great lengths to encourage sport in the civil service in the 1920s and 1930s in an attempt to break down barriers and foster his ideal of a unified service (O'Halpin, 1989, pp. 156–7). More importantly, perhaps, in thinking about leaders as role models/exemplars we should emphasize the cognitive dimension of leadership as seen in Howard Gardner's (1995) book about the way in which the most successful leaders, in his view, are successful to the extent that they communicate ideas and tell and embody persuasive 'stories' about what the institutions they head stand for or aspire to, or where they should be going and how they will get there. Biographical case studies can potentially illustrate both the particular 'stories' different leaders are telling as well as the dynamics and effects of this style or form of leadership in a generic sense.

This type of leadership is bound up with the definition and articulation of a public service's or agency's core values and 'institutional purpose' in a broad sense. Selznick (1957) and Hargrove (1994) emphasize that the central task of leadership is to infuse an organization with values and an institutional philosophy (Selznick's term is organizational 'myth') beyond the technical task(s) at hand. Nurturing an organizational culture is a central leadership task and administrative biography should be alert to, and try to illustrate, the processes through which it is defined, transmitted, challenged, defended and changed at different times and in different circumstances. The best biographical work will weave the collective through the individual, looking at the complex ways in which an organization's culture develops over time and shapes (and is shaped by) individual behaviour and experience (Clifford, 1978). A concern for organizational culture also underlines the importance of group biography, looking at the interplay and the interconnections of a number of individuals in a particular community, place, milieu or context – exploring group dynamics and the interactions of a 'power elite', background characteristics, and criss-crossing career paths (Nadel, 1984, pp. 191–6). It may be that if, in the manner of anthropology or ethnology, we want to portray the culture and values of a wider bureaucratic 'society', then we may in the end find a group or network rather than an individual focus more useful (whether we are looking at Treasury mandarins, Foreign Office diplomats, agency chief executives, local authority professionals, police chief constables, or whatever).

An historical perspective is vital in bringing out the connections between the life-story of the subject(s) of biographical research, and their institutional location and historical scope in terms of the character of the system, the prevailing administrative traditions and culture, political and environmental pressures and constraints, and the general circumstances of the period. Individuals and institutions are thus not mutually exclusive – both are a necessary focus. Portraying individuals, groups and organizations across time will highlight the way in which leadership provides a key link between organizational history and the present, and show how the tasks of leaders are very different at different times in the history of an organization (for example, the different styles and strategies associated with 'founding' and 'consolidating' leaders) (Hargrove, 1994, pp. 3, 281–3). Similarly, evaluation of leadership effectiveness centres on the relationship between an individual's skills and abilities, the task(s) faced, and the political environment and historical context. Historically-rooted analysis may also help to avoid the danger of developing an overly 'heroic' view of leadership or of particular leaders: the same leader may be seen to succeed in one context and fail in another, in different historical circumstances, and long time-frames of analysis lend a perspective to the varying potency and powerlessness of individual action (Leavy and Wilson, 1994, pp. 186–7). Leavy and Wilson describe leaders as 'tenants of time and context' in their study of the interaction of leadership, context and history in the formation of organizational strategy. Their method of analysing, comparing and classifying leaders not so much on the basis of their personal attributes but in terms of their historical roles and the challenges that they faced during their tenure at the top (identifying 'builders', 'revitalizers', 'turn-arounders' and 'inheritors') could usefully be adapted for a public administration context.

In terms of the case study use of biographical research to explore key public administration issues and theories, there is an urgent need for British versions of the sort of high-quality American projects mentioned earlier. What can we hope to get from comparative biographical/historical case study analysis of administrative leaders? At the minimum level, there is the argument that useful lessons can emerge from studying examples of acknowledged leaders: 'learning from great figures of the past' by looking at their personal qualities, their methods, their successes and their failures (Chapman and O'Toole, 1994, pp. 65, 76). (It should be noted that failures are not usually popular subjects for biographers – not least because there is usually far less readily available source material on them – but from a political scientist's viewpoint unsuccessful leaders may be just as important as the successful (Edinger, 1964, p. 424).) Comparative biography may be able to pick out the ingredients – the skills, qualities, traits, career-experiences, and so on – that are associated with effective administrative leadership (Riccucci, 1995). In terms of 'learning lessons', however, moving from description and generalization, through theory, to prediction is more problematic. Barber (1977) drew on biographical sources to produce a psychology-based framework for analysing the 'presidential character' and predicting performance in the White House. But in the field of administrative biography the argument so far tends not to go beyond the conclusion that leadership is contingent or that there is no one best way for executives to bring about positive change to public policy.

Through case studies we can also explore and assess the impact of individual background and personality on administrative behaviour and leadership. The challenge is to pin down how much individuals and personal characteristics matter, and to identify the conditions or circumstances in which they do make a difference. To take an example: biographical case studies could help us understand whether women manage or lead in a distinctive way, providing (as some claim) 'caring-sharing' or 'connective' leadership, or avoiding 'win–lose competition' (Cooper and Wright, 1992, pp. 188, 206, 210). We could equally use cases to ask whether 'imported' private-sector business managers act and lead in a special way when they move across into public-sector positions, or to examine the role of individuals at key turning points and 'critical junctures' in institutional development and change (an important issue in so-called 'new institutionalist' approaches).

Analytically, the general issue could be stated in terms used by Greenstein (1970, pp. 41ff): establishing *actor* and *action* indispensability. Is the action one that would have been performed by any actor in the same situation or role? 'The biographer,' Greenstein (1970, p. 68) argues, 'frequently seeks to establish whether some action of his protagonist was a necessary condition of a historical outcome (action dispensability), and, if so, whether the action is one that needs to be explained in terms of the protagonist's personal characteristics (actor dispensability).' Political science-based biographers would recognize that this approach would have to be institutionally-informed, as in Burch and Holliday's (1996, pp. 266–8) argument about assessing individual actions and impacts against what might be predicted or expected on the basis of their institutional identity or location. At times, individuals may well 'conform to type', but there may be critical occasions when they go beyond their 'institutional self'. Recognizing that leadership opportunities are highly contextual and that institutions constrain and channel leadership is not, however, a surrender to 'structure' in the familiar structure/agency debate (Jones, 1989, p. 5).

Finally, there is the evaluation of biographical case studies in the light of theories of leadership, and vice versa. Immediate progress could be made simply in terms of case study exploration of basic models and debates such as 'transformational' leadership (innovative and visionary change-agents or entrepreneurial leaders) versus 'transactional' leadership (the 'busy fixers' operating the existing system), or with the model of the 'administrative conservator' (a 'guardianship' role: the bureaucratic leader concerned to preserve 'institutional integrity' (Terry, 1995)) (see Theakston, 1999, on these leadership models as applied to Whitehall). Through the cases we could analyse the circumstances and situations (including political and historical factors) in which particular types or styles of leadership were possible or effective (or ineffective) and the results achieved (Doig and Hargrove, 1987). We could also examine possible national and sectoral factors conditioning administrative leadership: for example, are administrative entrepreneurs of the American kind more likely to be found outside the traditional Whitehall mandarinate and among the ranks of agency chief executives, 'quangocrats' and local authority professionals or chief executives (Jones, 1988, p. 216; Ioannou, 1992)? The result should be more theoretically-aware biographical case studies as well as developments and refinements on the theoretical level.

Outline of the Book

Norma Riccucci, in Chapter 2, certainly illustrates the first of the four kinds of administrative biography referred to earlier. Aiming to place her examples of US 'execucrats' in a positive light and demonstrate their valuable contributions to society, her six figures are also exemplars for what is possible in skill and craftsmanship in terms of executive leadership in the US federal government context. Each of the other three kinds of biography are also present as possibilities in her study. 'Ideas in good currency' are a political resource for innnovative execucrats (as well as entrepreneurial politicians), the six individuals she studies working within 'invisible colleges' or networks of research, advocacy and policy entrepreneurship. In an historical sense, the contributions of these executives can be seen against the ebb and flow of the politics of their time. And by taking the individual career as the unit of analysis, Riccucci provides case studies that can be used to identify contingent factors that influence effectiveness and ineffectiveness, and success and failure, providing also a valuable framework for systematically understanding how top bureaucrats achieve policy objectives and exercise leadership in the Washington system.

Chapters 3, 4 and 5 focus on Whitehall and the British civil service. 'It is not given to any civil servant to be more than a footnote in the history books', Sir Robert Armstrong, Secretary to the Cabinet and Head of the Civil Service in the 1980s, once commented (Harris, 1989). He was too modest, and his own role in Mrs Thatcher's Whitehall made him, at the very least, a sometimes controversial 'footnote' (Theakston, 1999). The important roles played by Sir Maurice Hankey, Sir Warren Fisher and Sir Horace Wilson in interwar government and administration have long been recognized by historians, and Geoffrey Fry's survey in Chapter 3 presents some interesting new evidence (including the interview testimony of 'insiders') relating to the activities, style and impact of these three Whitehall 'giants'. The fact that each of them operated at permanent secretary level for twenty years (rising to the top of the ladder aged only 39 or 40 – in comparison to today's top officials, typically appointed in their late forties or early fifties), meant that they virtually physically embodied the 'institutional memory' of the 'permanent government' of the mandarinate, and added to their power and influence. Administrative biography can illustrate how an individuals's approach and style may over time come to be seen as moulding an organization's 'character' (Spann and Curnow, 1975, p. 379), as seen with the example of Hankey's military background – with its emphasis on order, hierarchy and security – which may have had an important influence on his design and running of the Cabinet Secretariat (an organization also powerfully influenced by Hankey's successors, such as Norman Brook (Theakston, 1999)). Biographically, 'early successes' and formative career experiences can profoundly affect casts of mind and outlooks – how important is the conventional Whitehall apprenticeship as a ministerial private secretary in producing (and reproducing) the traditional 'mandarin' style, and will the fact that in the 1980s ambitious younger officials anxious to catch the eye of their superiors were often deployed on efficiency scrutinies ('Rayner's Raiders') contribute towards a more managerial, hard-edged and innovative approach as they reach the top?

June Burnham and George Jones, in Chapter 4 analysing the development of the Prime Minister's Office, adopt a longitudinal approach, looking at individuals and the different circumstances they faced, assessing what they counted for and attempting something like the 'biography of an institution'. Their focus is on 'innovators' in Downing Street, the people who 'did things differently' and made significant contributions to changing the ways in which premiers were assisted in the late nineteenth and twentieth centuries. Their cases include politicians (Gladstone, Lloyd George, Harold Wilson), a key civil service private secretary (Leslie Rowan), and a more shadowy figure (Ronald Waterhouse). They argue that prime ministerial support is essential for significant and perhaps permanent changes in the institutional structures and processes of the Number 10 operation. The strong impression is left of a system which was fluid and disjointed in the time of Gladstone and Lloyd George, but which later became more bureaucratic, regularized and institutionalized, constraining – though not removing – the scope for prime-ministerial innovation.

David Richards, in Chapter 5, presents a series of vignettes depicting various categories of senior civil servants ('can-doers', 'overtly political', 'also-rans', 'traditionalists', and 'black-balled') to illustrate the issues and the controversy around the alleged 'politicization' of Whitehall in the Conservative years in the 1980s and 1990s. He concludes that the mandarinate of today is in important ways different from that of 1979, and his chapter raises important questions about the political flexibility of the new-style higher civil service and its future under the New Labour government of Tony Blair.

Kester Isaac-Henry, in Chapter 6, also adopts a longitudinal methodology, reviewing the experience and exploring the changing role of all the chief executives of Birmingham City Council over the last 25 years, an approach which brings out the interconnections between individual personality, skills and style on the part of successive office-holders; institutional factors; and the changing environment. In the context of the debate about transactional versus transformational leadership, Isaac-Henry makes the important point that radical, vision-driven bureaucratic leaders or 'change-agents' usually need political consent and support. Effective chief executive leadership, he argues, involves achieving objectives and missions determined by the elected politicians and Council leaders. In a sense, behind the transformational bureaucrat we must look for the transformational political leader.

In Chapter 7, Christopher Lord's case study of Lord Cockfield and the Single Market initiative provides fascinating insights into the scope for policy entrepreneurship in a transnational institutional setting. 'Political' and 'administrative' leadership are blurred in the European Commission, with a fragmented (even chaotic) bureaucracy and the powers and sensitivities of member-states and the European Council further complicating the picture. The notion that an individual Commissioner might 'make a difference' is thus problematic. Cockfield, however, is convincingly portrayed by Lord as a creative policy technician and entrepreneur. If 'transactional' leadership involves delivering the preferences of political superiors more effectively (and in the Brussels context complex bargaining strategies are essential even for this), 'transformational' leadership from inside the institutions of the EU means persuading the politicians to want something different, or else locking them into a process where the outcome is different from what they originally wanted. Cockfield's aims, methods and achievements fit this latter agenda-setting and mobilizing model, though Lord also acknowledges the central importance of Cockfield's relationship with Commission President Jacques Delors.

In Chapter 8, Stephen Harrison and Gerald Wistow analyse another policy entrepreneur, Roy Griffiths, and assess the origins, conduct and implementation of his two key reports on British public services – on National Health Service management (1983) and on community care (1988). Griffiths undoubtedly had a radical and fundamental long-term impact on these two important services, and Harrison and Wistow conclude that his personal role was vital: the reforms made would probably not have happened without him. The chapter can be read on a number of levels and illustrates three of the catagories of biography outlined above. Thus, it provides insights into the processes by which ideas (in this case about better management in the NHS and a more client-focused approach in social services) are translated into public policy. Griffiths was not an original thinker – rather his achievement was more one of brokering, packaging and making politically palatable existing ideas. As administrative history, the chapter provides evidence about the interrelationships and attitudes of key political, bureaucratic and interest-group actors in a period of major policy change. And as a political science case study, the chapter explores and assesses the characteristics of successful policy entrepreneurship.

Finally, in Chapter 9, Elizabeth Mellon investigates the nature and formation of public sector managers' values, exploring the differences and similarities between the private and the public sectors, and within the latter between regular managers and agency chief executives – the agents, she suggests, of a broader cultural change in the British civil service, who may well be able to safeguard the best of the traditional public service ethos while also ensuring a more proactive approach towards management reform and modernization. Her case study of Derek Lewis – the head of the Prison Service agency sacked in controversial circumstances in 1995 – bears out her general argument and also illustrates the process of and varied influences on value-formation and reinforcement (family background, education, work environment, and so on). The chapter presents a valuable and fascinating blend of quantitative survey data and qualitative interview material – the mix of statistics and biography perhaps showing the way forward for other studies.

References

Barber, J. D. (1977). *The Presidential Character*. 2nd edn (Englewood Cliffs, NJ: Prentice-Hall).

Batchelor, J. (ed) (1995). *The Art of Literary Biography* (Oxford: Clarendon Press).

Beattie, A. (1993). 'Biographies of 1992 and the limits of biography', *Parliamentary Affairs* 46, 430–4.

Bellavita, C. (1991). 'The public administrator as hero', *Administration and Society* 23, 155–85.

Benn, T. (1989). *Against the Tide: Diaries 1973–76* (London: Hutchinson).

Brundage, A. (1988). *England's 'Prussian minister': Edwin Chadwick and the Politics of Government Growth, 1832–1854* (London: Pennsylvania State University Press).

Burch, M. and I. Holliday (1996). *The British Cabinet System* (London: Prentice-Hall).

Burns, J. M. (1978). *Leadership* (New York: Harper and Row).

Chapman, R. (1988). *Ethics in the British Civil Service* (London: Routledge).

Chapman, R. (1994). 'Document based studies in executive leadership – the case of the British civil service', paper to the SOG 'Ten Years of Change' conference, University of Manchester.

Chapman, R. and B. O'Toole (1994). 'The heroic approach in the historiography of public administration in the United Kingdom', *Yearbook of European Administrative History* 6, 65–77.

Clifford, J. (1978). '"Hanging up looking glasses at odd corners": ethnobiographical prospects', in D. Aaron (ed.), *Studies in Biography* (Cambridge, Mass.: Harvard University Press).

Cooper, T. L. and N. D. Wright (eds) (1992). *Exemplary Public Administrators* (San Francisco: Jossey-Bass).

Davidson, R. (1972). 'Llewellyn Smith, the labour department and government growth 1886–1909', in G. Sutherland (ed.), *Studies in the Growth of Nineteenth Century Government* (London: Routledge and Kegan Paul).

Doig, J. and E. Hargrove (eds) (1987). *Leadership and Innovation* (Baltimore: Johns Hopkins University Press).

Eckstein, H. (1975). 'Case study and theory in political science', in F. Greenstein and N. Polsby (eds), *Handbook of Political Science vol. 7: Strategies of Inquiry*. (Reading, Mass.: Addison-Wesley).

Edinger, L. J. (1964). 'Political science and political biography: reflections on the study of leadership (I)', *The Journal of Politics* 26, 423–39.

Gardner, H. (1995). *Leading Minds* (London: HarperCollins).

George, A. (1979). 'Case studies and theory development: the method of structured, focused comparison', in P. G. Lauren (ed.), *Diplomacy* (New York: Free Press).

Greenstein, F. I. (1970). *Personality and Politics* (Chicago: Markham).

Hargrove, E. (1994). *Prisoners of Myth: The Leadership of the Tennessee Valley Authority 1933–1990* (Princeton: Princeton University Press).

Harris, J. (1977). *William Beveridge: a Biography* (Oxford: Clarendon Press).

Harris, J. (1988). 'William Beveridge in Whitehall: maverick or mandarin?', in R. MacLeod (ed.), *Government and Expertise* (Cambridge: Cambridge University Press).

Harris, R. (1989). 'Most Public Servant', *Sunday Times Magazine*, 3 Dec. 1989, 57–8.

Hubback, D. (1988). 'Sir Richard Clarke 1910–1975: a most unusual civil servant', *Public Policy and Administration* 3, 19–34.

Ioannou, A. (1992). *Public Sector Entrepreneurship: Policy and Process Innovators in the UK*. Ph.D. thesis, London School of Economics.

Jones, B. (ed.) (1989). *Leadership and Politics* (Lawrence, Kan.: University of Kansas Press).

Jones, G. W. (1988). Book review of Doig and Hargrove. *Journal of Public Policy* 8, 214–16.

Leavy, B. and D. Wilson (1994). *Strategy and Leadership* (London: Routledge).

Lewis, E. (1980). *Public Entrpreneurship* (Bloomington: Indiana University Press).

Lowe, R. and R. Roberts (1987). 'Sir Horace Wilson, 1900–1935: the making of a mandarin', *Historical Journal* 30, 641–62.

Murphy, W. (1969). 'Populist in the pulpit', *Yale Law Journal* 78, 725–30.

Nadel, I. B. (1984). *Biography: Fiction, Fact and Form* (London: Macmillan).

O'Halpin, E. (1989). *Head of the Civil Service: a Study of Sir Warren Fisher* (London: Routledge).

Part, A. (1990). *The Making of a Mandarin* (London: Andre Deutsch).

Peden, G. (1983). 'Sir Richard Hopkins and the "Keynesian revolution" in employment policy, 1929–1945', *Economic History Review* (series 2) 36, 281–96.

Peltason, J. (1964). 'Supreme court biography and the study of public law', in G. Dietze (ed.), *Essays on the American Constitution* (Englewood Cliffs, NJ: Prentice-Hall).

Pimlott, B. (1990). 'The future of political biography', *Political Quarterly* 61, 214–24.

Quinlan, Sir M. (1995). 'Leadership in the public sector', lecture at Templeton College, Oxford.

Riccucci, N. (1995). *Unsung Heroes: Federal Execucrats Making a Difference* (Washington, DC: Georgetown University Press).

Seldon, A. (1996). 'Ideas are not enough', in D. Marquand and A. Seldon (eds), *The Ideas that Shaped Post-war Britain* (London: Fontana).

Selznick, P. (1957). *Leadership in Administration* (New York: Harper and Row).

Spann, R. and Curnow, G. (1975). *Public Policy and Administration in Australia: A Reader* (Sydney: Wiley).

Stivers, C. (1992). 'Beverlee A. Myers: power, virtue and womanhood in public administration', in T. L. Cooper and N. D. Wright (eds), *Exemplary Public Administrators* (San Francisco: Jossey-Bass).

Sutherland, G. (ed.) (1972). *Studies in the Growth of Nineteenth-century Government* (London: Routledge and Kegan Paul).

Terry, L. (1995). *Leadership of Public Bureaucracies* (London: Sage).

Theakston, K. (1999). *Leadership in Whitehall* (London: Macmillan).

Winnifrith, J. (1970). 'Edward Ettingdean Bridges – Baron Bridges', in *Biographical Memoirs of Fellows of the Royal Society*, vol. 16 (London: Royal Society).

2
Excellence in Administrative Leadership: an Examination of Six US Federal Execucrats

Norma M. Riccucci

Introduction

The literatures of public administration and organizational studies abound with theories of, and approaches to leadership and management. From the early writings of Chester Barnard (1938) to the present-day treatises of such scholars as Denhardt (1993), Lynn (1987; 1984), Cayer (1989), Bryson and Crosby (1992), and Faerman *et al.* (1990), students of public administration and administrative behaviour have been stocked with 'methods of effective leadership', 'ingredients for managerial success', and the like. The array of leadership theories reflects, in part, the fundamental disagreements about the precise meaning of leadership (Cayer, 1989; Gortner, Mahler and Nicholson, 1987). Despite the lack of an orthodox approach to studying leadership, several contemporary scholars of organizations have advanced frameworks for the study of leadership that coalesce the common components of leadership theories, thus providing a synthesized foundation for examining effective leadership in public institutions. One such theorist is Denhardt (1993), who, through in-depth discussions with public managers in Australia, Canada, Great Britain and the United States, proffers five characteristics of effective leadership: (1) a commitment to values; (2) serving the public; (3) empowerment and shared leadership; (4) pragmatic incrementalism; and (5) a dedication to public service.

This study relies on Denhardt's framework in examining the leadership behaviours of six high-level career servants in the US federal government. In examining leadership behaviours, the study employs biographical profiles, which allow us to take a closer look at the career

17

paths and personal lives of federal executives; this, in turn, tells us a good deal about what makes these bureaucratic officials tick. As was pointed out in chapter 1, biographical case studies have become a popular as well as useful method for examining the leadership behaviours of civil servants (also see: Doig and Hargrove, 1987; Riccucci, 1995; Lewis, 1980; Cooper and Wright, 1992; Hargrove and Glidewell, 1990).

Characteristics of Effective Administrative Leadership

As noted, there is a plethora of leadership theories that have guided research on effective leadership in American bureaucracies. Denhardt's framework, because of its versatility and pragmatic value, serves as a useful foundation for studying federal administrative leadership.

Commitment to Values

According to Denhardt (1993: 21), effective leadership depends upon the ability of an executive to develop 'a pervasive commitment to the mission and values of the organization'. Values, in large part, refer to the leader's ability to act professionally, with the utmost integrity, in the delivery of public goods and services. A commitment to values also means that leaders have a clear vision and direction for the organization; the organization and its mission are placed above all other interests.

Serving the Public

Effective leaders, according to Denhardt, will set as a high priority, service to the general public. They should hold themselves to high standards of performance and accountability, which will ultimately lead to high-quality services. And, the emphasis is not on serving one's profession, personal career aspirations or even the personal and political interests of elected officials, but rather on the organization's constituents and, more broadly, the general public. As Denhardt (1993: 124) points out, the 'values of service and quality are constantly on the minds of the best contemporary managers'. He goes on to say that the rights of the citizenry must never be overlooked or trammelled.

Empowerment and Shared Leadership

Effective leaders and managers are committed to teamwork, whereby all employees in the organization participate in the efforts to achieve common goals. Effective leaders will work hard to empower their staff, thus instilling a strong sense of commitment in all workers to the organization's goals and missions. Beyond the internal staff, effective leaders will also be successful in cooperating fully with other groups and policy players. It is also critical for leaders to take risks and allow their employees to take risks. As Denhardt (1993: 136) points out, 'at the core of the strategy of empowerment are individuals throughout the organization assuming responsibilities for their own actions and being prepared to take risks in what they believe is in the best interest of their organization'.

Pragmatic Incrementalism

Effective leadership depends upon the ability of the execucrat to achieve goals one step at a time (i.e., achieving small wins incrementally). It requires the use of several different strategies that fit the situations at hand, as well as practical knowledge of the inner workings of the systems that government executives operate in. According to Denhardt, pragmatic incrementalism also requires leaders to take into account the personal concerns and interests of constituents, the general public and employees.

A Dedication to Public Service

Effective administrative leaders are committed to government service. They maintain high ethical standards and insist that their staff act similarly. There is a strong intrinsic desire on the part of the effective leader to work for the public service; opportunities to work for the private sector at high salaries may avail themselves, but effective leaders instead are virtually 'driven' to the public service. This is due in large part to the professional and personal fulfilment realized by serving the broader public good.

Six Successful Federal Execucrats in the US

There is a layer of high-level civil servants in the US federal bureaucracy responsible for decisions and policies that affect the lives of the American people in vital ways. They are the 'execucrats', the career *execu*tives/bureau*crats*, who are not elected nor appointed to office, but rather have made a career as public servants. Despite popular sentiment about government workers as being lazy, slothful and ineffective, execucrats represent a cohort of public servants who defy these negative stereotypes.

The Denhardt framework, described above, provides a useful set of lenses through which to examine the effectiveness of execucratic leaders.

Six execucrats serve as the basis for this inquiry into effective administrative leadership.

Eileen Claussen and the EPA

With the exception of a brief consulting stint, Eileen Claussen has worked for the federal government since she graduated from Washington, DC's George Washington University with a BA in English Literature. By 1972, she accepted a post with the US Environmental Protection Agency (EPA), where she would spend the next 25 years of her career. Claussen explained that she wasn't interested in a career in private industry, even though the pay would be better, because

> the work, although interesting, was not as challenging and fulfilling as government jobs. I never saw the end results of my work.... Unlike my work in the private sector, I have a good idea of my work's impact and its implications. And I believe that public servants can have an impact if they are really trying to make a difference in our society. And, this is why I opted for a career in the public service; I really wanted to contribute something worthwhile to our society.

Claussen started out as a program analyst at the GS-13 level in EPA's Office of Solid Waste Management and almost immediately began to move up the EPA hierarchy into various management-level positions. This was due in large part to her initiative, analytical expertise and her utter determination to accomplish EPA's environmental goals, no matter which Administration has occupied the White House.

By 1986, Claussen was promoted to Director of EPA's Office of Atmospheric Programs, the position she currently holds. In this capacity, she has led her office in a number of major environmental victories, both national and international. Most notably, Claussen was one of the persons instrumental in negotiating and renegotiating the Montreal Protocol, an international agreement forged in Montreal, Canada in 1987 to curb the production of CFCs and other toxic chemicals. Signed by the US and 23 other nations – industrialized as well as Third World – the Montreal Protocol was the first global agreement to regulate the use of CFCs; it represented a major achievement in international diplomacy.

Claussen played a pivotal role in the signing of the treaty, and also in 'selling' it to the Reagan Administration, which was a friend of big business and, thus, not supportive of any environmental regulation. Claussen was particularly well suited for the role, because she had proven herself to be a skilful and professional negotiator around domestic environmental issues. Indeed, not only was she successful in working with various officials at the EPA (e.g., the Administrator, Lee Thomas), but she also forged important linkages with both environmental and industry groups, which saw her as an honest, trustworthy negotiator with outstanding management and leadership skills (Doniger, 1992; Fay, 1992).

After years of negotiations, it finally seemed to all parties that an international accord was extremely close to being struck. But an unexpected twist of events, precipitated by the US, threatened to obstruct the entire agreement. Any international agreement would require each nation's head of state to sign off on the Protocol. When Claussen and the other US delegates returned home for President Reagan's authorization, they were astonished to learn that he and some of his key advisers were devising ways to stave off an international accord. Instead of supporting an international effort, key Reagan officials advanced an alternative, 'market-based' approach to curbing ozone depletion. They suggested that people could wear hats and sunglasses and also use suntan lotion to protect themselves from the sun's ultraviolet rays. The plan was dubbed by opponents as the 'Rayban Plan'.

Claussen, teamed with officials from the State Department, embarked on a massive interagency campaign to defend and promote the international environmental accord. While Claussen recognizes the importance of standing by Administration policy, she saw the so-called 'Rayban Plan' as nothing more than a disingenuous attempt by Reagan officials to eschew government regulation over CFCs. Claussen's sense of loyalty and commitment to the EPA and its mission – combating environmental abuse – won out. An important strategy that Claussen employed was to educate the public as well as to garner its opposition to the Administration's plan. The media were viewed as an obvious conduit here, and so the *Washington Post* was contacted. Over the next several days, political cartoons and editorials lampooning the Administration's Rayban Plan appeared in the *Post* as well as other newspapers.

Needless to say, the Rayban Plan failed. Ultimately, the Reagan Administration was willing to concede to a 50 per cent reduction in CFC production. When Claussen and the US team returned to Montreal, their position was somewhat watered down, but it was now formally backed by President Reagan. The Montreal Protocol on Substances that Deplete the Ozone Layer was signed on 16 September 1987 by 24 of the 64 nations in attendance. (Delegates from most of the other 40 countries did not sign the Protocol because they had not been granted the authority by their governments to do so.)

Dr Vince Hutchins and Maternal and Child Health (MCH)

Dr Vince Hutchins has spent virtually his entire life working to improve the lives of mothers and children. He retired from government service in 1992, but he has a long, productive career that winds its way through medical school, private practice, the military during the Korean War, graduate work in public health, academia and then government service.

Vince Hutchins graduated from medical school in 1952 just around the time of the Korean War. After spending one year as an intern at the Edward Sparrow Hospital in Lansing, Michigan, Hutchins was drafted for military service. He served on Navy transport ships at the tail end of the Korean War, where he tended to the medical needs of service persons and their dependants, who were being transported from San Francisco to military bases in the Pacific. When he finished his military tour in 1955, he started a private practice in San Francisco and worked mainly with children and families.

During this time, Dr Hutchins developed a broader commitment to improving the system of health care for mothers and children in the society at large. So, in 1967, at the age of 39, Hutchins began a programme of study in public health. Within one year, he had earned an MPH from the University of California's School of Public Health at Berkeley and had already left private practice.

By 1971, Dr Hutchins entered government service as a GS-15 to become the Regional Medical Director for Health Education and Welfare's (HEW) Maternal and Child Health Service. He continued to move up the MCH hierarchy and by 1977, Dr Hutchins was promoted to Director of the Maternal and Child Health Bureau. He served as Director of this division or bureau, under its various names within both HEW and Health and Human Services (HHS), from 1977 until his retirement in 1992.

One of Dr Hutchins's many responsibilities as head of the MCH Bureau was working with other units and agencies within the federal government that have some role in MCH care programmes or services. This was often challenging for Dr Hutchins because of the highly political, fragmented nature of the federal bureaucracy. Yet, as several persons pointed out, Dr Hutchins was very skilful in working with the other players, inside and outside of government, and in managing and coordinating efforts with them in order to promote the interests of mothers and children (Koop, 1993; Will, 1993; Katz, 1993; Weiss, 1993). As Dr Mary Hughes (1993), formerly of the March of Dimes, has said:

Vince was very effective at getting disparate groups together and even different units of the bureaucracy to work together toward a common goal. Vince is a born networker and born team leader.... Vince was one of the few people who would get [various] departments talking to one another, because he was an excellent team player and leader.... His team approach was key to his ability to fostering innovation, change and improvement in MCH care policy in such a fragmented, disjointed environment.

Cultivating good ties with political appointees and members of Congress has also been important to Dr Hutchins in his ability to influence MCH care policy. It appears that most of the time, his relationship with political appointees has been quite congenial. As Dr Rae Grad (1992), Executive Director of the National Commission to Prevent Infant Mortality, noted, Dr Hutchins worked well with political appointees

because he has no ego.... The only time I sensed any friction was when political appointees would try to push their own political agenda on Vince rather than the mothers and babies' agenda. But, Vince was never put off by this, getting into a huff. He would just bring everything back to what the goal was – mothers and babies.

In addition to the formal responsibilities and duties as Director of the Maternal and Child Health Bureau, Dr Hutchins also spent a good deal of his time counselling and mentoring young health professionals on their careers. One of Dr Hutchins' key staff persons, Dr Merle McPherson (1993), noted that 'Vince's management style was one that was very supportive and interactive. He had an open-door policy and was very good at mentoring.'

Dr Hutchins recognized the importance of mentoring his staff. He noted that 'it is hard to get these professionals to work for federal government, because they don't see federal executives as having any power. They have been more apt to work for state governments, because they view this as the center of power [for MCH care] policies and programs.' Dr. Hutchins disagreed somewhat with this perception, because he believes that federal execucrats do have the ability to positively change public policy.

Dr Hutchins's personal philosophy regarding how federal career execucrats can influence MCH care policies in this country revolves in part around risk-taking. He said that there is a philosophy that I believe in of not asking for permission to do something, but then being willing to have your hand slapped occasionally. And, if you are able to share the hand slap with friends and colleagues, you can avoid trouble.... Risk-taking, within certain parameters, of course, is key. Seasoned bureaucrats have a responsibility to teach the younger bureaucrats how to do these things. Part of the fun of working in government is to see how far you are willing and able to go, even though we're rarely rewarded for risk-taking behavior. But you must be willing to put your wrist out and get it slapped. This is crucial if you want to get things to work in the federal government.

As a manager, Dr Hutchins was also very willing to allow his staff to take risks. As one of his former Deputy Assistants (McPherson, 1993) noted,

Vince had a very flexible management style, where he encouraged us to take risks and this is important in our profession. It allowed us to be creative in finding ways to do things. And this was the bottom line for Vince. Getting the work done for mothers and children, regardless of what administration was in or what hierarchy was in place.

Vince Hutchins is a leader in the field of MCH care. Although he retired from government service in 1992, he continues to work toward improving MCH in the US. Currently, he is the Executive Director of the National Ready to Learn Council, a non-profit organization that focuses on issues of health, child care, parental care and neighbourhood concerns.

Steven Marica and the Small Business Administration (SBA)

Born in Utica, New York in 1948, Steve Marica spent most of his formative years in and around Washington, DC. His family moved to the nation's capital in the early 1950s, when his mother landed a job with the Department of Interior's geological survey unit, where she remained until her retirement in 1979. Despite his mother's career as a public servant, and growing up in the nation's hub of political activity, Marica had no particular aspirations to join the public service.

Upon graduation from high school in 1966, Marica enrolled in Virginia Tech College, where he majored in business management with the expectation of entering into a private sector career. Job prospects in private industry at the time of his graduation were not very high, so after a short stint as a clerk in a hardware store, Marica joined the federal government as an investigator for the US Civil Service Commission (CSC). His major responsibility was to investigate the backgrounds of persons being considered for jobs with the federal government.

After about six months at the CSC, Marica moved on to a more challenging job: investigator for the US Department of Treasury's Internal Revenue Service. He started out as a GS-7 in the Internal Security Division, which investigated IRS employees suspected of illegal activities and taxpayers who attempted to corrupt IRS employees through, for example, bribery or extortion. By January of 1986, Marica was ready for another career move; he applied and was hired for his current position, Assistant Inspector General (IG) for Investigations at the SBA. As Assistant IG for Investigations, Marica conducts administrative as well as criminal investigations into alleged wrongdoings of the people and businesses over which his agency has jurisdiction. This includes over 3,800 SBA employees as well as the quarter of a million or so individuals and small businesses with loans and contracts administered by the SBA. The total value of these loans and contracts is about $25 billion.

When Marica first arrived at the SBA, he completely revitalized the Investigations Division of the Office of Inspector General (OIG), changing the focus from administrative to criminal investigations. Prior to his arrival, the Division had focused primarily on administrative cases, such as abuses to time and attendance, travel reimbursements, and so forth. Marica took a variety of steps to improve the expertise, image, status and, hence, morale of the IG's investigators. In order for this to occur, Marica recognized that the IG's investigators would need the proper training, and so he saw to it that the investigators were trained at the Federal Law Enforcement Training Center at Glynco, Georgia, where most federal law enforcement officers receive training. In addition, Marica set up an annual in-house training programme for SBA investigators in order to further hone and improve their skills.

In line with the emphasis on criminal investigations, Marica initiated the use of the special deputation process, which allows special agents to execute arrests and to carry firearms under certain conditions. He believed that, although most of the crimes investigated by SBA special agents were classified as 'white-collar crimes', many of the cases were more efficiently conducted through the use of more 'traditional' methods such as surveillance, consensual electronic monitoring, undercover operations and search warrants.

Marica continued to stress professionalism. To this end, he created an investigators' handbook to ensure consistency of operations, established a Management Information System to allow for better oversight of cases, and requested and received authority to pay investigators administratively 'uncontrollable' overtime, whereby the agents would not need to secure approval in advance for overtime pay. He also identified a need for US Attorneys and SBA programme managers to have quicker access to management at the OIG's Investigations Division. In effect, Marica was instrumental in decentralizing the division for the purpose of enhancing responsiveness.

These and other efforts helped to create a sense of identity and pride within the division, and the agents responded by enthusiastically attempting to meet the established goals. Ultimately, as many point out (Hurd, 1992; Marchetta, 1992; Jones, 1993), productivity increased dramatically.

Marica's concern for equity did not stop here. He is a firm believer in equal employment opportunity and, as such, has been very successful in recruiting and hiring women and persons of colour into investigator positions. Consequently, there are more women and people of colour working as investigators in the SBA's OIG than ever before. He believes diversity has enriched and strengthened the agency.

Marica treats his staff as professionals and, hence, they act in a professional manner. This is the basis of Marica's management and leadership style, and it has paid off. Several have commented that Marica's style 'breeds a tremendous amount of loyalty. He makes it clear that if you perform for him, then he will do anything in his power to make your job as rewarding as possible' (Hurd, 1992). One of his investigators commented that

> Steve's workers naturally respect him and his abilities, and so they have the tendency to follow what he does and listen to him out of respect. They do things for him because they genuinely want to. He establishes a climate of trust and loyalty and so there is not a lot of foot dragging or low lives. (Marchetta, 1992)

Marica continues to move his office aggressively into criminal investigations. He has proven himself to be an experienced, accomplished criminal investigator, manager and leader in his field.

Edward Perkins, US Ambassador to South Africa

Edward Perkins was born on 8 June 1928 in the small Southern town of Sterlington, Louisiana. In large part because of the racist conditions in the South, Perkins' family moved to Portland, Oregon when he was just 12 years old. He would spend the next several years of his life in this north-western city, which proved to have a significant impact on his future career. It was here that certain opportunities became available to Perkins, chances that would not have existed for him in the South. In particular, while he was in high school, he developed an earnest interest in international affairs. He and a few of his friends would meet regularly after school and their part-time jobs at the local community centre to discuss world affairs. They became so enthusiastic about their informal discussions that they formed an international affairs club. Perkins was designated the programme chair and was responsible for bringing in a number of international relations' experts from the entire north-west region of the US to speak to the club and other interested members of the community.

Perkins' early interest in international affairs eventually led him to a career as a Foreign Service Officer (FSO) for the US State Department. He started at the bottom of the ladder, like most FSOs, working abroad in US embassies. Just before leaving for his first assignment in Bangkok, Thailand, he completed his undergraduate studies at the University of Maryland, where he earned, in 1967, a BA with a specialization in public policy. When he was restationed in the US in the early 1970s, he earned master's and doctoral degrees in Public Administration from the Washington, DC campus of the University of Southern California.

Perkins' work as an FSO began in East Asian affairs but later shifted to African affairs. This paved the way for his first ambassadorship. In 1985, President Reagan appointed Perkins Ambassador to the Republic of Liberia. It was a particularly challenging assignment to say the least because of the 1980 coup which overthrew the government. Perkins was so successful in just a short amount of time that in 1986 he was called upon by President Reagan to serve as Ambassador to South Africa.

This ambassadorship was also challenging because of the harsh resistance black South Africans had toward the US government at the time. In particular, Reagan's much-criticized 'constructive engagement' policy, which called for 'friendly,' behind-the-scenes negotiations rather than open criticism and punitive (e.g., economic) sanctions, did not endear US officials to blacks in South Africa. So Perkins was under very close scrutiny from the outset. Notwithstanding, Perkins ploughed ahead with several incisive, pragmatic strategies.

One was getting to know *everybody* in South Africa – whites, blacks and even the leaders of banned black groups – and to develop clear and open lines of communication with them. This was a significant milestone for US foreign policy in that no other US Ambassador before him was willing to work with the black community in South Africa. Because of his willingness to reach out and actually *listen* to them, black South Africans became very receptive and responsive to Perkins. Needless to say, this strategy was very unpopular with white South Africans.

In addition, Perkins lent his support to politically-charged events in South Africa. One such event was an ecumenical protest by black South African bishops against a newly issued law which barred demonstrations against the government for its practice of mass detentions without a trial. At the time, some 30,000 people – mostly blacks, including an estimated 10,000 children – had been detained without a trial. Perkins was one of only three foreign ambassadors to participate in the protest.

Perkins' participation in this as well as other demonstrations was galvanizing. In particular, it established his credibility with black South African leaders and the black press. Further, it sent a very clear message to the white-controlled government of South Africa: that a window was open for Americans to change the oppressive racial system through their ambassador; that Perkins would not, as ambassadors had done before him, 'lower his voice' in deference to white leaders, but rather would make it known that change was on the horizon and that he would be an active participant in bringing it about.

Ultimately, it was these and other strategies that helped chip away at South Africa's racist policies. Many have acknowledged Perkins' exceptional work in South Africa, commenting that his leadership, negotiation and communication skills helped promote positive internal changes in South Africa. Secretary Shultz (1993), summed it up in this concise fashion:

> Ed was very well qualified for post, [because] he understood the issues, the problems and the opportunities [in South Africa]. And he understood American foreign policy so he could express that well ... In the end, Ed made a difference in South Africa because he is a first-class professional.

Helene Gayle and the Centers for Disease Control and Prevention (CDC)

Born on 16 August 1955 in Buffalo, New York, Helene Doris Gayle is the third of five children. She was very much influenced and inspired by her hard-working parents, Jacob, a small business owner, and Marietta, a social worker. Reflecting on the values they instilled in her, Gayle has said that 'both of my parents felt strongly that, to make a contribution to the world around us is one of the greatest things you can do'. What a presage this would be for Gayle, who would eventually go on to impact the global war against one of the deadliest diseases of the twentieth century, AIDS.

Gayle began working on her medical degree at the University of Pennsylvania in the late 1970s. By the age of 25, she had earned both an MD from that university as well as a Masters of Public Health (MPH) from Johns Hopkins University. Her interest in public health had been sparked by a desire to be involved in the social as well as political aspects of medicine.

After graduation, Dr Gayle began a paediatric residency at the Children's Hospital National Medical Center in Washington, DC, where she developed skills and expertise in the different specialities within paediatric medicine. Three years later, Dr Gayle was selected to participate in the CDC's very prestigious two-year epidemiology training programme, the Epidemic Intelligence Service (EIS). This programme is an apprenticeship of sorts, in that the participants go through hands-on training in epidemiology.

Upon completion of her training in the EIS, Dr Gayle joined CDC's Division of HIV/AIDS. Her early work at CDC involved examining the risks of HIV transmission from mother to child, and among adolescents and college students. Dr Gayle's work eventually took on a more international focus, and she was promoted to Chief of International Activity within the Division of HIV/AIDS. In this capacity, she has been involved in epidemiological research in over 20 countries, including Zaire, Jamaica, South Africa, the Ivory Coast and Thailand. Most of Dr Gayle's efforts in the international AIDS arena have been centred around women and children.

Dr Gayle can be credited with several accomplishments around AIDS research and public policy; one, in particular, stands out. She has been very successful in bringing communities and community-based organizations served by the US federal government *vis-à-vis* AIDS more into the public policy process. She has been very instrumental in getting disparate groups, including minority, gay and church communities, involved so that they have a better understanding of what the government does around AIDS. This has also fostered the CDC's ability to better understand and ultimately serve the divergent needs and interests of these groups.

One of the reasons why Dr Gayle has been so successful at building bridges and fostering communications between the federal government and various communities is her expertise in interpersonal relations. Rashida Hassan (1994), Executive Director of a non-profit organization which provides services to African Americans on sexual health issues, explains it in this fashion:

> Helene has been very effective in establishing a dialogue with community-based groups in order to keep us involved in the policy process [around AIDS]. And she is so effective because first and foremost, she has a personal commitment to the issue areas which goes beyond her government job. . . . Also, she was not afraid to make it clear to the federal government that they were not getting just a Dr Helene Gayle, but they were getting a black female physician who was very dedicated to her work and the black community. We have been pleased to discover that the government has not neutralized her, that she still retains her African heritage and she has not relinquished this identity to the government bureaucracy. This has made a big difference to us and our clients, especially since there are very few women of color in government for us to talk to.

Another aspect of building bridges with community-based groups involves cultivating good relationships with the other critical policy players, in particular political appointees. Dr James Curran (1994), Associate Director of CDC for AIDS, has commented on this. He said that

> Helene has the unique capacity to get people to work together in part. . . . because she understands not only the scientific issues but she is also able to see other people's points of view; she is able to walk in their shoes and this is a very valuable asset. It is also important that she is not politically motivated. She is committed to the public's health and not any particular philosophy of government.

Dr Gayle has found her work in the area of AIDS very painful at times because of the human suffering that this deadly disease inevitably brings. But she has remained involved in AIDS because of her commitment to working with and helping those afflicted with it. Dr James Curran of the CDC summed up Dr Gayle's commitment to the battle against AIDS in this fashion. He said that 'the thing that men and women of all races and cultures should know about Helene is that she is an excellent example of a dedicated scientist and public servant. She truly enjoys working for the government and she has made enormous contributions to our efforts to fight AIDS' (Curran, 1994).

William Black and the Bank Board

Bill Black knew from an early age that he wanted to be a lawyer. When he was in middle school, he was required to prepare and give a speech on his career goals. In his speech, Black said that he wanted to go on to high school and become an expert debater and then go on to college to become a lawyer. Black had little idea as to what law was at the time because no one in his family had ever been a lawyer. What really inspired him was the career of the pre-eminent American lawyer, Clarence Darrow. Darrow became an important role model for Black because of his uncompromising commitment to justice and fairness.

Black did eventually become a lawyer. Along the way, just as he had planned, Black acquired excellent debating skills not only in high school but in college as well. These skills proved to be critical later in his career, especially in his efforts to combat the savings and loan (S&L) crisis. Black also picked up a BA in economics along the way. His formal training in economics would also prove to be an invaluable asset in his efforts to restore order to the ravaged S&L industry.

Black's first involvement with the S&L industry was as a lawyer for Squire, Sanders & Dempsey, a large commercial law firm in Washington, DC. This law firm performed contract work for the Federal Home Loan Bank Board (the Bank Board), which, up until 1989, was the federal agency responsible for regulating S&Ls. In 1983, Black was assigned to a crucial S&L case, and his handling of the case led to an important victory for the Bank Board. In fact, it was precedent-setting. The Bank Board was so impressed by Black's victory that it offered him a position as head of litigation. In April of 1984, Black accepted the position, and it was in this and other capacities that Black would aggressively attack the mismanagement and corruption pervading the S&L industry.

One of the first steps that Black, along with Ed Gray, Reagan's appointee to head the Bank Board, took was to *re*-regulate the thrift industry. Black played a critical role here because of his expertise in law, accounting and economics. Specifically, Black was relied upon to write and enforce a new rule which would restrict direct investment powers of S&Ls. It was Gray's predecessor, Richard Pratt, who in the early 1980s removed various restrictions over what S&Ls could invest in. Pratt's move enabled S&Ls to invest in risky, fraudulent ventures.

Black and Gray faced an incredible amount of resistance here, not only from the thrift owners, but also from the Reagan Administration, which was averse to *any* type of re-regulatory endeavour. In addition, Charles Keating, Jr, owner of Irving, California's Lincoln S&L, cashed in some chips with Congress by persuading enough members of the House of Representatives to sign a resolution asking the Bank Board to delay implementation of the new direct investment rule. Gray and Black, however, refused to back off and began enforcing the new rule.

As the Bank Board began closing or taking over failed S&Ls, angry thrift operators turned up the heat on Congress to stop Black and Gray. The House Speaker at the time, Rep. Jim Wright (D.-Tex.) was particularly sympathetic to these pleas, since Texas S&Ls – where some of the most egregious forms of abuse and fraud were being committed – were the target of the Bank Board's crackdown. Wright turned out to be a major obstacle to Black, doing anything he could to stop him. He even prevented Black from testifying before Congress on the condition facing the S&L industry in Texas. This turned out to be a big mistake for Wright. Black went to the media and 'blew the whistle' on him. This was an effective strategy for Black, and it ultimately led to an investigation into Wright's improprieties around Texas S&Ls. On 31 May 1989, Wright resigned from Congress.

Keating's S&L was next on Black's list. Lincoln's S&Ls were snowballing, and in fact its collapse would ultimately cost the American taxpayers over $2.5 billion. But Keating, painfully aware of what Black did in Texas, did everything he could to keep his failing S&L open. One of Keating's major tactics was to muscle five US senators to intervene on his behalf. The senators, who came to be known as 'the Keating Five', had all received generous political contributions from Keating (DeConcini, D.-Ariz., $55,000; Riegle, D.-Mich., $76,000; McCain, R.-Ariz., $112,000; Glenn, D.-Ohio., $200,000, and Cranson, D.-Calif., $889,000).

Black blew the whistle on the Keating Five. In fact, Black's courage and willingness to stand up to Keating and the five senators was a watershed in the S&L scandal. An investigation was subsequently triggered into the Keating Five, and the federal home loan banking system was also reorganized. Black made a lot of enemies as a result of his efforts, but he was also responsible for containing Americans' tab in bailing out the failed S&L industry. Ed Gray (1994) summed it up rather well when he said: 'Bill Black deserves to be called a patriot in that he is a person who strongly cares about the public's well-being. Real patriotism is when you put the public interest ahead of your own. And this is exactly what Bill did.'

Administrative Leaders: Exemplars of Excellence

The six execucrats profiled in this study have demonstrated themselves as effective leaders and managers in government. But what exactly are some of the characteristics of effective leadership that they possess? Denhardt's (1993) framework described earlier is a useful vehicle for analysing the execucrats' effective leadership behaviours. His framework offers five attributes of effective leadership:

1 commitment to values;
2 serving the public;
3 empowerment and shared leadership;
4 pragmatic incrementalism, and
5 dedication to public service.

Table 2.1 provides an appliqué of Denhardt's framework to the six federal execucrats examined in this study. As we can see, there are some commonalities between and among the execucrats. But each, in his or her own unique way, exhibits the five qualities of effective leadership. For example, each execucrat demonstrated a strong *commitment to values*, as seen by their unyielding commitment to, and clear vision for the mission and goals of their agencies. Moreover, each was unwilling to compromise their values around achieving the goals of their agencies for the sake of personal, material or political gain. Ambassador Perkins, for instance, was absolutely unflappable and would not be deterred by the white-controlled, pro-apartheid government in his efforts to change the internal racial policies of South Africa. Likewise, Bill Black challenged the third most powerful person in the US – House Speaker, Jim Wright – in pursuit of his agency's goal of ending and cleaning up the corruption that ravaged the S&L industry.

In addition, each execucrat was resolute in their commitment to *serving the public*. This was *the* primary consideration in their work. For example, Claussen fully understands the realities of the effects of the depleting ozone on the health and well-being of not just Americans but of all people. Skin cancer (sometimes resulting in death) and eye cataract cases (sometimes resulting in blindness) are on the rise world-wide due to the depleting ozone layer. Well aware of the hazards associated with ozone depletion, Claussen was relentless in her efforts to cut through the political posturing by the Reagan Administration, which sought the counter-goal of protecting big business from CBC regulations.

The six execucrats profiled in this study also understood the importance of *shared leadership and empowerment*. Steve Marica, for example, empowered his staff, professionally, psychologically and bodily, to become the best criminal investigators. His agents, as a result, remain

Table 2.1 Denhardt's attributes of effective administrative leadership as they apply to six federal execucrats

Execucrat	Commitment to Values	Serving the Public	Empowerment & Shared Leadership	Pragmatic Incrementalism	Dedication to Public Service
Eileen Claussen	Clear vision for agency; strong values for clean environment; professional integrity; strong sense of ethics.	Everyone benefits from clean environment; protect public from disingenuous plans (e.g. 'Rayban Plan'); non-partisan.	Shared power; teamwork in negotiations.	Good working relationship with Congress, business groups and environmental groups; forges ties with political appointees; different strategies for different groups.	Has worked entire career as a public servant.
Vince Hutchins	High degree of professionalism; clear vision around MCH care; committed first and foremost to promoting health of mothers and children; high degree of ethics and morality.	Public health is a priority; protects interests of mothers and babies; does not play partisan politics.	Empowers staff, mentoring, coaching; takes risks and encourages staff to take risks.	Pragmatic, hands-on approach to MCH care; knowledgeable of political networks affecting MCH care; good working relationship with Congress and MCH care constituency.	Most of his career working for mothers and children.
Steven Marica	Strong clear vision of OIG's responsibilities; ethical; strong sense of professionalism and integrity.	Strong commitment to rooting out corruption and protecting public.	Empowers staff as criminal investigators; instils sense of loyalty, professionalism and high morale in staff.	Small steps taken towards revitalizing Investigations Division of OIG.	Has worked entire career as a public servant.

Edward Perkins	Emphasis on professionalism; goal oriented; sound insight into international relations.	Promotion of change in South Africa; keeping Americans informed.	Instils sense of professionalism; takes risks.	Series of small steps taken to promote change in South Africa.	Has worked entire career as a public servant; formal education in public administration.
Helene Gayle	Clear vision around steps to take in combating AIDS; strong commitment to preventing spread of AIDS among women and children.	From early childhood has held a value in promoting public health.	Works with and in teams; empowers community groups to help in battle against AIDS.	Building bridges incrementally to ensure public and community group participation in fighting the spread of AIDS.	Entire career has been in government.
William Black	Strong sense of morality; values revolve around restoring control to failed S&L industry; clear vision for Bank Board.	Challenged powerful political establishment to minimize America's tab in bailing out failed S&L industry; strong sense of patriotism.	Risk-taker; worked closely with small teams.	Incremental gains around cleaning up S&L industry.	Recognizes important role of government in serving justice to American people.

loyal not to him personally, but to him as the embodiment of the agency's goal to root out corruption in American business.

Hutchins also empowered his staff to promote MCH care and provided the necessary mentoring and coaching for them to be exemplars in the MCH care field. Hutchins also took risks and encouraged his staff to take risks; this is an essential characteristic of effective leadership in that it promotes innovation and creativity. Hutchins was quite remarkable in this sense, because risk-taking rarely occurs in the public sector – the rewards are virtually non-existent, while the punishments for making mistakes can sometimes be quite high.

Dr Gayle was also extremely effective in her empowerment strategies. She was successful in empowering church-based and minority communities to not only better understand the government's involvement in AIDS prevention, but to also get these groups more directly involved in the battle against AIDS.

In working to meet the goals or their agencies, no execucrat had a single, definitive strategy. Rather, each took a series of small, pragmatic steps which led to incremental gains. (According to Denhardt's taxonomy, this attribute is *pragmatic incrementalism*.) For example, Bill Black began with efforts to re-regulate the failed S&L industry. Next, he targeted S&Ls in the state of Texas, where some of the most egregious crimes were being committed. Black then blew the whistle on House Speaker Wright, who aggressively sought to deter his efforts. Next, Black targeted Keating's S&L; when Keating and five US senators decided to play hardball with Black and the Bank Board, Black blew the whistle on them.

Similarly, Marica moved forward to change the nature and duties of the OIG's Investigation Division by taking small, successive steps. First he worked on the image and morale problems of the IG's investigators. Next, he ensured the investigators would receive the proper training in criminal investigations. He also redesigned the special agents' credentials in order to distinguish them from the generic identification cards, which were previously furnished to *all* personnel of the OIG.

Finally, each of the six execucrats profiled here showed an unwavering *dedication to public service*. In fact, each could have opted for higher-paying careers in the private sector, but instead, they chose government in order to serve the broader public good. Drs Gayle and Hutchins, for example, are highly trained, competent physicians who could earn enormously higher salaries in private practice. But rather, they chose the public service. Dr Gayle, carrying a message instilled in her by her parents at an early age, works hard to 'make a contribution to the world around us'.

Administrative Leaders Making a Difference

The biographical profiles of six federal execucrats provide an in-depth look at the actual behaviours of, and strategies employed by, effective administrative leaders. Denhardt's framework facilitated this examination. Although broad inferences cannot be made from the six execucrats profiled here, insight is gained into some of the factors and attributes that contribute to effective administrative leadership in government. Moreover, this study suggests that effective governmental leaders can positively affect the quality of life not just for Americans, but for people in every part of the world. Future studies of execucrats via comparative biography are encouraged, in that they can lead to further insight into the actual leadership behaviours of administrative officials.

References

Barnard, Chester I. (1938) *The Functions of the Executive* (Cambridge, Mass.: Harvard University Press).

Bryson, John M. and Barbara C. Crosby (1992) *Leadership for the Common Good: Tackling Public Problems in a Shared-Power World* (San Francisco: Jossey-Bass, Inc.).

Cayer, N. Joseph (1989) 'Qualities of Successful Program Managers'. In Robert E. Cleary and Nicholas Henry (eds), *Managing Public Programs* (San Francisco: Jossey-Bass).

Cooper, Terry L. and N. Dale Wright (eds) (1992) *Exemplary Public Administrators* (San Francisco: Jossey Bass).

Curran, Dr. James. Personal interview, 8 Feb. 1994.

Denhardt, Robert B. (1993) *The Pursuit of Significance: Strategies for Managerial Success in Public Organizations* (Belmont, Calif.: Wadsworth Publishing).

Doig, Jameson W. and Erwin C. Hargrove (eds) (1987) *Leadership and Innovation: a Biographical Perspective on Entrepreneurs in Government* (Baltimore: Johns Hopkins University Press).

Doniger, David. Personal interview, 22 July 1992.

Faerman, Sue R., Robert E. Quinn, Michael P. Thompson and Michael R. McGrath (1990) *A Framework for Excellence* (Albany, NY: Governor's Office of Employee Relations).

Fay, Kevin. Personal interview, 24 July 1992.

Gortner, Harold F., Julianne Mahler and Jeanne Bell Nicholson (1987) *Organization Theory: a Public Perspective* (Chicago: the Dorsey Press).

Grad, Dr Rae K. Personal interview, 24 Sep. 1992.

Gray, Ed. Personal interview, 10 March 1993.

Hargrove, Erwin C. and John C. Glidewell (eds) (1990) *Impossible Jobs in Public Management* (Lawrence, Kan.: University Press of Kansas).

Hassan, Rashida. Personal interview, 23 Feb. 1994.

Hughes, Dr Mary. Personal interview, 9 June 1993.

Hurd, Dave. Personal interview, 21 Sept. 1992.

Jones, Debbie (SBA's Special Agent in Charge, Los Angeles, California). Personal interview, 1 July 1993.

Katz, Ruth. Personal interview, 19 April 1993.

Koop, Dr C. Everett. Personal interview, 22 April 1993.

Lewis, Eugene. (1980) *Public Entrepreneurship* (Bloomington, Ind.: Indiana University Press).

Lynn, Laurence E., Jr (1987) *Managing Public Policy* (Boston: Little, Brown and Company).

Lynn, Laurence E., Jr (1984) 'The Reagan Administration and the Penitent Bureaucracy'. In Lester M. Salamon and Michael S. Lund (eds), *The Reagan Presidency and the Governing of America* (Washington, DC: the Urban Institute Press).

Marchetta, Steven (former Special Agent, SBA). Personal interview, 22 Sept. 1992.

McPherson, Dr Merle. Personal interview, 10 June 1993.

Riccucci, Norma M. (1995) *Unsung Heroes: Federal Execucrats Making a Difference* (Washington, DC: Georgetown University Press).

Shultz, Secretary George P. Personal interview, 24 Nov. 1993.

Weiss, Marina. Personal interview, 20 April 1993.

Will, Madeleine. Personal interview, 22 April 1993.

3

Three Giants of the Inter-war British Higher Civil Service: Sir Maurice Hankey, Sir Warren Fisher and Sir Horace Wilson

Geoffrey K. Fry

'The anonymity of the Civil Service may or may not be a valuable convention of the Constitution; it is one that the historian of modern Britain accepts at his peril.' So wrote Max Beloff (1975, p. 227), who was of the belief that the inter-war period was 'the one in which the Higher Civil Service in Britain probably reached the height of its corporate influence' (p. 210). Administrative historians may well need all the encouragement that they can get, especially from such a distinguished source, in their often demanding pursuit of scholarly tasks, but surely few relatively modern interpretations of inter-war British politics fail to mention, for instance, Sir Maurice Hankey, Sir Warren Fisher, Sir Horace Wilson, Sir John Anderson, Thomas Jones and Sir Robert Vansittart. Even the erratic A. J. P. Taylor did so in his famous textbook, *English History 1914–1945*, written many years ago. One is spoilt for choice in writing about the giants of the inter-war Higher Civil Service, and in selecting Hankey, Fisher and Wilson for special attention one does so on the basis that they were at the top of the British machinery of central administration for either all or almost all of the inter-war years.

Sir Maurice Hankey: Secretary of the Cabinet

Of Sir Maurice Hankey (1877–1963), Stephen Roskill wrote from personal experience that a major problem faced by Hankey's biographer was 'the sheer quantity of material left behind by him. Indeed one may doubt whether any person, with the possible exception of Sir Winston Churchill, has bequeathed to posterity such a vast accumulation of minutes, memoranda, letters and publications. They must in all amount to many millions of words. Furthermore, no one, except once again Churchill, was so near to the centre of national and international politics over so long a period' (Roskill, 1970, p. 26). Hankey kept a diary comprising 'four large leather bound volumes, fitted with strong locks'. He began to keep it in 1915 and 'up to 1923 he kept it with regularity'. On the suggestion of Ramsay MacDonald, when he first became Prime Minister in 1924, Hankey resumed keeping a diary, and the last entry was dated 31 August 1942 (Roskill, 1970, p. 24). In addition, once Hankey's eldest son entered the Foreign Service in 1927, he began to write him long letters about current affairs and his own work. These letters filled 'many gaps in the final volume of the diary' (Roskill, 1970, p. 26). It may be that one detects in Roskill's observations even a touch of resentment at the scale of work involved. Whether this perception was justified or not, Roskill prevailed, producing a three-volume study characterized by scholarly excellence.

The future Lord Hankey was educated at Rugby and then the Royal Naval College at Greenwich. Of Hankey, Roskill wrote:

> After serving in the Royal Marine Artillery at sea and in the Admiralty's Department of Naval Intelligence he became Naval Assistant Secretary to the Committee of Imperial Defence early in 1908. Four years later he was appointed Secretary to that body, and after the outbreak of war in 1914, when the C.I.D. was placed in a state of suspense, he became successively Secretary of the War Council, the Dardanelles Committee, and the War Committee, which were in turn the supreme British authority for the direction of the war under Asquith's Ministries. When in December 1916 Lloyd George formed the War Cabinet he appointed Hankey as its Secretary and he served the War Cabinet and the Imperial War Cabinet in that capacity until, in October 1919, the former was dissolved – after having held 650 meetings. Hankey then continued as Secretary of peacetime Cabinets under Lloyd George, Bonar Law, Baldwin, Ramsay MacDonald and Neville Chamberlain. In addition, he once again acted as Secretary of the Committee of Imperial Defence from June 1920 when its first post war meeting took place. Furthermore in June 1923 he undertook the additional responsibility of Clerk of the Privy Council, and continued to hold all three appointments until he retired at the end of July 1938. (Roskill, 1970, p. 17)

Asquith described Hankey in a letter to him in November 1918 as having been in a true sense what Lazare Nicholas Carnot was called, 'the organizer of victory' in the First World War (Roskill 1970, p. 632). Lloyd George endorsed this verdict when commending Hankey's services to the House of Commons in 1919: '[Hankey] was the first to recognize before this War that if a great war ever came it would be a matter not merely of fighting men, but for the organization of the whole sources of a country, and he it was who initiated, organized, and inspired that war book that is one of the most remarkable productions any man could peruse. Going through it now, one can see how he forecast things which were perhaps not visible except to very searching minds like his at the time, and which have become part of the horrible realities of war' (Hansard, 6.8.1919, col. 419) In his diary, Hankey gloated about 'my overwhelming triumph'. He wrote: 'I initiated and forced through all our preparations for war . . . half the structure of our innumerable War Depts. has arisen out of my conception; and my creation; . . . I have been the confidant and consultant first of one great war Prime Minister and then of another; . . . I have steered the great ship of state round one dangerous headland after another into a port of security.' Thus, Hankey felt able to claim that the war machine of the British government was as much his creation as the German machine was that of Helmuth von Moltke or Albrecht von Roon (Roskill, 1970, p. 630). Hankey's high estimate of himself was certainly shared by A. J. Sylvester, his Private Secretary for many years, who later wrote that 'in my judgement he was the finest civil servant who ever functioned in Whitehall. He was solely dedicated to his work, which he performed with machine like efficiency and integrity. He had a most amazing memory, never spared himself and did not spare others. In his work he was ruthless, had very little consideration; little if any humour, and little or no sentimentalism in his nature . . . He was very abstemious, hated the limelight, avoided most kinds of social engagements and distractions, and disliked the Press. He was a very happy family man, and very simple in all his tastes . . . I really grew up with him. I was with him from 1914 till 1921, through the fateful years of the First World War, including the Allied Conferences at home and abroad, the Peace Conference, and the aftermath – including the Great Strike of 1919 . . . Then for the first time in the history of this country records were kept of the proceedings of the Cabinet, made by Hankey' (Roskill, 1970 pp. 632–3).

'Hankey's greatest achievement was the creation of the Cabinet Secretariat which first came into existence in 1916,' Sir George Mallaby

later wrote. Previously 'the only official record of Cabinet proceedings
...was the Prime Minister's letter to the Sovereign. Responsibility for
executing decisions lay with individual Ministers in the Cabinet: the
danger of confusion and negligence was considerable. With the onset
of war in 1914 the consequences of misunderstandings could well
have been disastrous. Hankey saw clearly the need for some effective
articulating machinery and to him must go the chief credit for the
formation of the Cabinet Secretariat. He laid down the principles
which have continued to guide its performance... [It] has remained
right at the centre of power and inevitably the Secretary of the Cabinet
has more direct contact with the Prime Minister than any other official
could hope to have' (Mallaby, 1981, pp. 485–6). None the less, in the
period between October and December 1922, it had taken all of Hankey's skill to keep the Cabinet Office and his own role in being. 'I have
been fighting all day with my back to the wall for my position,' Hankey confided to his diary for 25 October 1922, 'I am up against the
whole hierarchy of the Civil Service, who have taken advantage of
Lloyd George's fall to try and down me. Luckily their representative
was [Sir] Warren Fisher, a personal friend and gentleman.' Andrew
Bonar Law, as the incoming Conservative Prime Minister, committed
himself to bringing the Cabinet Secretariat 'in its present form to an
end'. There was Press coverage to the effect that 'Sir Maurice Hankey's
share in the direction of the country has been distinctly unconstitutional' in the words of *The Daily Mail* for 28 October 1922, while *The
Times*, the day before, had described the Cabinet Secretariat as 'a Prime
Ministerial Department for the conduct of important international
affairs apart from, or even in subversion of, well tried constitutional
practices and safeguards.' So, Sir Eyre Crowe and the Foreign Office felt
threatened, and Sir Warren Fisher, whom Hankey misjudged, turned
out to have been planning for some time to absorb the Cabinet Secretariat into the Treasury and, thus, to make Hankey an official there.
Bonar Law was looking for symbolic economies in public expenditure,
and wished all along 'to continue the system of recording Cabinet conclusions, which he thought essential to businesslike procedure'. Hankey provided an economy plan at the outset of the controversy, and
the Cabinet Secretariat survived as an independent entity, though
in a slimmed down form, and Hankey survived too (Roskill, 1972,
pp. 304–29).

'Hankey's mind was capacious, his memory large and exact, his per-
sistence relentless, and his tenacity invincible: characteristics of many
public servants,' Sir George Mallaby observed.

But Hankey had supplementary qualities which brought him into the ranks of the really great administrators. He had more than the usual allotment of tact with those volatile politicians who were his daily masters. He served with equal success men as widely dissimilar in temperament as Asquith, Lloyd George, Bonar Law, Baldwin, Ramsay MacDonald, and Neville Chamberlain. If he did not like all of them to an equal degree, they all trusted his integrity and used him to sort out some of the rough animosities which constantly arise between ambitious men. They relied also upon his prodigious memory and his extraordinary application to the problems which confronted them. On questions of defence in particular his opinion and advice were constantly sought, and he had no hesitation about responding. (Mallaby, 1981, p. 485)

Hankey recognized 'as early as 1932 that the time had come when there was no alternative to rearmament' (Roskill, 1974, pp. 660–1) and advised accordingly. In the 1930s, down to his retirement in 1938, Hankey's workload was very heavy, and it apparently amused him that he would be succeeded by three men, although he was unenthusiastic about Sir Edward Bridges, a Treasury official; and, hence, the preferred choice of Sir Warren Fisher, replacing him as Secretary of the Cabinet (Roskill, 1974, pp. 352–8). For his part, Bridges believed that, by the mid-1930s, Hankey had become too self-important, and he was to boast about having rationalized Hankey's administrative arrangements. In retrospect, Hankey himself felt that he had been in his various posts for too long (Roskill, 1974, p. 366) After being given a peerage in1939, he joined Neville Chamberlain's War Cabinet as Minister without Portfolio, and once Churchill became Prime Minister, Hankey was made Chancellor of the Duchy of Lancaster and then Paymaster General before being dismissed in 1942. Though Hankey did not devote the remainder of his time to writing up his experiences, he did produce several publications (e.g. Hankey, 1945; 1946; 1961; 1963) which were less rewarding to read than might have been expected, ironically at least partly as the result of the constraints imposed upon Hankey by the all-embracing interpretation of the scope of the Official Secrets legislation that, when Secretary of the Cabinet, he had himself pioneered (Naylor, 1984).

Sir Warren Fisher: Head of the Civil Service

To describe Sir Norman Fenwick Warren Fisher (1879–1948) as a 'distinctly controversial figure', as one of his successors as Permanent

Secretary to the Treasury and Head of the Civil Service, Lord Bridges, later did (Bridges, 1964, p. 169) was to put the matter mildly. 'I have no doubt that a great deal of the ferment and disputation arose out of Fisher's ways and his habit of talking in an unguarded way about what he regarded as the demerits of those – quite a large number – whom he held in no high repute', Bridges observed, adding that '[Fisher] did more than any other man in the last fifty years to give cohesion to the Civil Service and to help to turn the Treasury into a proper instrument to be the central department of the British Civil Service' (Bridges, 1964, p. 175). The present writer lost track of the number of times that he was told that he had effectively settled the controversy over Fisher in a long footnote in his book, *Statesmen in Disguise*, published in 1969 (Fry, 1969, pp. 52–4) and by the analysis of Fisher's contribution to the development of the Higher Civil Service contained elsewhere in that book. The research done, though, and some further investigations, suggested that there was scope for a biography of Fisher, and, twenty years later, another scholar, Eunan O'Halpin produced such a biography, primarily based on private papers as well as Public Record Office documents, and one that was impressive (O'Halpin, 1989).

Fisher, born into a family with independent means, was educated at Winchester and at Oxford where he obtained a Second Class Honours degree in Greats, before being successful in the Administrative Class examination and being appointed to the Board of Inland Revenue in 1903. According to Sir Horace Hamilton, Fisher soon attracted the attention of Sir Robert Chalmers, who had become Chairman there in 1907, and, after two years as Chalmers' Private Secretary, was assigned to prepare for the introduction of super tax, in which work he displayed drive and organizational ability. This led to him being noticed by Lloyd George who, according to Fisher, was partly responsible for him being seconded in May 1912 to the National Health Insurance Commission for England, when once more, Fisher was said to have shown his capacity to strengthen and develop a new organization. In May 1913, he returned to Somerset House as a Commissioner of Inland Revenue, becoming Deputy Chairman of the Board in October 1914, and Chairman in August 1918 (Hamilton, 1959, pp. 252–3). Sir Edward Playfair, who began his career there, was clear that Fisher's 'shortish but vital' period at the Inland Revenue was important. According to contemporaries, Fisher had 'completely changed the spirit of the place. Before he came, all Inspectors regarded taxpayers as natural enemies. He changed all that, and introduced the concept that it was their duty always to help the taxpayer. There was a short piece written by him to that effect which was the first paragraph of all manuals of instructions. He also, by a typically clever trick, won the heart of the Inspectors by having them made HM Inspectors...It was a brilliant piece of work by a brilliant young man' (letter to author: 13.7.69). On 1 October 1919, Fisher went to the Treasury as Permanent Secretary, a post which he held for exactly twenty years. Sir Horace Hamilton observed:

> By the time that he reached the Treasury in 1919 [Fisher] had had the experience of administering one of the largest and most important departments of State under war conditions and had already shown a striking capacity for improvising staff arrangements to meet new and urgent requirements. It was also of value that Fisher had become accustomed to deal personally with members of the various classes of...the Inland Revenue staff and he had become acquainted with representatives of the Civil Service staff as a whole by his membership of the [Ramsay Committee] which evolved the Whitley scheme for the Civil Service. Moreover, his membership of the [Bradbury] Committee on Staffs had presented him with an exceptionally favourable chance to view the Service as a whole and in detail and he was able to assist in formulating recommendations which have proved of lasting value in the sphere of Establishment questions. Fisher came therefore to the Treasury well equipped to face the postwar problems of that department. (Hamilton, 1951, p. 9)

'In any gathering [Fisher] was the most remarkable creature there', Sir Thomas Padmore recalled. Fisher had 'a striking appearance, a considerable presence'. He was 'larger than life'. Sir Thomas and also his wife, who had similarly worked with Fisher, believed that 'nobody was ever indifferent to Fisher. He had, and inspired, strong views.' Fisher was 'a powerful figure, an intense personality. His personal popularity was as high as it could be. Fisher was liked by almost everybody and adored by large numbers of people. Fisher was particularly kind to the younger officials. He had no sense of rank, no stuffiness. He was madly informal. Everybody called him Warren. Fisher had enormous charm. He had time for everybody. He never made you feel that he was too big for you.' Sir Thomas Padmore added that 'Fisher's flamboyant personality came out in his behaviour before Royal Commissions and the like. He was aggressive and forthright...Fisher's evidence might sound more forthright than it was. Fisher had great charm in his way of putting things.' The Padmores believed that Fisher's 'immense charm' meant that he was 'loved throughout the Service' (interview: 25.11.69). This would surely be true of nobody, and just to cite one example within the Home Civil Service, Sir Philip Allen, later a Permanent Secretary, was no admirer of Fisher, whom he saw as having his favourites (interview: 17.10.88), and, to put the matter mildly, Fisher had plenty of critics in the Foreign Office. One diplomat who was a friend, Sir Owen O'Malley, also believed that Fisher 'tended to dominate any gathering,' possessing 'great adroitness in presenting a case'. He found him to be 'a charming companion', but Lady O'Malley (Ann Bridge) recalled being irritated by Fisher's sentimentality. Sir Owen added that 'Fisher was not a quarreller. He wove a web of charming "love and trust". Fisher was a little too clever in thinking himself a judge of character'. Fisher himself was 'an elusive character: a heavyweight phantom, of tremendous self confidence somehow mixed with diffidence. Fisher was absorbed by and eaten up with his profession. He had immense intelligence, streets ahead of even [Sir Richard] Hopkins as regards brain power in the practical sense. Fisher had a lion-like courage. He was not afraid of Cabinet Ministers, lectured them and told them what they could and could not do' (Interview: 9.4.70).

Sir Thomas Padmore said that 'the job was everything to Fisher' who 'worked very long hours (10–8: c.f. Sir John Anderson 9.30–6)', his outside interests being limited to reading and to music (interview: 25.11.69). With his marriage a shell, Fisher, always controversial, attracted rumours about his private life, some of which suggested that he was homosexual, which his bigrapher dismissed as unfounded and in some contrast with Fisher's reputation in the Civil Service as a womanizer, which he also believed to be undeserved (O'Halpin, 1989, p. 12). Sir Owen O'Malley observed that 'Fisher was fond of women, but not excessively so'. He was not 'bed ridden' (interview: 9.4.70). One notes that in a letter dated 14 September 1939, which is in my possession, the Chairman of the Council of Women Civil Servants wrote to Fisher on his retirement, reminding him that 'you once described yourself . . . as a feminist' and thanking him for the interest that he had taken in advancing the career interests of women in the Civil Service.

When Sir Warren Fisher became Permanent Secretary to the Treasury in October 1919 he inherited a recently revised structure which divided it up into what were in effect three different departments – Finance, Establishments, and Supply Services – each headed by a Controller with a status equivalent to a Permanent Secretary elsewhere. Fisher's position, which involved 'the general supervision and coordination of the work of the Treasury as a whole', he found to be 'deliciously vague, floating somewhere rather Olympian'. Fisher did his best to work the scheme, but 'it was an extremely unwieldy and top hampered and unsatisfactory arrangement.' The scheme was modified in 1927 when the Finance and Supply departments were merged, but otherwise Fisher worked under the 1919 scheme until 1932, when the Treasury reverted to a divisional form of organization with a Permanent Secretary, a Second Secretary, and three Under Secretaries in charge of the divisions (Hamilton, 1951, pp. 10–12). Sir John Winnifrith recalled that

> in charge of each of these divisions he put a man of the highest cal-ibre. In my time [they were] Sir Frederick Phillips – Finance, Sir Alan Barlow – Supply, and Sir James Rae – Establishments. Co-ordinating all three divisions was the Second Secretary – Sir Richard Hopkins. Fisher himself rarely intervened in Finance and left this almost entirely in the hands of Hopkins and Phillips. I think he would have admitted that he really didn't understand the problems except inso-far as they involved high policy where he could contribute on the broad issues. Much the same was true of Establishment work. Inevit-ably he took the keenest interest in advising the Prime Minister and Ministers in charge of departments about the making of senior appointments. He also interested himself in the major policy issues in regard to conditions of service in the Civil Service, particularly pay. An interesting sidelight was his close and friendly relationship with W. J. Brown, the strong leader of the Civil Service, Clerical Asso-ciation and the most powerful figure on the Staff Side of the National Whitley Council.

Sir John Winnifrith wrote that 'of the advice given to the Chancellor of the Exchequer on day to day business' there tended to be 'little writ-ten comment by Fisher ... That [did] not mean that Fisher had played no part in the formulation of some of this advice either by himself taking the initiative in discussing the matter with senior colleagues or as a result of their seeking his advice. He was, in fact, far better with the spoken than with the written word. When occasionally he composed a memorandum to the Chancellor it was often disappointing, far too long and with far too little substance.' Sir John thought that 'in the Treasury generally at this time his reputation was that of a good man to work for and with; in particular his willingness to delegate made for good relations with his colleagues. My own impressions may be coloured by the fact that he was particularly charming to the juniors who, as Private Secretaries, had to take his instructions on the business of Treasury Ministers. He was always anxious to find out your own views and had something of a mission in seeking to train them in what he regarded as the right attitude to the duties of a civil servant' (letter to author, 27.1.70). Fisher had eventually introduced an arrangement whereby the Treasury did not recruit directly from the Administrative Class examination. Fisher's idea was to use the Treasury as 'a sort of clearing house, or general staff' (Hamilton, 1951, pp. 12–13). Sir Thomas Padmore recalled how he and Edward Playfair were picked out from the Inland Revenue: 'P. J. Grigg, then Chairman of the Inland Revenue, told Fisher and Jimmy Rae that Padmore and Playfair were promising, and they were sent along to be interviewed by Rae and Bridges with a view to one of them being transferred. Rae told Fisher that the Treasury should have both, and so they did. Padmore had his doubts, but Grigg told him to get in and he would go up the promotion ladder' (interview: 26.11.69). The arbitrary nature of such arrangements scarcely needs emphasizing, and, for all Fisher's rationalization of Civil Service practice in, for instance, making the Permanent Secretary the Accounting Officer in departments (Hamilton, 1951, pp. 18–22), Fisher's behaviour all too often invited criticism, most obviously in his role as Head of the Civil Service.

'There were Heads of the Navy, Army, Air Force. Why not of the Civil Service?' That was how Sir Horace Wilson saw this particular controversy in later life. He thought Lord Bridges' appraisal of the manner in which Fisher conducted himself as Head of the Civil Service to be 'nonsense', observing:

It is true that he distinguished very clearly between the Heads of Departments and other senior officials as to their records and merits or demerits and once he had made up his mind he tended to act upon it, as and when opportunity offered. He was determined (and here he seemed to be like a crusader) to form a *Civil Service*, as distinct from a group of separate departments, and as part of this objective he insisted on the doctrine that each Minister was entitled to the best help that could be given him even though this involved – as it often did – making appointments of senior officials from outside the department where the vacancy occurred. As part of this, he consulted Heads of departments from time to time about their up and coming staff, and about their knowledge of those in other departments with whom they came into contact. Thus, it was not the case of his individual judgement but a considered opinion. (letter to author: 25.1.70)

Sir John Winnifrith stated that:

> I have no doubt that, in his own mind, he was clear that his task [as
> Head of the Civil Service] was to ensure an effective machine serving
> the Government of the day with fidelity, impartiality and efficiency
> and he persuaded himself that all the appointments he recommended
> to the Prime Minister of Permanent and Deputy Secretaries, Finance
> and Establishment Officers, were made with this object in view. One
> criticism which one often heard was that he was too much influ-
> enced by a comparatively narrow circle of senior colleagues. Another
> criticism was that he liked to see the familiar faces of his best known
> colleagues appearing in new settings as Permanent Secretary in dif-
> ferent departments. All this, I suppose, boils down to an allegation
> that he liked to have in the most important positions those whom
> he thought would best carry out his policy of ensuring a Civil Service
> of the sort described above. I think Lord Bridges's criticism was justi-
> fied in Fisher's last years of office ... Those who raised the criticisms
> I have mentioned distinguished [between] his attitude in his earlier
> and later years and I have no doubt that, in his earlier years, there
> was fairly considerable support for his ruthless pruning of some of
> the dead wood. (letter to author: 27.1.70)

Sir Edward Playfair recorded P. J. Grigg's opinion that people of Playfair's generation 'tended to judge Fisher by his later years. But, if we had
known him as he was before 1930, we would have recognized him as
the greatest civil servant of his time' (letter to author: 18.7.69).

'His role as Head of the Civil Service was Fisher's prime interest,'
Sir Thomas Padmore emphasized (interview: 25.11.69), and Sir Owen
O'Malley believed that 'Fisher certainly fancied himself in this role. He
loved the honours part of it, being himself fond of the velvet clothes of
the KCB' (interview: 9.4.70). 'That Fisher as Head of the Civil Service
could intervene in Foreign Service matters was greatly resented', Sir
Thomas Padmore recognized, describing it as 'a running sore, partly
following from the feeling that the Office was a senior department
compared with the Treasury. The Office feared that the Treasury would
look at foreign policy issues from a financial standpoint' (interview:
25.11.69). There was more to it than that. Sir Owen O'Malley observed
that 'nobody in the Diplomatic Service had ever heard of Treasury
control over appointments. Sir Eyre Crowe would not have tolerated
interference. Fisher's imperial designs did not begin until the Francs
case of 1928' (interview: 9.4.70). This case involved currency speculation

by Foreign Office civil servants (Cmd. 3037, 1928) who included O'Malley, who subsequently persuaded Fisher that he should be allowed to continue with his diplomatic career (O'Malley, 1954; Bridge, 1971). Sir Owen O'Malley recalled that what was perceived as being the pretentious nature of the remarks in the White Paper about the proper conduct of civil servants caused Fisher to be the subject of amusement in the Foreign Office for some time afterwards, although one diplomat, Sir Percy Loraine, went to the trouble of securing an official ruling that he was responsible only the Crown and to the Foreign Secretary (interview: 9.4.70; Waterfield, 1973, pp. 143–5).

Sir Owen O'Malley did not doubt that Fisher had been instrumental in securing the Permanent Under Secretaryship of the Foreign Office for Sir Robert Vansittart in 1930 (interview: 9.4.70), though Fisher's biographer assembled evidence which suggested that while Fisher wanted Vansittart to have the post, the appointment was the result of the preference for Vansittart on the part of the Labour Prime Minister, Ramsay Macdonald (O'Halpin, 1989, pp. 183–4). Sir Anthony Eden later placed on record a discussion with Fisher in 1935 in which the then Head of the Civil Service asserted the right to be involved in Ambassadorial appointments. Eden said that he threatened to resign from the National Government rather than put up with Fisher's interventions (Avon, 1962, pp. 319–20). Fisher's biographer disputed this account, while observing that it was highly likely that Fisher would have expressed strong opinions as to who should go where (O'Halpin, 1989, pp. 249–50), although on what informed basis has to be a mystery. Fisher and Sir Horace Wilson were portrayed in Eden's memoirs as trying in May 1937 to undermine Vansittart's position as Permanent Under Secretary because his influence over Eden was 'too great' and 'hampered all attempts of the Government to make friendly contact with the dictator states' (Avon, 1962, pp. 447–8). Eden's Private Secretary, Oliver Harvey, though, recorded in March 1937 that 'A.E. spoke about his lack of confidence in Van's judgement' and that 'Van's refusal to go to Paris [as Ambassador] when offered it, and urged by both A.E. and the P.M. in December and January last, made his position a weak one' (Harvey, 1970, p. 22). Harvey observed in May 1937 that 'A.E. spoke to [the] Chancellor [Neville Chamberlain] about Van and the necessity of replacing him. [The] Chancellor agreed to such action being taken but said that it would obviously be wise to wait a little. He asked A.E. who he wanted instead A.E. said "Alec Cadogan". [The] Chancellor said Warren Fisher [was] strongly opposed to this and wished to see [Sir] Findlater Stewart from the India Office appointed. [The] Chancellor added he did not favour A.C. A.E told me afterwards he could not possibly have an outsider who was not a trained diplomat and would insist on A.C.'

Fisher's biographer noted that in his memoirs Eden got the timing of Fisher pressing the claims of Findlater Stewart wrong, mixing it up with the changes which led to the actual replacement of Vansittart by Cadogan with effect from the beginning of 1938, with the former being made Chief Diplomatic Adviser to the Government (O'Halpin, 1989, p. 263). The same writer observed that Fisher's prejudice against Cadogan was based on the fear, borne out later, that as head of the Foreign Office he would seek to separate it from the Home Civil Service, whereas Fisher favoured integration (O'Halpin, 1989, p. 254). Of course, Eden's objection to Findlater Stewart that 'it made no sense to bring someone who was inexperienced in international diplomacy into the most responsible advisory position in the Foreign Office' (Avon, 1962, p. 521) ran counter to Fisher's generalist philosophy.

Fisher's role as Head of the Civil Service, with the powers that it gave him in relation to senior appointments in the Service and in relation to the honours system, had been seen by some as constitutionally unsound in the 1920s and it was the subject of a two-day debate in the House of Lords as late as 1942, in which Lord Hankey participated. Lord Addison was one who disliked the patronage that Fisher had exercised, and repeated the opinion put to him that 'there was not much chance of promotion for a man ... during the several years between the two wars unless he happened to be *persona grata* with the Head of the Treasury' (125 H.L.Deb. 5s. c.252). The scale of controversy was compounded by Fisher's supposed interventions in the determination of foreign policy in the 1930s. Frank Ashton-Gwatkin, from the department concerned, later alleged that Fisher used his position as Head of the Civil Service 'so as to interfere in the ... submission and non-submission of Foreign Office advice to the Cabinet. This nefarious system was an important contributory cause of the weaknesses of Foreign Office authority in the thirties and one of the reasons Foreign Office warnings about Germany and the warnings from British Representatives abroad did not reach the Cabinet in an effective form. It was also one of the principal reasons the Prime Ministers, Baldwin and then Neville Chamberlain, began to turn for advice on foreign affairs to Sir Horace Wilson ... rather than to the Foreign Office experts. Neither of these men had any profound knowledge of foreign countries' (Ashton-Gwatkin, 1950, p. 27). The only instance of Fisher intervening to prevent Foreign Office material being submitted to the Cabinet was in November 1931, and

Vansittart and Sir John Simon, the then Foreign Secretary, took a similar view of its worth (O'Halpin, 1989, p. 186).

The bracketing together of Fisher and Wilson as if they were both Appeasers like, indeed, Ashton-Gwatkin himself, was misleading. As Sir Thomas Padmore observed: 'From the outset Fisher was convinced that no accommodation was possible with the Nazi regime. He was passionately in favour of rearmament' (interview: 25.11.69). Subsequent research has borne out how influential Fisher was in promoting rearmament (Peden, 1979a; Peden, 1979b). Fisher remained a figure of controversy, though, even after leaving the Treasury to become eventually a Special Commissioner for London, falling out with the Home Secretary, Herbert Morrison, and being required to resign in 1942 (Hamilton, 1959, p. 255). Fisher could not have endeared himself to the post-war Labour government either by writing in 1946 that he feared that 'we shall end up as a Corporative State which is Fascism; and where then will be our individual liberty?' (Fisher, 1946). Fisher died in 1948, having left an imperious stamp on the development of the Civil Service.

Sir Horace Wilson: Mandarin turned Emissary

Whatever controversies Sir Warren Fisher was involved in or aroused, it was not his fate to be listed as one of the *Guilty Men* as numbered in the notorious pamphlet of that title published in 1940, and written by Michael Foot and two other journalists. The name of Sir Horace Wilson (1882–1972) was listed as one of the fifteen. 'When Mr Chamberlain flew to Germany to meet Hitler [in 1938], he did not take with him the Foreign Office experts,' the pamphleteers observed, for Chamberlain was 'content to be accompanied by the gentleman who was then known as Industrial Adviser to the Government. This figure is never seen without an umbrella (and it is still in dispute whether he gave the habit to Chamberlain or Chamberlain to him). His name is Sir Horace Wilson. He deserves a prominent part in this narrative. For his was the policy, his the philosophy of life, his the ideology which dominated the mind of Mr Chamberlain during the whole of his fateful Parliament' ('Cato', 1940, p. 86). The polemicists continued:

> Sir Horace's rise to power is a wonderful story. His father was a furniture dealer. His mother kept a boarding house. Sir Horace was born in a Bournemouth back street. He went to the local board school. In the course of time he got into the Civil Service, as a Second Division man. That is to say, he did not enter the service in the top grade,

which is expected to provide civil servants who plan the execution of policy. The second grade of the Civil Service is designed to provide the executive. It is an easy standard to achieve. The examination for the grade is open to those who have reached the advanced stages of a secondary school education. ('Cato,' 1940, pp. 87–8)

This form of sneering at lower middle-class persons making their way seems a familiar feature of British life, Michael Foot himself, by this stage a committed socialist, having been born to social privilege. Wilson entered the Patent Office as a Boy Clerk in 1898 and passed into the Second Division in 1900. In 1904, he enrolled as a 'night school' student at the London School of Economics and Political Science, where he obtained a B.Sc. (Economics) degree in 1908 (Armstrong, 1986, pp. 914–15).

Anybody describing this as an 'easy' route to career advancement was a fool, though in strict career terms, Wilson was fortunate to be at the Board of Trade when promotion was rapid. The staff numbers there increased by more than eightfold between 1900 and 1914. Wilson benefited by becoming involved in 1907 in what was, in effect, a policy planning unit at the Board of Trade; and in 1911 by becoming Registrar of the Industrial Council, a new body set up by the Chief Industrial Conciliator, Sir George Askwith; and then, during the First World War, encouraged by Askwith again, becoming Secretary of the Committee on Production, the government's central arbitration tribunal. When the Ministry of Labour was created out of the Board of Trade in December 1916, Wilson was well placed to advance further, initially at the expense of Askwith who had offended Lloyd George (Lowe and Roberts, 1987, p. 645). In correspondence with the present writer about Sir Warren Fisher, Wilson recalled: 'I had 4 promotions (Staff Officer grade as it was then called) before the First World War and two at the end of the War: these were to Principal and Assistant Secretary – both on the same day!' Sir Horace added: 'To P[rincipal] A[ssistant] S[ecretary] followed in 1919 – part of a general re-grading. I do not think Fisher had anything to do with these. He will have heard of me from Sir James Masterton Smith, who became Per[manent] Sec[retary] to the M[inistry] of L[abour] in 1919 or 1920, and perhaps from some of the Treasury officials with whom I had dealings, but I do not remember any contact with Fisher until I was appointed Per[manent] Sec[retary] in place of Masterson Smith, transferred to the Col[onial] Office, to the M[inistry] of L[abour] in August 1921' (letter to author: 25.1.70).

Masterton Smith had been originally appointed in 1920 to consider whether the Ministry of Labour should be abolished, and, as within 16 months overwork had adversely affected his health, not surprisingly he recommended the Ministry's retention to the Treasury (Lowe, 1986, p. 41). With Masterton Smith departing and with Sir David Shackleton, a former Chairman of the TUC, who had also had Permanent Secretary rank within the Ministry of Labour, being moved sideways to the honorific role of Chief Labour Adviser in 1921 (Lowe and Roberts, 1987, p. 645), the way was clear for Horace Wilson to become Permanent Secretary at the age of 39.

'Wilson had in the highest degree many of the attributes of a great public servant; intelligence, clarity of mind and expression, skill in conciliation, impartiality, and integrity,' Sir Robert Armstrong later wrote; 'The attribute which made him especially valuable to Ministers was his ability to see issues plain and clear, and then to present them plainly and clearly to his political chiefs. His experience as a negotiator led him to believe that, given a modicum of good will, there was no problem or dispute which could not be resolved by the use of an appropriate form of words; and his skill in devising such formulae was one of the qualities which most commended him to the Ministers with whom he was associated, though it was sometimes felt that he was not always sufficiently mindful of the longer term implications of the formulae which he produced' (Armstrong, 1986, p. 916).

As Permanent Secretary at the Ministry of Labour between 1921 and 1930, that department's foremost historian believed that Wilson displayed 'considerable strengths and serious weaknesses'. He recruited many talented officials from other departments which remedied the Ministry's wartime shortcomings and the limitations of Treasury control, while his friendship with Sir Warren Fisher helped to secure the Ministry's future (Lowe, 1986, p. 64). Sir Horace Wilson's recollection was that 'like other heads of departments, I must have had discussions with Fisher from time to time. In 1923, F[isher] and I worked at the tidying up of the administration of the Poor Law [and] related affairs of Unemployment Insurance, for which I was responsible at [the] M[inistry] of L[abour]. Fisher, who was always working at the tidying up of Govt. administration, just as I was working at my own similar problems at the M[inistry] of L[abour], probably found me a congenial spirit in this. A Report of a C[ommi]tee at this time formed the basis of the Poor Law Act – N. Chamberlain I think' (letter to author: 25.1.70). Rodney Lowe believed that Wilson's knowledge of industry enabled him to escape being a complete prisoner of contemporary economic orthodoxy. As

Wilson wrote to Baldwin in 1925: 'We cannot be sure that improvement is in sight and will come in the happy way that it did after the smaller depressions of the pre-war period; we cannot afford to sit still and hope for the best.' However, Lowe observed of Wilson, 'his vision – although clear – was very restricted ... His tragedy was that, having had the courage to face problems others evaded, he was unable to suggest any lasting remedies. He was not an original thinker, nor, in the nineteenth century sense, a "zealot". He was a compromiser, seizing on policies not for their inherent worth but because they temporarily satisfied the bargaining positions of the interests involved' (Lowe, 1986, p. 64).

When J. H. Thomas was appointed to the post of Lord Privy Seal in the Labour government of 1929–31 with special responsibility for dealing with the unemployment problem, Sir Horace Wilson was put at the head of the team formed to assist him. Initially, Wilson retained his post as Permanent Secretary at the Ministry of Labour, but then in 1930 he became Chief Industrial Adviser to the Government, a post located at first in the Treasury, and which he retained until 1939. J. H. Thomas remained an admirer of Sir Horace Wilson's administrative skills, especially as displayed, this time on behalf of the National Government, at the Imperial Economic Conference at Ottawa in 1932 (Thomas, 1937, pp. 271–2). Wilson was involved in the attempts to reorganize British industry on more efficient lines, notably in relation to the Lancashire cotton textiles industry, but, when Baldwin became Prime Minister once more in 1935, Wilson was asked to join his staff as his personal adviser, with an office next door to the Cabinet Room. In this role, which still carried the title of Chief Industrial Adviser, Wilson was involved over the whole range of public policy, including the Abdication Crisis of 1936. When Neville Chamberlain became Prime Minister, Wilson was asked to 'stay around for a bit' (Armstrong, 1986, p. 915), and Wilson, who eventually became Permanent Secretary to the Treasury and Head of the Civil Service in succession to Fisher in 1939, gained for himself what one enemy called 'a more powerful position in Britain than almost anybody since Cardinal Wolsey' (Brown, 1943, p. 229).

'H.W.'s interference in our affairs wants watching, but it will be just as well to keep in with him and look after him', Sir Alexander Cadogan, the Permanent Under Secretary at the Foreign Office, wrote about Sir Horace Wilson on 10 January 1938 (Dilks, 1971, p. 34). Years later, Cadogan reflected: 'Horace Wilson had become an institution ... and I came to the conclusion that we must make the best of him – for which I was doubtless criticised by members of my own Service. If I had tried to fight against him, I should only have been removed.' Cadogan never regretted the attempt at cooperation. He remained on friendly terms with Wilson to the end of his life. Cadogan observed that 'so far from feeling that Horace Wilson made things difficult between Prime Minister and Foreign Secretary, I always found him extremely helpful, when the pressure of work was heavy, in ensuring that I was fully acquainted with the thought of the Prime Minister and vice versa, and that neither was drifting into any misunderstanding of the other's mind.'

When shown the relevant passages of Cadogan's diary, Sir Horace Wilson stated that he was by no means as influential in 10 Downing Street as Cadogan had suggested (Dilks, 1971, p. 53). However, as Chamberlain's adviser, Wilson seemed to be far too influential for the tastes of Anthony Eden, when Foreign Secretary, and J. P. L. Thomas, Eden's Parliamentary Private Secretary, who normally acted as an intermediary between them. After a discussion with Wilson on 20 January 1938, in the weeks leading down to Eden's resignation, Thomas wrote that 'Wilson had been working up the Prime Minister in no mean fashion' in the dispute between Chamberlain and his Foreign Secretary about the British response to an initiative from the American President Roosevelt. Thomas recorded that 'the interview (with Wilson) was stormy. I said that if A.E. did resign it might well be that the whole of this American business might leak out from the American end and that the country would then know that the P.M. preferred to turn down the help of a democracy in order that he might pursue his flirtation with the dictators untrammelled. H.W., who was in a towering rage – the first time I have ever seen him in this state – warned me that if America produced the facts he would use the full power of the Government machine in an attack upon A.E.'s past record with regard to the dictators and the shameful obstruction by the F.O. of the P. M.'s attempts to save the peace of the world' (Avon, 1962, pp. 562–3).

When Eden did resign in February 1938, Thomas recorded a telephone call from Wilson in which the official 'presumed that . . . Anthony would resign for reasons of health'. Thomas asked 'why, when Anthony was so thoroughly fit'. Wilson was said to have replied: 'Because it would be better for him and what is more it would be better for you if you persuaded him to do so' (Avon, 1962, p. 595). Arrogance was present in the behaviour of both Chamberlain and Eden, but, if Thomas's accounts were accurate, that Wilson chose to display this characteristic too was unfitting in a higher civil servant, not least in one with no training in foreign policy matters. It was interesting to note, though, that Eden's successor as Foreign Secretary, Lord Halifax, who broadly shared Chamberlain's outlook on foreign policy, and, having none of

Eden's commitment to the Foreign Office as an institution, tended to see Wilson, while irritating at times in his interventions, as being one of the 'minor characters' in policy making (Birkenhead, 1965, p. 425).

Several of Sir Alexander Cadogan's fellow officials did not take this tolerant view, and Keith Feiling, the author of a masterly biography of Neville Chamberlain, published only a few years later, recognized what he called

> the feeling of the Foreign Office that the Prime Minister preferred the amateur advice of Sir Horace Wilson . . . to their own expert counsel. This impeachment must, in great part, be admitted. He had found Wilson's judgement indispensable at the Ottawa Conference, and succeeded, as it were, to his services since he had been seconded in Baldwin's time, to work under the Prime Minister, who, for that matter, we must suppose, is entitled to seek advice in any quarter where he thinks he will find it best. Broadly speaking, Chamberlain was too masterful a man to look much for policy to others, but true it is that he valued the measuring of any nice question by an intellect the tranquillity and firmness of which he admired, and whose precision of expression he found congenial. To a certain extent, I think, it reflected his own solitariness. But, however that may be, though neither unnatural nor unprecedented, in some phases the friction thus created did no good to the common weal. (Feiling, 1946, pp. 327–8)

Those believing Sir Horace Wilson to be a sinister figure inevitably included the Edenites. As late as 27 August 1939, one of them, Oliver Harvey of the Foreign Office, professed himself to be 'terrified of another attempt at a Munich and selling out on the Poles. Horace Wilson and R. A. Butler are working like beavers for this' (Harvey, 1970, p. 307). If so, they were not successful, and, for instance, Wilson's behaviour in the face of Gennan overtures relayed through the Swedish businessman, Birger Dalherus, on 31 August 1939, was firmly negative (DBFP 1919–39, 3rd series, VII, 1954, pp. 441–2). Similarly, on the day before war was declared, Wilson, when told by Prince Philip of Hesse that Ribbentrop was seeking the agreement of the British government to Wilson going to Berlin to meet Hitler and himself in secret, replied to Hesse that the British government could not agree to any conversations until the German forces had been withdrawn from Poland and the status quo restored (DBFP 1919–39, 3rd series, IX, 1955, p. 539). That Wilson was singled out in this way was an indication of his prominence, and within British politics as late as February 1940, Thomas Jones could write that 'Horace Wilson is envied because of his power' (Jones, 1954, p. 455). None the less, this power could not survive Chamberlain's fall three months later. Wilson went to his office next to the Cabinet room as usual on the first day after what Hugh Dalton called 'the Great Change', and, according to him, Wilson found Brendan Bracken and Randolph Churchill installed there: 'they stared at Sir Horace but no one spoke or smiled. Then he withdrew, never to return to that seat most proximate to power' (Dalton, 1957, pp. 320–1).

'I feel that Winston [Churchill] has dishonoured the Premiership and the Civil Service in his treatment of me,' Sir Horace Wilson told Thomas Jones after leaving the Permanent Secretaryship of the Treasury in 1942 at the formal retiring age of 60 (Ellis, 1992, p. 465). That Wilson's successor, Sir Richard Hopkins, was more than two years older than him emphasized that Wilson was unwanted even in a situation of total war. The only subsequent role that Wilson played in public life was as Independent Chairman of the National Joint Council for Local Authorities' Administrative, Professional, Technical and Clerical Services between 1944 and 1951. NALGO's official historian was full of admiration: 'Sir Horace's qualities had failed with Nazi Germany – but they were to prove invaluable in the less paranoid atmosphere of English local government. To his new task, he brought not only personal charm, clarity of mind, and the diplomatic skill to find a way through every impasse, but also a vast experience of industrial relations and Whitleyism – acquired in nine years as Permanent Secretary to the Ministry of Labour and another nine as the government's Chief Industrial Adviser. He led the new National Council superbly' (Spoor, 1967, p. 230).

Though it was his association with Appeasement that laid low Sir Horace Wilson's reputation, he was by no means universally admired in his earlier career, certainly in the Labour Party. In 1930, Hugh Dalton had written dismissively that 'Horace Wilson (of all people) has been set up as Industrial Adviser' (Pimlott, 1986, p. 129). Clement Attlee was also hostile to Wilson, who believed that this antipathy was related to the role that Wilson had played in the General Strike of 1926 and his opposition to the repeal of the Trade Disputes Act of 1927, while Attlee had also been involved in the controversy over the Mosley memorandum in 1930 (Lowe and Roberts, 1987, p. 642). In 1940, Attlee made Wilson's exclusion from Downing Street 'a condition' of the Labour Party joining the wartime Coalition Government (Ellis, 1992, p. 465). 'We should require the influence of Sir Horace Wilson to be eliminated', Hugh Dalton had grandly informed R. A. Butler in the early days of the War. Butler expressed surprise that the Labour Party saw Wilson as being important. Dalton added: 'If we read that [Wilson] had been appointed Governor of the Windward Islands and had already left England in order to take up this most respected position, we should be favourably impressed' (Pimlott, 1986, p. 297). Wilson found Churchill's antagonism harder to bear than that of Attlee and Labour (Ellis, 1992, p. 465). John Colville wrote of Churchill at the time that 'the P.M. seems to have made an exception of Horace Wilson in the general forgiveness he has bestowed on the Men of Munich' (Colville, 1985, p. 226); but then no other official had been as publicly prominent in pursuing Appeasement as Wilson had been, and many of the Appeasers were Churchill's fellow Conservative parliamentarians.

Wilson proved to be a comfortable target, not given to hitting back at critics even during his lengthy retirement. According to A. J. P. Taylor, in conversation with the present writer in 1974, Wilson had come to blame him for his continuing troubles, being in the habit of pointing from Bournemouth towards the Isle of Wight and saying that 'he lives over there', a reference to Yarmouth, where the wealthy socialist historian had one of his homes. Taylor seemed to be at a delusions of grandeur stage, but Wilson was certainly unwise to have helped Martin Gilbert and Richard Gott with their book, *The Appeasers*, which first appeared in 1963, which proved hostile to him. The book was dedicated to Taylor, who repeated some of its findings in a general history of England (Taylor, 1965, pp. 475–6). Sir Orme Sargent, later to be head of the Foreign Office, was only stating the obvious when he commented in 1941 of Horace Wilson that 'he had suffered greatly from Chamberlain pushing him into something for which he had no qualifications and by which his reputation and his future were bound to be compromised' (Colville, 1985, p. 394).

The Controversial Giants

Sir Horace Wilson was plainly one of the four outstanding men in the inter-war Higher Civil Service in the opinion of one of his contemporaries, H. E. Dale, and as 'none of the four entered the Service by the ordinary portal of the Administration Class examination' and three were dead by the time that Dale wrote in 1941 (Dale, 1941, p. 97), it was evident that Sir Maurice Hankey, Thomas Jones, Sir John Anderson, Sir Robert Vansiltart and Sir Warren Fisher did not qualify. It may be that being left by Fisher in the backwater that was the Ministry of Agriculture and Fisheries had displeased Dale, whose account need not be treated as dispassionate because it was beautifully written. Dale did not disguise his opinion that nobody with even a modest level of private means would be a higher civil servant in the first place, and certainly not in the Home Civil Service, which had been his fate (Dale, 1941, p. 77). The Foreign Office remained socially exclusive, but Dale's picture of the Home Civil Service including scholarship products modifies perceptions of social exclusivity. Sir John Anderson's father owned a stationer's shop in Edinburgh, though he became more prosperous later (Wheeler-Bennett, 1962, pp. 1–3). The father of Thomas Jones was drawn from 'the ranks of the Welsh petit bourgeoisie', being the manager of the company shops and farm in mining village (Ellis, 1992, p. 6). In later career, a senior Treasury Knight told Hankey that Jones was 'flying very high in contemplating the Permanent Secretary' of the Board of Education in 1924. One of Jones's contemporaries said that 'he would never get to the top . . . because he was not an Oxford man', and would therefore never be considered for one of the plum jobs by Warren Fisher and the oligarchy in control (Ellis, 1992, p. 264). There was not much evidence that Jones was an outstanding administrator, and he did reach the status of Deputy Secretary of the Cabinet. That Sir Horace Wilson made it to the top meant that there was no caste system in Fisher's Civil Service, but not, of course, that social advantages did not matter. They did not always work in favour of the official. Sir Owen O'Malley recalled that Sir Robert Vansittart 'had married money and could afford not only to live in grand style but also to have his own Secret Service' (interview: 9.4.70). It was understandable that, as Foreign Secretary, Eden was apprehensive about his Permanent Under Secretary's independent authority (Rose, 1978, p. 183). O'Malley did not find Vansittart's eventual displacement to be sinister: 'On the German question anybody had to turn against Van in the end. His behaviour was so stupid. He wrote ghastly memoranda in a would be funny style, and it was not surprising that the Cabinet got fed up with it and eventually kicked him upstairs' (Interview: 9.4.70).

If Vansittart was put in his place, Sir Warren Fisher and Sir Horace Wilson came to fail to recognize theirs. Wilson was described by the admiring Thomas Jones as conducting himself as 'a sort of deputy P.M.' (Ellis, 1992, p. 416), and by making his personal association with the policy of Appeasement and with Neville Chamberlain so public, he was open to severe criticism once the former failed and the latter fell. Sir William Strang, who was head of the Foreign Office between 1949 and 1953, later wrote that criticisms of Wilson were misplaced because he was only acting as a civil servant under political direction (Strang, 1956, pp. 126–7). Strang, though, had also accompanied Chamberlain to Munich, but he attracted none of the opprobrium that Wilson did because, unlike him, he was present as an official not as a political emissary. A remark of R. A. Butler's that Wilson was 'the uncrowned ruler of England' (Roberts, 1991, p. 52) was not only inconsistent with another and lower estimate of Wilson's importance. Plainly, as Prime Minister, Chamberlain was such a ruler. Harold Nicolson, formerly of the Foreign Office, observed at the time of Munich that 'Chamberlain had disregarded the advice of the experts like Vansittart who was consistently right, and listened to Sir Horace Wilson, whose advice was never inconvenient' (Lees-Milne, 1981, p. 112). If Chamberlain had wanted pro-Appeasement advice from the Foreign Office he could have found it from Cadogan, Strang and Ashton-Gwatkin, as well as Gladwyn Jebb, among others (Newman, 1976, p. 62). It could be added too that Sir Nevil Henderson, a career diplomat whom Nicolson called 'a complete Nazi', gave Chamberlain advice that was 'never inconvenient' from his post as British Ambassador in Berlin, to which Vansittart had recommended his original appointment (Rose, 1978, p. 203). As for Vansittart, while his attitude towards Nazi Germany was consistently hostile, he had been partly responsible for the Hoare–Laval Pact of 1935. This had 'shocked the Foreign Office', Sir Owen O'Malley recalled; 'Van had overestimated Mussolini in his attempt to use the Italian dictator as a counterweight to Hitler' (interview: 9.4.70).

'I think you will find it worth your while, as I did, to glance through the attached prophetic despatch by [Sir Horace] Rumbold [Britain's Ambassador in Berlin, 1928–33] of five years ago,' Sir Maurice Hankey wrote to Sir Horace Wilson in March 1938. 'It shows in the light of other events, how clearly Hitler has adhered to *Mein Kampf* and provides some guide to the future' (Gilbert, 1973, p. 433). There had been similar warnings from Rumbold's successor, Sir Eric Phipps, but Wilson, like the National Government he advised, chose to believe that appeasing Hitler was the best course of action. Baldwin once said of Wilson to Thomas Jones, 'you know what a sane view he takes' (Jones, 1954, p. 31). This was not an observation that could so easily have been made about Fisher, and, certainly, Vansittart, but then sanity was not one of Hitler's characteristics. Like Chamberlain, Wilson was out of his depth dealing with Hitler. This was illustrated in late September 1938 when, in his emissary role, Wilson, having been earlier given a demented private rehearsal (DBFP 1919–39, 3rd series, 11, 1949, pp. 554–7), praised a crazed public speech by Hitler in Civil Service prose. Wilson also emphasized that he shared the interest aroused in Britain by Hitler's suggestion that 'England and Germany [could act as] bulwarks against disruption, particularly from the East' (DBFP 1919–39, 3rd Series, 11, 1949, pp. 564–7). Thus, Wilson associated himself with those on the Conservative Right who believed the Soviet Union to be a greater danger to Britain and its interests than Nazi Germany, which, in the immediate future, was always unlikely to be the case.

For many years afterwards, the reputations of the inter-war higher civil servants concerned suffered if they had not taken what was deemed to be the Keynesian line on combating mass unemployment or a Churchillian one on rearmament and Appeasement. That, at one time, Sir Warren Fisher managed the remarkable feat of sharing some of the opprobrium heaped on Wilson was explained by his capacity to make enemies in and around the Foreign Office (Murray, 1946; Legge-Bourke, 1950; Ashton-Gwatkin, 1950; Selby, 1953), and by his taste for intrigue, which he eventually indulged even against Vansittart (Rose, 1978, pp. 201–2, 209–10, 266, 267). This alienated those who saw Vansittart in heroic terms (e.g. Colvin, 1965), but Vansittart himself seemed to bear no malice (Vansittart, 1958, p. 350). Towards the end of his life, Fisher actually wrote what would have been a good pastiche of the supposed Churchillian line had he not been plainly serious (Fisher, 1948, pp. 212–13). The reality was that Britain had more than one formidable potential adversary and no reliable allies in the 1930s. Fisher was among those in favour of appeasing Imperial Japan (Watt, 1965, pp. 83–99; O'Halpin, 1989, pp. 227–31, 239–40, 292), and one notes that, at the time of the Manchurian crisis of 1931–3, Churchill took the view that Britain had serious enough problems in Europe without getting involved in the Far East (Bassett, 1952, pp. 564–7). Fisher thought that even the threat of force towards Italy in 1935 was 'too dangerous' (O'Halpin, 1989, p. 255), and we have already noted Vansittart's behaviour. On rearmament, Sir Horace Wilson observed that Fisher 'worked hard at the problems of rearmament and was in close touch with Ministers and the Chiefs of Staff as soon as it became apparent (after 1933) that the political climate was becoming more favourable for a more progressive rearmament policy' (letter to author: 25.1.70). One historian, who paid fulsome tribute to Fisher's contribution to national defence, believed that Fisher was 'as virulently and obsessively anti-German as Vansittart himself' (Watt, 1965, p. 102). Sir Horace Wilson dismissed this as 'nonsense. Of course [Fisher] knew, and disliked, the Nazi policy and their methods of attaining power, but he knew that there was no ready made and simple method of coping with them' (letter to author: 25.1.70). None the less, it is hard to believe that Fisher had suddenly come to the views that he expressed in an address in Manchester on

11 March 1940, which described the War as one of 'Christ against anti-Christ' and which portrayed the character of the German people as being imbued with 'Prussian barbarism'. Prussianism being a 'many centuries old and deep rooted creed whose principal articles of faith and conduct are brutality, bestiality, bullying, fraud, plunder and cunning' (Fisher, 1940, pp. 507–9). Sir Thomas Padmore emphasized that 'Fisher never changed his mind about Appeasement of Nazi Germany which he thought mad and profoundly wrong. Fisher never departed a centimetre from this view. Fisher was bitterly opposed to Munich, and he was convinced throughout that his old friend, Wilson, and his old Chancellor of the Exchequer were pursuing a crazy policy' (interview: 25.11.69).

Hankey believed Fisher to be 'rather mad' (O'Halpin, 1989, p. 229) and his behaviour in the defence field was cavalier, though none of the three giants of the inter-war Higher Civil Service fully observed the mores of the constitutional convention of ministerial responsibility. The biographical studies of Hankey and Fisher have proved invaluable, as would one of Sir Horace Wilson, and it was unsurprising that the Fulton Committee of 1966–8 was initially interested in commissioning biographical studies of great civil servants. It was told early on that Sir John Wheeler-Bennett had found great difficulty in pinpointing the precise contribution made by Sir John Anderson (PRO: BA 1/2), but the Committee persisted with the idea (PRO: BA 1/17) until it took the academic advice that its envisaged time-scale did not permit studies of a high standard (PRO: BA 1/4). Sir Thomas Padmore did see Sir Edward Boyle and Sir James Dunnett from the Committee to give his views on Sir Warren Fisher, a note of which was circulated (PRO: BA 1/18). Fisher had then recently been the subject of criticism in a popular book by Samuel Brittan, who deemed Fisher to be a 'distasteful figure' because of his behaviour and his emphasis on being Head of the Civil Service and disregard for economic questions despite being Permanent Secretary to the Treasury (Brittan, 1964, pp. 48–9). Sir Horace Wilson said of Fisher that 'like the rest of us he was disturbed by the continuance of heavy unemployment due to many causes quite beyond the sphere of the Treasury but there was little he could do personally.' Of Keynes's various schemes, Wilson considered that Fisher 'would know that in the then political climate in the UK those ventures were impracticable' (letter to author: 25.1.70). Sir Thomas Padmore said that 'it would be misleading to say that Fisher was unconcerned by unemployment. It was the great public issue of the age. For the Jimmy Thomas circus, Fisher provided the best Civil Service brains he could spare: that was how he saw his contribution' (interview: 25.11.69). The Keynesian era was the aberrant one we can now see, but, if Sir John Winnifrith was right about Fisher not having many economic ideas (letter to author: 27.1.70), to judge from his evidence to the Tomlin Commission on the Civil Service in 1930 (Tomlin evidence, pp. 1267–94), Fisher would not have seen this as a disqualification for being Permanent Secretary to the Treasury. Similarly, Fisher could suggest himself to Chamberlain in 1936 as a successor to Vansittart at the head of the Foreign Office (Neville Chamberlain Papers: NC/7/11/29/19), lack of expertise in foreign policy not being a problem.

'Fisher's main achievement was to do more than any other man to make the Civil Service a Service,' Sir Thomas Padmore told the Fulton Committee, adding: 'During the [Second World] War the idea of a unified Service took tremendous strides but on foundations which he laid down, although it was true that to some degree those developments would have taken place anyway' (PRO: BA 1/18). In actual fact, in obvious reaction to the powers exercised by Fisher and Wilson, the Eden Reforms of 1943 anticipated the removal of the Foreign Office from the remit of the Head of the Civil Service (Cmd. 6420, 1943). It has to be said, too, that none of Fisher's successors seemed so obsessed with securing for the Civil Service a status comparable with that of the Armed Forces (Hamilton, 1951, pp. 28–9), a strange reading of their respective functions and the relationship with the Crown. With this ambition was linked Fisher's odd emphasis on promoting Civil Service sport (Hamilton, 1951, pp. 35–6). Always concerned about the quality of the people at the top of public life, and with continuing faith in his ability to identify the high fliers, despite, for instance, the Christopher Bullock episode, to the end Fisher thought on the grand scale, and in a book dedicated to him and (so the author, Richard Greaves, told this writer) full of his ideas, Fisher even envisaged the staffing of the whole of the public sector, hugely enlarged by 1947, as being run as one from the centre (Greaves, 1947, p. 211). This did not come to pass, but in terms of its philosophy of administration, the Civil Service persisted with the Fisher inheritance. For, it was Fisher, not the Northcote–Trevelyan Report, as the Fulton Committee seemed to think, nor Fisher's eventual successor, Sir Edward Bridges, as Brittan seemed to believe (Brittan, 1964, pp. 49–50), who patented the all-rounder style of general administrator. Whether a Civil Service organized even in broad terms on the Fisher model was better than a more devolved structure for the performance of the actual work was not a question that was effectively confronted for more than half a century after Hankey, Wilson and Fisher himself had left the scene.

References

Armstrong, Sir R. (1986). 'Sir Horace John Wilson' in Lord Blake and C. S. Nicholls, eds, *The Dictionary of National Biography 1971–1980* (Oxford: Oxford University Press).

Ashton-Gwatkin, F. (1950). *The British Foreign Service* (Syracuse, NY: Syracuse University Press).

Avon, Lord (1962). *The Eden Memoirs. Facing The Dictators* (London: Cassell).

Bassett, R. (1952). *Democracy and Foreign Policy* (London: Longmans, Green).

Beloff, M. (1975). 'The Whitehall Factor: the Role of the Higher Civil Service 1919–1939' in G. Peele and C. Cook, eds, *The Politics of Reappraisal 1918–1939* (London: Macmillan).

Blrkenhead, Lord (1965). *Halifax. The Life of Lord Halifax* (London: Hamish Hamilton).

Bridge, A. (1971). *Permission to Resign* (London: Sidgwick and Jackson).

Bridges, Lord (1964). *The Treasury* (London: Allen and Unwin).

Brittan, S. (1964). *The Treasury under the Tories* (Harmondsworth: Penguin).

'Cato'. (1940). *Guilty Men* (London: Gollancz).

Colville, J. (1985). *The Fringes of Power. The Downing Street Diaries* (London: Hodder and Stoughton).

Colvin, I. (1965). *Vansittart in Office* (London: Gollancz).

Dale, H. E. (1941). *The Higher Civil Service in Great Britain* (London: Oxford University Press).

Dalton, H. (1957). *The Fateful Years. Memoirs 1931–1945* (London: Mueller).

Dilks, D., ed. (1971). *The Diaries of Sir Alexander Cadogan 1938–1945* (London: Cassell).

DBFP 1919–1939 (1949). *Documents on British Foreign Policy 1919–1939.* 3rd series, vol. II, 1938, eds E. L. Woodward and R. Butler (London: HMSO).

DBFP 1919–1939 (1954). *Documents on British Foreign Policy 1919–1939.* 3rd series, vol. VII, 1939, eds E. L. Woodward and R. Butler (London: HMSO).

DBFP 1919–1939 (1955). *Documents on British Foreign Policy 1919–1939.* 3rd series, vol. IX, 1939, eds E. L. Woodward and R. Butler (London: HMSO).

Ellis, E. L. (1992). *T.J.: A Life of Dr Thomas Jones* (Cardiff: University of Wales Press).

Felling, K. (1946). *The Life of Neville Chamberlain* (London: Macmillan).

Fisher, Sir W. (1940). 'Facing the Facts'. *The Nineteenth Century and After,* CXXVII, 507–12.

Fisher, Sir W. (1946). 'Safeguards of Freedom are Being Whittled Away'. *Daily Graphic,* 5 Nov.

Fisher, Sir W. (1948). 'The Beginnings of Civil Defence'. *Public Administration,* 26, 211–16.

Francs Case (1928). *Report of the Board of Enquiry appointed by the Prime Minister to investigate certain Statements affecting Civil Servants.* Cmd. 3037 (London: HMSO).

Fry, G. K. (1969). *Statesmen in Disguise. The Changing Role of the Administrative Class of the British Home Civil Service 1853–1966* (London: Macmillan).

Gilbert, M. (1973). *Sir Horace Rumbold, Portrait of a Diplomat* (London: Heinemann).

Gilbert, M. and Gott, R. (1963) *The Appeasers* (London: Weidenfeld and Nicolson).

Greaves, H. R. G. (1947). *The Civil Service in the Changing State* (London: Harrap).

Hamilton, Sir H. P. (1951). 'Sir Warren Fisher and the Public Service'. *Public Administration*, 29, 3–38.

Hamilton, Sir H. P. (1959). 'Sir Norman Fenwick Warren Fisher' in L. G. Wickham Legg and E. T. Williams, eds, *The Dictionary of National Biography 1941– 1950* (Oxford: Oxford University Press).

Hankey, Lord (1945) *Government Control in War* (Cambridge: Cambridge University Press).

Hankey, Lord (1946). *Diplomacy by Conference. Studies in Public Affairs* (London: Benn).

Hankey, Lord (1961). *The Supreme Command 1914–1918*. 2 vols. (London: Allen and Unwin).

Hankey, Lord (1963). *The Supreme Control at the Paris Peace Conference 1919* (London: Allen and Unwin).

Harvey, J., ed. (1970). *The Diplomatic Diaries of Oliver Harvey 1937–1940* (London: Collins).

Jones, T. (1954). *A Diary with Letters 1931–1950* (London: Oxford University Press).

Lees-Milne, J. (1981). *Harold Nicolson. A Biography 1930–1968* (London: Chatto and Windus).

Legge-Bourke, Sir E. H. A. (1950). *Master of the Offices* (London: Falcon Press).

Lowe, R. (1986). *Adjusting to Democracy. The Role of the Ministry of Labour in British Politics 1918–1939* (Oxford: Clarendon Press).

Lowe, R. and Roberts, R. (1987). 'Sir Horace Wilson 1900–1915: the Making of a Mandarin'. *Historical Journal*, 30, 641–62.

Mallaby, Sir G. (1981). 'Maurice Pascal Alers Hankey, first Baron Hankey' in G. T. Williams and C. S. Nicholls, eds, *The Dictionary of National Biography 1961– 1970* (Oxford: Oxford University Press).

Murray, Lord (1946). *Reflections on Some Aspects of British Foreign Policy between the two World Wars* (Edinburgh: Oliver and Boyd).

Naylor, J. N. (1984). *A Man and an Institution. Sir Maurice Hankey, the Cabinet Secretariat, and the Custody of Cabinet Secrecy* (Cambridge: Cambridge University Press).

Newman, S. (1976). *March 1939: the British Guarantee to Poland* (Oxford: Clarendon Press).

O'Halpin, E. (1989). *Head of the Civil Service. A Study of Sir Warren Fisher* (London: Routledge).

O'Malley, Sir O. (1954). *The Phantom Caravan* (London: Murray).

Peden, G. C. (1979a). 'Sir Warren Fisher and British Rearmament against Germany'. *English Historical Review*, XCIV, 29–45.

Peden, G. C. (1979b). *British Rearmament and the Treasury 1932–1939* (Edinburgh: Scottish Academic Press).

Pimlott, B., ed. (1986). *The Political Diaries of Hugh Dalton 1918–1940 and 1945– 1960* (London: Cape).

Roberts, A. (1991). *'The Holy Fox'. A Biography of Lord Halifax* (London: Weidenfeld and Nicolson).

Rose, N. (1978). *Vansittart. Study of a Diplomat* (London: Heinemann).

Roskill, S. (1970). *Hankey. Man of Secrets*, vol. 1, 1877–1918 (London: Collins).

Roskill, S. (1972). *Hankey. Man of Secrets*, vol. 2, 1919–1931 (London: Collins).

Roskill, S. (1974). *Hankey. Man of Secrets*, vol. 3, 1931–1963 (London: Collins).

Selby, Sir W. (1953). *Diplomalic Twilight* (London: Murray).

Spoor, A. (1967). *White Collar Union. Sixty Years of NALGO* (London: Heinemann).

Strang, Lord (1956). *Home and Abroad* (London: Deutsch).

Taylor, A. J. P. (1965). *English History 1914–1945* (Oxford: Clarendon Press).

Thomas, J. H. (1937). *My Story* (London: Hutchinson).

Tomlin Evidence (1929–31). *Royal Commission on the Civil Service 1929–1931. Minutes of Evidence* (London: HMSO).

Vansittart, Lord (1958). *The Mist Procession* (London: Hutchinson).

Waterfield, G. (1973). *Professional Diplomat. Sir Percy Loraine* (London: Murray).

Watt, D. C. (1965). *Personalities and Policies* (London: Longman).

Wheeler-Bennett, J. W. (1962). *John Anderson. Lord Waverley* (London: Macmillan).

4
Innovators at 10 Downing Street
June Burnham and G. W. Jones

Introduction

The objective of the research reported here was to discover who were the innovators at 10 Downing Street – who were the politicians or officials who made significant contributions to changing the way prime ministers were assisted between 1868 and 1997. In looking for motives for change we concentrated our attention on the innovator, but external factors could not and should not be ignored. There are institutional and contextual constraints on all would-be innovators, such as the number of staff that can legally be publicly funded; the expectations of party, parliament and monarch; and relationships with colleagues and rivals in Cabinet and departments. People who were influential at 10 Downing Street were not isolated from the colleagues they worked with and for. An equally vital caveat is that our set of five characters – Gladstone, Lloyd George, Waterhouse, Rowan and Wilson – were chosen from a mass of evidence for the 'quantum-leap' nature of their innovations. This selection left out not only those who introduced what we decided were comparatively minor reforms, such as filing systems in the 1920s or some specialized functions in the 1940s, but may also have omitted some quiet revolutionaries still to be discovered.

Gladstone

Gladstone was prime minister in four governments: 1868–74; 1880–5; 1886; and 1892–4. His office arrangements were more varied than those of his great rival, Disraeli, but the basic structure was initially similar. Between 1868 and 1874 he had two paid secretaries – one dealing with more political matters, and the other with more official business.

Disraeli during his short first administration of 1868 had made similar arrangements that look typical of the assistance given to prime ministers from 1812 to 1868. Disraeli took to No. 10 the two secretaries who had been working for him as Chancellor of the Exchequer and Leader of the House of Commons at No. 11. One was a close confidant, Montagu Corry, focusing mainly on political and policy issues and very much a personal appointee who stayed with him in and out of office; the other was from the Treasury and carried out mainly administrative and routine tasks. On Disraeli's return to government in 1874 he brought back Corry, and used two private secretaries from the Treasury to assist with the more routine work until his retirement in 1880.

In Gladstone's later administrations he always had more staff in No. 10 than had Disraeli, increasing their number to four and five. Some were paid to assist him when he held additional ministerial portfolios, like Chancellor of the Exchequer. Though presented as a man of the people, Gladstone was connected through his wife and his closest political confidant, Lord Granville, to the 'gilded youth and noble chaps' he recruited to his service (the phrase used by Bryan Keith-Lucas). Of the 14 people he appointed to private-secretary positions – some in more than one administration – 8 had been educated at Eton, 3 at Rugby, Marlborough or Harrow. Four civil servants employed at Gladstone's No. 10 had close connections with Liberal politics. They were easily able to act as intermediaries between Gladstone and the Whig grandees who were so prominent in his cabinets.

His family merged into the secretariat. Where Disraeli treated Corry as his surrogate son, Gladstone treated his family as surrogate secretaries. Mrs Gladstone copied letters in busy periods; his son, Henry, when at home from India, and his daughters, Mary and Helen, sorted and replied to correspondence, Mary dealing especially with minor church patronage matters; and another son, Herbert, handled relationships with the Liberal Party – as an MP he acted essentially as a Parliamentary Private Secretary for the Prime Minister and was later Chief Whip (Matthew 1990). Gladstone had a more extensive network of aides than had Disraeli. Together his office staff and family formed for Gladstone, especially as he grew older, 'an interlocking protective cocoon' (Jenkins 1995: 460).

Assiduous and industrious, Gladstone enthusiastically immersed himself in the work of government. A true innovator at 10 Downing Street he thought about what had to be done and how it could be done better by organizing and recording the flow of paper and decisions. His predecessor in 1868, Disraeli, 'never possessed the drive, energy or application which were the qualities of Pitt, Peel, Palmerston, or Gladstone'. Disraeli 'was not an energetic Prime Minister, and he expected his three private secretaries . . . to do a great deal of his work for him' (Blake 1966: 543; 682). In contrast Gladstone did not devolve 'manual labour' to his secretaries so he could do less, but so he could achieve more. In a letter to one of his secretaries Gladstone wrote: 'No man . . . could dream, until by experience he knew, to what extent devolution can be carried – how it strengthens the feeble knees, and thus sustains the fainting heart' (Hamilton 1898: 79). The routines he set up for the orderly processing of paperwork seem to have been his own initiative, since he followed them not only out of session but out of government, according to his secretaries J. A. Godley and Henry Gladstone (Godley 1931: 87; Thomas 1936: 94–5). Order was 'a means of increasing power and efficiency for good' (Hamilton 1898: 78). But orderly recording appealed to Gladstone for its own sake too, and for its contribution to his future reputation (Matthew 1982: lxxxiii; 1978: xcix).

Gladstone acted as his own office manager, and his disciplined methods of working imposed a routine on the practice of his secretaries. 'He had thought out numerous methods of saving time and trouble in office work, insisted on their strict observance, and observed them strictly himself' (Godley 1931: 87). He devolved to his aides the selection and answering of letters that could receive standard replies – items he termed 'rubbish' – but conducted spot checks on these weeded items. The secretaries folded incoming letters neatly and put on them a note of the correspondent, date and topic, and suggested a reply. Gladstone would write a few replies himself, or write tops and tails on Downing Street notepaper, between which the secretaries would add a filling; the rest he left to the secretaries to answer. The secretaries would copy and index non-trivial replies, including all to Cabinet ministers, as a permanent record. The only letters that were not to be opened by the secretaries were those contained inside other envelopes and those sent by Mrs Thistlethwayte in specially marked envelopes. (Descriptions of the way correspondence was dealt with can be found in Hamilton 1898: 80–3; Leveson Gower 1940: 160–4; Godley 1931: 87–98; Ramm 1952: x–xiii; Bahlman 1972: xvii–xxii). Gladstone filed himself only letters that he indicated by refolding to a narrow strip, and he had one or two locked drawers forbidden even to his principal private secretary (Godley 1931: 138).

Gladstone ran an office that served both prime minister and Cabinet. He was unique among Victorian prime ministers in his systematic recording of Cabinet agenda and decisions: the documentation more thorough than under later prime ministers until Lloyd George set up the Cabinet Secretariat in 1916 (Matthew 1982: xxxiii). He was innovatory in preparing an orderly list of items for Cabinet to discuss, indicating on the list whether the item had been discussed, and noting succinctly on the agenda paper the points discussed and decisions made. He would plan for the summer recess a series of Cabinet meetings to outline the forthcoming legislative programme (Ramm 1952: xiv). He wrote memoranda about Cabinet items like modern briefs to prime ministers from No. 10 or Cabinet Office officials, perhaps to clear his own mind or as a basis for Cabinet discussion. The notes he squeezed into the space between the items on his agenda formed the basis of his report to Queen Victoria on the Cabinet meeting. These reports were so hastily written the Queen reproved him for describing as a decision something which should have been described as a submission of advice. The Leader of the Lords, Granville, wrote to Gladstone on 17 July 1880 that the Queen had commended his (Gladstone's) daily reports of House of Commons sittings as 'a lesson of how things should be done' (Ramm 1952) – which suggests her criticism of his Cabinet reports was as much personal as constitutional. Gladstone for all his office efficiency was not as effective at dealing with the Queen as the slapdash Disraeli, who could send the charming Corry as his representative even to report on Cabinet.

Yet, despite Gladstone's expressed wish to devolve work to his staff, he took a close interest in church patronage, a task later prime ministers saw as suitable for a junior member of staff, save for the final touches. Leveson Gower noted that when a church appointment had to be made 'the whole business of State seemed to be put aside whilst he [Gladstone] poured forth a perfect avalanche of letters inquiring at great length and in minute detail... [he] was hardly able to give his full mind to any other matter' (1940: 165; and see Stephen 1964: 145–62). However, one particular secretary was always assigned to handle correspondence on church appointments, and there was an attempt at specialization of other functions too. In the early 1870s West, the principal private secretary, dealt with matters 'unofficial but political, and especially all questions affecting patronage', while Gurdon dealt with Treasury matters, Civil List and Royal Bounty (West 1899: 333).

In Gladstone's first administration Gurdon drew up a 'Book of Knowledge' about procedures in the office, to guide new staff, since, Gurdon explained, the Prime Minister and staff had no department to fall back upon. There were no permanent staff to provide continuity. The Book gave information on routine matters, like the proper wording for announcements, for responding to requests from clergymen for appointments and for arranging journeys. It was revised by Hamilton in the 1880–5 administration, as a notebook of about 100 pages. There was nothing like it in Disraeli's time and it seems not to have survived Gladstone's period, or indeed into his fourth administration, being taken away by Hamilton in 1885 and left to his family (Bahlman 1972: xxiii). Like other 'innovations' in the central offices, including many of Gladstone's careful recording mechanisms, it was not passed on to new occupants of No. 10.

Matthew claimed 'Gladstone thus ran an embryonic "cabinet office", probably more formally organized and certainly more fully recorded than that of his predecessors' (Matthew 1978: xcix; and see Ramm 1952: xiii–xiv). Under Disraeli No. 10 was uncoordinated and chaotic. Gladstone increased the staff and taught them efficient management routines that gave him more time for the important business of running the Cabinet. He introduced Cabinet agenda, briefs and minutes, all handled by himself and his secretaries from No. 10. Gladstone made more efficient the system left by Disraeli and made it look like a precursor of the modern Prime Minister's Office and Cabinet Office.

Lloyd George

Whereas Gladstone had a passion for order in the conduct of business, Lloyd George thrived on disorder: 'a man quite without system' (Turner 1977: 173). As prime minister from 1916 to 1922 he moved from adviser to adviser regardless of their formal positions, and without giving them clear allocations of responsibility. Contemptuous of red tape, he felt unorthodox methods were required to win the war, and was determined his will would prevail. His style was a reaction to the leisured and orderly arrangements of Asquith.

Lloyd George maintained a team of private secretaries like those of his predecessors, but added two new sets of advisers. The first was based on the Cabinet Secretariat, located in Whitehall Gardens across Whitehall from Downing Street. The second was his Private Secretariat in temporary huts in the gardens of No. 10, often known as the 'Garden Suburb'. Although each of these three clusters of advisers was assigned main tasks there was great overlapping in what the people in them did, depending on whom Lloyd George trusted at a particular moment. These new groups took away from the core group of private secretaries two key tasks: providing secretarial support for the Cabinet, and providing advice to the Prime Minister about important issues, initially about waging the war and later about producing peacetime settlement.

Two secretaries in the traditional core of No. 10 remained with Lloyd George for his whole term of office: the principal private secretary, J. T. Davies, and Frances Stevenson, who acted as the Prime Minister's personal secretary. Davies was Lloyd George's private secretary when he was Chancellor of the Exchequer and Minister for Munitions. Stevenson was his personal secretary in those posts, previously a tutor to his daughter, and his mistress. Stevenson was the first female private secretary and the first prime-ministerial mistress installed at No. 10. The others in the core group had either worked for Lloyd George in government or were acquainted with him or his friends. It was very much a team personally attached to Lloyd George. They replaced Asquith's team and left when Lloyd George left. Their functions were those of the traditional secretaries at No. 10. The principal handled the more important issues and contacts, including relations with the press, parliamentary questions, honours and personal matters. Frances Stevenson handled casework and personal correspondence (interviews G. Davies and M. G. Stenhouse, J. Eastwood, G. Shakespeare, A. J. Sylvester). The number three, William Sutherland, became notorious for his exercise of patronage, selling of honours, spreading malicious gossip against enemies of the Prime Minister, and manipulating the press on behalf of his master. But all would deal with any task.

Under Lloyd George the core group of secretaries gave up carrying out certain functions it had performed before. Bonar Law, Leader of the House of Commons while Lloyd George was prime minister, used to write the daily letter to the King about its proceedings. Whereas Asquith used to go to the Palace in a frock coat and silk hat to tell the King what had happened at Cabinet, Lloyd George did not go, which the Court resented (interview A. J. Sylvester). Lloyd George wanted to concentrate on running the government.

The function of servicing the Cabinet was transferred by Lloyd George in 1916 to the Cabinet Secretariat, based on the team of officials under Maurice Hankey that had serviced the Committee of Imperial Defence and Asquith's War Council. Hankey and other members of the Secretariat prepared the Cabinet's agenda, provided briefs on the topics under discussion, wrote its minutes and conclusions, and arranged for their distribution throughout Whitehall. Hankey was 'a formidable influence in central government, on military policy and on inter-allied diplomacy' and 'reinforced LG's command at critical moments' (Morgan 1974: 103). His deputy, Tom Jones, acted as 'a fluid person moving about among people who mattered and keeping the P.M. on the right path so far as possible' (Ellis 1992: 188). Jones linked Lloyd George with many Welsh interests and with both employers and trades unions, and had a significant role in the making of the government's policy on Ireland. Although located in the Cabinet Secretariat, Jones, like Hankey, carried out tasks similar to those being carried out by people in No. 10 and in its garden.

Lloyd George's other main innovation, and it was seen as an innovation at the time, was to set up the Prime Minister's Secretariat – a 'think-tank' providing him with policy advice, especially to keep a check on what the departments were advising and doing, or not doing. Lloyd George has been described as 'the first British premier to hire a "brains trust" . . . for personal assistance' (Morgan 1974: 105). It was staffed by people known to Lloyd George or to his close friends, or linked to interests he wished to influence, like the press. They brought him expertise in special areas and contacts with key groups. During the war the Secretariat focused on economic aspects of the war like food control, agriculture, shipping, munitions supply and liquor control, and after the war on different aspects of peacemaking in Europe and Ireland, and on Imperial matters, providing advice for the Prime Minister for the many conferences he attended. Its work largely involved collecting statistics, analysing and assessing policies, and making policy proposals, all to inform and assist the Prime Minister (Davies 1951; Turner 1980).

After the war there was considerable hostility to these innovations. Both the Cabinet Secretariat and the Prime Minister's Secretariat were seen as examples of Lloyd George's presidential ambitions. He was described as an 'Imperial Caesar' and the two secretariats were regarded as institutions that enabled him to exert his will over ministers and departments. They resented his intrusions through these unaccountable secretariats into their domains. His interventions were seen as unconstitutional, subverting both collective Cabinet government and the individual responsibility of ministers by enhancing the personal administrative resources at the service of the Prime Minister. Many critics conflated the two secretariats, not recognizing the distinction between the one that served the Cabinet and the other that served the Prime Minister alone. Both seemed a buttress for the aggrandizement of an untrustworthy and corrupt prime minister.

On the fall of Lloyd George Bonar Law abolished the Prime Minister's Secretariat and had the garden huts dismantled. The Cabinet Secretariat, though much reduced, survived the reaction against Lloyd George and his works. Hankey managed to beat off an attempt by Warren

Fisher to bring it under the Treasury's responsibility. It continued and later developed into a most important institution of central coordination in government, the Cabinet Office.

The chaotic and fluid arrangements for providing assistance to Lloyd George reflected his temperament, style and mode of working. He preferred to have many advisers and to talk to them rather than read long memoranda. He was a dynamic force, working 16 hours a day, demanding of his staff, expecting everything to be ready in five minutes but, as with Churchill later, attracting their loyalty as a leader who could win the war and get things done. He created a tense atmosphere in the office, enjoying intrigue and tensions created by crises. Lloyd George was a 'throbbing engine'; he seemed to possess superhuman power and exuded a charismatic atmosphere as he entered a room (interviews G. Davies and M. G. Stenhouse, G. Shakespeare, A. J. Sylvester).

The irony is that the innovations of Lloyd George, which did so much between 1916 and 1922 to increase the Prime Minister's power, served in the longer run to undermine it. On the one hand, his interventions so angered ministers and their departments that the memory of his enhancement of the resources available to the Prime Minister could always be counted on for use in arguments against strengthening the staff of the Prime Minister and creating a Prime Minister's Department. On the other, the setting up of the Cabinet Secretariat ultimately curbed the power of the Prime Minister, since it became the guardian of collective decision-making in government, ensuring that all departments concerned with an issue put in their views to Cabinet, and that when Cabinet had decided, its decisions, and not those of only the Prime Minister were sent around the departments as their marching orders. Had Lloyd George not innovated by creating the Cabinet Secretariat at a distance from No. 10, its functions would have remained with the Prime Minister's secretaries. They would have been the focus for coordination in British government. But Lloyd George's imperious methods and flouting of conventions made a similar strong premiership hard to sustain in the future. In the shorter term his immediate successors were committed to purge public life of Lloyd George's improprieties, and that meant some of his innovations (Morgan 1974: 167).

Ronald Waterhouse

Ronald Waterhouse looks one of the most important private secretaries in the evolution of 10 Downing Street. He seems a man of immense significance as an innovator in the development of the private office.

He was the first principal private secretary since the 1830s to continue in office under prime ministers of different parties. Between 1922 and 1928 he served the Conservative Bonar Law (1922–3), the Conservative Stanley Baldwin (1923–4), the Labour Ramsay MacDonald (1924) and Stanley Baldwin again (1924–8). He was the last of the old-style personal and political appointees, ushering in, as a transitional figure, the new-style civil servants who were to hold the post after him to the present day.

Waterhouse studied 'the art and usages of a Private Secretary', aware of Disraeli's comments on the relationship between a minister and his secretary being like 'the married state', and Charles II's eulogy of his secretary Godolphin, 'Sydney is never in the way, and never out of the way'. He read the writings of and references to his predecessors 'who had left a mark', like Cowper for Melbourne, Corry for Disraeli, Godley for Gladstone, and Sandars for Balfour. He read about Murray of Broughton, secretary to Prince Charles Edward, and about Louis de Bourrienne, secretary to Napoleon. He proposed some precepts about the role of the private secretary.

> He must be susceptible as a chameleon to every shade of atmosphere; reticent though not backward in coming forward; tolerant and patient yet decisive and forceful; receptive to great men and adaptable to fools...He must remember that a case is more often lost through being unpalatably presented than because it is inherently wrong...and that to win a race by eighteen lengths may prove evidence of stupidity, when it could have been won by half a neck without either chagrin to the opponent, or the disclosure of strength.... He comes into contact with all the prominent actors upon the political stage and is in confidential relationship with the controlling constitutional force behind the Throne...but above all he must remember that while the world knocks at his threshold it is not to him, but to his office, that sycophancy bows. (Waterhouse 1942: 186–9)

Waterhouse's reflections on his role, as recorded by his wife, show him as essentially a courtier, adept at winning the confidence of those he served, discreet, unscrupulous, economical with the truth, and not to be trusted by others. In Roy Jenkins' judgement: 'There remains something slightly odd about Waterhouse' (1988: 188).

The oddness is all the more striking because, despite his long tenure, many felt he was not up to the job, even those who recommended him to others and kept him for so long in their service (Montgomery Hyde

1973: 148). Robert Blake observed that Waterhouse as Law's principal private secretary was 'not a very happy choice'. Waterhouse 'was indifferent at paper work, and wrote in a convoluted style which on occasions is so stilted as to be scarcely comprehensible.... He inspired little trust in the members of Bonar Law's family or his immediate entourage.' Law 'personally rather disliked him, and indeed said on one occasion that he did not care to have him in the same room'. The mystery intensifies since Law not only tolerated Waterhouse as his secretary from March 1920 to March 1921 while he was Lord Privy Seal and Leader of the House of Commons, but 'asked for his services again on becoming Prime Minister eighteen months later' (Blake 1955: 402).

Other staff at No. 10 said he was useless. A. J. Sylvester said he was not a worker, arrived late at the office, sat down, got up, walked to the palace to see the King's private secretary, walked back, and the morning was gone. In the afternoon he strolled to the Commons. He did virtually nothing. The women who worked as secretaries at No. 10 found him pleasant but lacking in intellect and character, and unreliable. Graham Vincent, who served in the private office with Waterhouse, said that despite his impressive presence, Waterhouse was hopeless – a 'runnel'. Vincent wondered why Waterhouse stayed so long (interviews A. J. Sylvester, G. Davies and M. G. Stenhouse, J. Eastwood, H. G. Vincent).

Waterhouse was a shipowner's son, went to Marlborough, was sent home 'in disgrace' and packed off to Cape Town, where he became a mounted policeman. He returned to London and sought to pass the Oxford entrance examinations by slipping the papers through a window to a college friend; he 'inadvertently' passed, but never stayed. Instead he joined the army, serving in Africa and India. In 1915 he was posted to the Intelligence Department of the War Office. But then his career took a different direction as private secretary to a series of figures in public positions.

Most of these posts were obtained through J. C. C. Davidson, a political 'fixer' with friends in MI5, who was by turn private secretary to Bonar Law and Baldwin. Davidson became an MP, a minister and Chair of the Conservative Party organization. Between Waterhouse and Davidson 'a great intimacy existed ... and they were constantly together' (Waterhouse 1942: 156). Davidson organized a position for Waterhouse as private secretary to Brigadier-General Sir Frederick Sykes, Chief of the Air Staff (Sykes 1942:219). When Sykes married Bonar Law's daughter, Isabel, Waterhouse was best man. In 1920, when Davidson had to go abroad, he asked Sykes to let Waterhouse take his place as private secretary to Bonar Law (Waterhouse 1942: 183–5). Waterhouse served Bonar Law until 1921, and briefly and uneasily Law's successor, Austen Chamberlain. He was then appointed private secretary and royal equerry to the Duke of York, which brought him into daily contact with the royal family.

When Bonar Law became prime minister in October 1922, Waterhouse was named principal private secretary; Davidson was Law's Parliamentary Private Secretary. But Davidson carried out the tasks usually associated with the principal private secretary. Davidson was the office manager, given the responsibility to 'clear up Downing Street' and abolish the 'garden suburb'. He had a free hand with the press and his word was accepted as Law's (James 1969: 139–40). In 1923, when he was appointed Chancellor of the Duchy of Lancaster, he continued in effect as Law's political secretary.

When illness compelled Law to resign in May 1923 Waterhouse played a key role in securing the accession of Baldwin. Waterhouse was the means of contact with the King, but Law's family did not trust Waterhouse and ensured Sykes, as his father-in-law's official representative, accompanied him on his mission. They were right not to trust Waterhouse. Despite having promised Law he would keep secret Law's personal inclinations, he gave the King's private secretary a memorandum, written by Davidson after discussions with Baldwin, that purported to give Law's arguments for Baldwin and against Curzon. Waterhouse also told the King the memorandum embodied Law's opinions. Waterhouse misrepresented Law, putting firm views where there was only indecision (Blake 1955: 519–27; Waterhouse 1942: 259–65; James 1969; Hazlehurst 1974).

Law's team at No. 10 had demonstrated their support for Baldwin, so the continuation of Waterhouse as principal private secretary to Baldwin seems less surprising than how in 1924 he came to serve MacDonald. Some No. 10 staff thought MacDonald, new to the job as the first Labour prime minister, lacked confidence and had decided he needed to keep someone with experience (interview, Davies and Stenhouse). Waterhouse would have been more acceptable than Davidson, or Tom Jones in the Cabinet Office. Waterhouse's wife asserted the idea came from Baldwin, aware that MacDonald's tenure of office would be short-lived – 'he would be acting as a kind of *trait-d'union*' – a link between two Baldwin administrations. Baldwin, MacDonald and Waterhouse were said to have agreed in the Cabinet room that the entire personal staff at No. 10 would stay (Waterhouse 1942: 295). Scepticism should be tempered by Morgan's observation that Baldwin and MacDonald in the 1920s 'based their careers' more on 'the gulf that divided them from Lloyd George' than 'their differences from each other' (Morgan 1978: 51). At first MacDonald was suspicious of Waterhouse and tried to do much himself. But gradually Waterhouse won his confidence and was used increasingly by the Prime Minister, especially for advice about dealing with the court (Waterhouse 1942: 296–306). When Baldwin returned to office in October 1924 Waterhouse stayed in place until 1928, when his affair with the secretary of Mrs Baldwin became known and he offered his resignation, which Baldwin accepted. He never held public office again, though Hugh Dalton in his diary entry for 12 February 1935 noted an approach by Waterhouse about returning as principal private secretary to the next Labour prime minister (Pimlott 1986: 186).

Waterhouse was not a civil servant. But by staying on for MacDonald he showed that a principal private secretary could serve prime ministers from different parties, an innovation that enabled the civil service to take over the position. After him the private office of the Prime Minister became the preserve of civil servants, and a clear distinction emerged between them and any personal and political staff located at No. 10. Yet Waterhouse doubted the advantages of this neat distinction. He noted the civil service drew 'an arbitrary line of demarcation between the departmental and the political duties involved, the former being essentially his, while the latter belonged exclusively to his colleague the parliamentary private secretary'. But to Waterhouse 'it seemed obvious that the extent or limit of his usefulness could only be decided by himself' (1942: 188). He felt he could better 'do good work for his political chiefs' through not being 'an official civil servant' (Pimlott 1986: 186). He noted 'there was a limit to adventuring in the public service' (1942: 220).

Leslie Rowan

Leslie Rowan was the private secretary most admired by those who worked at No. 10. He was there from 1941 to 1947, serving first Churchill as private secretary and then Attlee as principal private secretary. John Peck, his colleague, said: 'He was by far the most talented and best suited for the task of all those who served as Private Secretaries during the Churchill régime' (Gilbert 1994: 194–5). His innovations were to consolidate and develop a variety of practices that had emerged in the past, especially during the Second World War under Churchill, which continued as the model for running the office in later years.

Rowan was a professional civil servant, joining first in 1930 the Colonial Office and then in 1933 the Treasury, where he was assistant private secretary to the Chancellor of the Exchequer from 1934 to 1937. After his time at No. 10 he was briefly permanent secretary at the Ministry for Economic Affairs and then held a variety of key positions in the Treasury, as economic minister in Washington and as second secretary. He left the public service in 1958, at the age of 50, to go into business. He fitted the totally different styles and working habits of Churchill and Attlee. The former appeared disorganized, but rather he was unconventional, working long and unusual hours, and demanding personal attendance from a number of aides, while Attlee appeared more disciplined and self-contained, preferring office routine and working from papers. Churchill tried to get Rowan back to No. 10 in 1951, but by then he was too senior a figure in the Treasury to be a private secretary (interview J. Colville, Churchill's joint principal private secretary, 1951–5).

The views of those who served at No. 10, as Rowan's colleagues and as subordinates, indicate his contribution to the Prime Minister's Office and the qualities they valued. They felt he was the best: 'outstanding', 'exceptional', 'a good brain', 'the most able at handling the job'. He was like 'quicksilver'. He had 'a crucial role', and was of 'dominating importance', 'interested in all aspects of the work'. He was a good organizer, deft at staff management, arranging their tasks on a sound basis and keeping them happy with his gaiety and humour, and in high morale. He was 'a perfect civil servant', possessing a 'breadth of vision' and 'personal integrity' combined with 'push', 'drive', a capacity to take the initiative, and patience. He worked enormously hard. He had 'a belief in action', 'in getting things done'. He had 'a flair for coordination', and was able 'to pick up a piece of paper and see its effects on something else'. His style was of 'calm and collected efficiency' (interviews J. Addis, A. Bevir, J. Colville, G. Davies and M. G. Stenhouse, P. Kinna, J. Martin, S. Minto, J. Peck).

His colleagues praised him for how he tendered advice to the Prime Minister, about how to handle meetings, even about policy in papers from departments and ministers (interviews J. Addis, D. Jay). He had a discreet way of phrasing his advice as questions and suggestions: noting 'the prime minister may feel the argument in paragraph 4 is weak and may wish to ask...'; 'the prime minister would want to be sure of...'; pointing out what the Prime Minister might wish to pay attention to and inconsistencies. He tried to put himself in the mind of the Prime Minister, anticipating his likely reactions: agree, add something, stop. Churchill disliked his private secretaries giving him policy advice, and this indirect method probably enabled them to give it all the same;

while Attlee relied on his private office for advice and soon dispensed with special advisers on public relations and economic policy, such as Francis Williams and Douglas Jay.

Although with Churchill there was a rough division of work between the private secretaries, it was difficult to keep the staff contained within distinctive spheres of responsibility given the press of wartime events and the Prime Minister's demands, which required all secretaries to turn their hands to any task, except that Anthony Bevir was left to specialize in church and Crown patronage. With the more settled methods of Attlee and less need for instant wartime improvisation, Rowan was able to devise a more stable allocation of duties to each of the junior secretaries. One secretary dealt with foreign affairs, two with domestic matters, and another handled parliamentary questions and other issues such as Imperial topics, defence and civil aviation.

Rowan improved the working practices of the office to enable all the secretaries, including himself, to know what was going on. He started the 'dip': a long tray where the secretaries deposited their papers on their way to the Prime Minister. Any secretary could dip into the tray and see what was going up. Rowan had been taught by Norman Brook, at Attlee's request, how to process paper efficiently (letter from Professor J. Burke, Attlee's private secretary). Different coloured folders contained different types of work: urgent letters to the Prime Minister, Cabinet Office papers, important Foreign Office telegrams to be seen by the Prime Minister, and non-urgent telegrams. Papers were divided into those 'seen before but not dealt with' and 'new'. In this way the secretaries, and the Prime Minister, could see quickly what was essential and non-essential – what should go for the Prime Minister's personal handling.

Rowan was credited with starting 'the Bible'. It was more a work of reference than an office handbook, a compendium of precedents about how to handle different kinds of business, containing the formalities of constitutional lore and governmental procedure. It was suggested he began its production because precedents had to be sought from the more permanent junior staff at No. 10, like Miss Davies and Miss Stenhouse. From Gladstone's days the 'Bible' had been in existence but it soon became out-of-date and often forgotten, and had to be revised from time to time. Rowan carried out such a major revision that many colleagues thought he had created it.

Rowan motivated the other secretaries to follow his methods in much the same way as Gladstone had inspired his staff. They copied Rowan's approach, putting comments on papers the way he did, making positive contributions, all doing their best to help the Prime Minister shoulder his responsibilities. Attlee's quiet style gave him the chance to make changes, and to deploy staff more efficiently. Churchill's impatience to deal on any topic with whichever private secretary was nearest made it difficult to share out policy areas.

Rowan also kept No. 10 in touch with the Cabinet Office, meshing their activities together so they worked in effect as a single entity. When the No. 10 mess closed after the war in 1945, Rowan regularly went for lunch to the Cabinet Office mess and maintained close contact with Cabinet Office staff, especially Brook, the Cabinet Secretary. Brook would talk to Rowan two to three times a day on his way to and from the Prime Minister. From the vantage point of Rowan's room, next to the Cabinet room where Attlee worked, the secretaries were able to peer through the keyhole straight to where the Prime Minister was sitting and see what he was doing, and visitors to the Prime Minister had to pass through Rowan's room on their way to the Prime Minister. Rowan was the orchestrator of the communications network linking the Prime Minister both to the Cabinet and other ministers and to the Cabinet Office and other departments.

Although some thought Rowan's personal political views were reactionary, he was able to win the confidence of a Conservative and a Labour prime minister. He was justification of the success of the system begun by Waterhouse that a principal private secretary could serve chiefs of different political parties. Foreign observers were amazed that the same official could serve the Conservative Churchill at the Potsdam Conference one day and then a few days later after the general election of 1945 the new Labour prime minister Attlee.

Harold Wilson

Harold Wilson was prime minister 1964–70 and 1974–6. He came to the premiership determined to be an innovatory prime minister after thirteen years of Conservative government. He portrayed Alec Douglas-Home as reacting to events, whereas he wanted to take the initiative and turn No. 10 into a 'powerhouse'. Wilson had thought about the office of prime minister before taking office, and he was the first prime minister since Gladstone and Rosebery in the Victorian era to write about the Prime Minister's role in governance (1976; 1977). His innovations produced for the first time a clear division of No. 10 into four 'offices': the private office, the political office, the policy unit and the press office, which has persisted to this day. And under his last principal private secretary, Kenneth Stowe, this ensemble of offices became known officially as the Prime Minister's Office.

His quest was twofold: first to sustain his personal and political position against powerful rivals in the party and government; second to counteract what he believed would be a watering down by the civil service of Labour Party policies. So he brought into No. 10 a political 'retinue' (Pimlott 1992: 338) considerably larger than it had experienced since the days of Churchill and, before that, of Lloyd George. He maintained a sharp distinction between the responsibilities of civil servants and those of his political staff, a clear break with previous practice. It provoked conflicts about where the dividing line should be over such issues as rooms, handling of correspondence, use of notepaper, funding, and access to official papers, committees, visits, status and titles, as well as access to the Prime Minister himself. It took time for the delineation between the political and administrative to be negotiated: it could not be discovered and proclaimed at the outset.

Wilson, a stickler for constitutional propriety, wanted the civil service kept in what he felt was its proper place, subordinate to political control. His style of working was so admired by the civil service that he was said to be 'a civil servant's Prime Minister' (Pimlott 1992: 347), like Attlee, his model, under whom he had served in the 1940s. He conducted business in an ordered and efficient manner, dispatching his papers with clear decisions attached. While his staff might be engaged in bitter wrangles, he remained above their squabbles. He admired the civil service for its competence, but distrusted it too, especially the Treasury and others at the top for their policy inclinations, manipulation of senior jobs and patronage, and general conservatism. So he rejected its advice on who should be his principal private secretary, replacing Derek Mitchell prematurely in 1966 with Michael Halls, and on Halls' death in 1970 choosing Alexander Isserlis. Halls had been Wilson's junior private secretary at the Board of Trade in the 1940s, while Isserlis was the nephew of the wife of Sir Leslie Plummer, a left-wing MP friendly with Wilson. The civil service advised against both appointments, but Wilson insisted. He wanted officials sympathetic and loyal to him, not a civil-service plant. On his return to No. 10 in 1974 he retained Robert Armstrong, but in 1975 selected as his successor Kenneth Stowe, who was again not the civil service's choice. Wilson sought to diminish Treasury influence in the private office, widening its composition to staff from more earthy departments. He left the civil servants in the private office to do their jobs in ways they thought best. He moved his place of work away from the Cabinet room to his study on the next floor up, where the private office could not get at him as easily and he could hold conversations with political aides without the civil service knowing what he was up to.

The misgivings of the Prime Minister and of his political staff about civil servants extended to the Cabinet Office too. Burke Trend and John Hunt, Secretaries to the Cabinet under Wilson, were less present at No. 10 than Edward Bridges and Norman Brook had been, and there was less meshing together of the two networks. Hunt seems to have been regarded with greater suspicion by the political staff, as if he had his own agenda. Wilson distrusted the security services too and wanted to avoid the scandals that had destabilized Macmillan's government. From 1964 to 1967 he located his political ally, George Wigg, the Paymaster General, first in the Cabinet Office and then at No. 10 to provide him with advice about security and to warn him of possible scandals. But Wilson later let this innovation lapse.

To counterbalance the assistance from the civil service Wilson inserted a set of political aides and advisers into No. 10. Marcia Williams was its most assertive member, eventually called his political and personal secretary. She carved out a distinctive role, handling political matters with separate staff in separate rooms. Wilson brought in other political and personal helpers to No. 10, such as John Allan, Alfred Richman, George Caunt and others, who, together with the Parliamentary Private Secretaries, liaised with Labour MPs, party headquarters, local parties and his own constituency party, dealing with correspondence, organizing meetings and ferrying Wilson to and from party events (Williams 1972; 1975; Falkender 1983).

Tentatively at first, to avoid controversy over his enhancing of the prime-ministerial office, Wilson appointed the Oxford economics don Thomas Balogh as his policy adviser, located initially in the Cabinet Office and then in Wigg's former room in No. 10. Balogh headed a unit of economists, including Andrew Graham and David Piachaud, which gave the Prime Minister advice on policy proposals. It was low-profile and largely a countercheck on the Treasury and the bureaucratic view. In the 1974–6 government the group of policy advisers was formalized and publicized as the Policy Unit under Bernard Donoughue, an LSE political scientist. Donoughue headed a larger team of full and part-time staff, including Graham and Piachaud. Their status was regularized as temporary civil servants. They concentrated on domestic issues, especially economic, financial and social matters (Donoughue 1987).

Wilson enlarged the staff dealing with the media, ensured they were civil servants and separate from the private office staff, and brought in as head of the Press Office a non-civil servant. Wilson wanted someone who was both a journalist, familiar with media requirements and practices, and a political sympathizer. However, the first, Trevor Lloyd-Hughes, took seriously his role as a temporary civil servant and avoided anything that smacked of party-political propaganda. So Wilson brought to No. 10, as political press officer, Gerald Kaufman, a political correspondent and known Labour supporter, who worked closely with Marcia Williams. In 1974–6 the head of the Press Office was Joe Haines, a political writer from the Labour paper, the *Daily Mirror* (Haines 1977a; 1977b). He did not work well with Marcia Williams. Nor did he endear Wilson to the media, at one point breaking off briefings to them. He preferred to be a kind of political secretary, giving advice to the Prime Minister about policy and its presentation, and drafting speeches.

With Wilson's backing Marcia Williams transformed the recruitment patterns of the office support staff from personal selection from Kensington secretarial schools by the long-serving women secretaries at No. 10 to routine trawling of established civil servants from departments. Wilson's innovations changed the atmosphere at No. 10 from that of the family home of the Conservative era, in which civil servants, political and personal staff mingled, to a divided arena of mutually suspicious groups. Wilson liked to have advice coming at him from many angles, so that playing off one against the other, and testing the soundness of their contending propositions, he could reach his own decisions (Pimlott 1992: 347). It prevented anyone else becoming dominant. He liked to relax in his study and flat with political friends. They constituted what some called a 'kitchen cabinet', including at various times Marcia Williams, Thomas Balogh, Bernard Donoughue, Joe Haines, Gerald Kaufman, Albert Murray, and his favourite left-wing ministers, Barbara Castle, Richard Crossman, Peter Shore and Tony Benn. The set-up was reminiscent of that of Lloyd George and of Churchill, and similar to the 'court' of Margaret Thatcher (Urban 1996).

Wilson's first premiership was characterized by mutual suspicions between the political staff he brought to Downing Street and civil servants. As time went on they become used to each other's ways and needs and established a *modus vivendi*. When Heath became prime minister in 1970 a distinct political presence in Downing Street was more easily accepted, and in Wilson's second period, 1974–6, relationships between the two sides were more settled, as Armstrong and then Stowe achieved a rapport with the political staff, and Marcia Williams was less involved. The No. 10 he left was a structure of separate units, though with links across, and more distinct than formerly from the Cabinet

Office and Treasury, a change symbolized by the appearance of 'The Prime Minister's Office' after 1977 as an independent entry in the *Civil Service Yearbook*, and no longer a subsection of the Treasury. Most of Wilson's innovations became accepted as the norm and were carried on not only by his successor James Callaghan but also by the subsequent Conservative prime ministers, Margaret Thatcher and John Major.

Conclusion

Findings based on five innovators alone are bound to be tentative, and biased in favour of those types of innovation viewed in 1997 as worthy of attention. Yet certain conclusions can be drawn from the evidence in the paper, summarized in Table 4.1. First, any assumption that there was a single thread, however tangled, of evolutionary development from Disraeli to Major would be false. Innovations that Gladstone, Lloyd George or Wilson thought valuable fell or were pushed into disuse, sometimes to be reinvented later. Especially before continuity was ushered into No. 10 by Ronald Waterhouse there was no 'institutional memory' at senior level. Individuals were not constrained by institutions because they had to make their own arrangements. But neither did they have the benefit of inherited experience and steady improvement.

Second, the innovation with the most impact on the effective organization of the office – the taking over of the top official job by career civil servants ready to serve any PM – was not, as might have been thought, a consequence of the excellent neutral service its author provided, transcending party politics; it was the reverse. Perhaps we shall never elucidate the truth. But it is probably the only one of our five cases where the primary cause was not the personal interest of the innovator in improving the functioning of the office.

Third, three of the four deliberately innovative individuals were prime ministers; moreover, the fourth, Rowan, though seen as the brightest and best of the principal private secretaries, not only made the least contentious changes but was able to carry them out because the Prime Minister, Attlee, was amenable to them in a way Churchill was not. Solely prime ministers, it appears, can make wider changes that alter structures or have a large impact outside No. 10 and its links into the civil service network.

So, for the innovations discussed, the key factor shaping the way prime ministers were served was the Prime Minister. But it is too soon to conclude definitively that prime ministers can always get what they

Table 4.1 Innovators at 10 Downing Street, 1868–1997

Innovator	Posts	Innovations	Continuity of innovation*	Innovation exists in 1997‡	Primary factors and secondary factors
Gladstone	PM 1868–74 1880–5 1886 1892–4	No. 10 correspondence routines. Some specialization of tasks. Cabinet agenda and minutes. Cabinet Office briefs. 'PPS' to the Prime Minister.	× × × × ×	√ √ √ √ √	Personal interest in orderliness, efficiency, devolution. Future reputation. Extensive support network. Experience in office.
Lloyd George	PM 1916–22	PM's Secretariat. Cabinet Secretariat (Office).	× √	√ (policy unit) √	Personal demand for more advice and control of war effort and peacetime policy. Charisma, especially as war leader – could get away with it.
Water-house	Principal private secretary 1922–8	Continuity of service by principal private secretary under prime ministers from different parties. Civil service takes over No. 10.	× √	? √	Difficult to sack? Helped Baldwin into power? Provided experience for the inexperienced MacDonald? (not competence).
Rowan	Private secretary, then principal private secretary 1941–7	Specialization of tasks. Closer links to Cabinet Office. The 'Bible'. Efficient handling of PM's paper. The 'dip'. Briefing advice to prime minister.	√ √ (varies) ? √ √ √	√ √ ? √ √ √	Personal qualities as excellent civil servant and staff manager. Attlee offers the right conditions. Previous experience of No. 10 as junior secretary.

Table 4.1 (*Continued*)

Innovator	Posts	Innovations	Continuity of innovation*	Innovation exists in 1997‡	Primary factors and secondary factors
Wilson	PM 1964–70 1974–6	Separate political office. Policy unit. Political press office. Prime Minister's Office.	√ √ (after 1976) x √	√ √ x √	Personal idea of a powerhouse. Suspicions of political colleagues and press. Suspicions of policy stance and autonomy of senior civil servants. Introduced twice.

Notes: * A tick √ means innovation has survived without a break since this introduction.
‡ A tick √ means innovation is still, or is once again, in place in 1997.

want against countervailing pressures from bureaucracies, parliament and other institutions. The research looked at those who innovated, not those who might have done so but did not. All three reforming prime ministers were from the radical party of their day, willing to challenge the institutions of governance. They were forceful politicians with ideas of their own, backed up by political and personal supporters. Only Wilson of the three was in office after the development of a self-confident and unified bureaucracy. His innovations were not achieved without painful and inefficient battles against the conventions guarded by the civil service. It may be the exceptional individuals who overcome the constraints of the institutions. More research remains to be done.

References

Bahlman, D. W. R. (1972) (ed.) *The Diary of Edward Walter Hamilton 1880–1885* (Oxford: Clarendon Press).

Blake, R. (1966) *Disraeli* (London: University Paperback).

Blake, R. (1955) *The Unknown Prime Minister: the Life and Times of Andrew Bonar Law, 1858–1923* (London: Eyre and Spottiswoode).

Davies, J. (1951) *The Prime Minister's Secretariat* (Newport, Mon.: Johns).

Donoughue, B. (1987) *Prime Minister: the Conduct of Policy under Harold Wilson and James Callaghan* (London: Jonathan Cape).

Ellis, E. L. (1992) *T.J.: a Life of Dr Thomas Jones, CH* (Cardiff: University of Wales Press).

Falkender, M. (1983) *Downing Street in Perspective* (London: Weidenfeld and Nicolson).

Gilbert, M. (1994) *In Search of Churchill: a Historian's Journey* (London: Harper-Collins).

Godley, J. A. (Lord Kilbracken) (1931) *Reminiscences of Lord Kilbracken* (London: Macmillan).

Haines, J. (1977a) *The Politics of Power* (London: Jonathan Cape).

Haines, J. (1977b) *The Politics of Power*, rev. edn (London: Coronet).

Hamilton, E. W. (1898) *Mr. Gladstone. A Monograph* (London: J. Murray).

Hazlehurst, C. (1974) 'The Baldwinite Conspiracy', *Historical Studies*, 16.

James, R. R. (1969) *Memoirs of a Conservative: J. C. C. Davidson's Memoirs and Papers, 1910–37* (London: Weidenfeld and Nicolson).

Jenkins, R. (1995) *Gladstone* (London: Macmillan).

Jenkins, R. (1988) *Baldwin*, paperback edn (London: Collins).

Leveson Gower, G. G. (1940) *Years of Content, 1856–1886* (London: John Murray).

Matthew, H. C. G. (1978) (ed.) *The Gladstone Diaries, vol. 6, 1861–68* (Oxford: Clarendon Press).

Matthew, H. C. G. (1982) (ed.) *The Gladstone Diaries, vol. 7, 1869–71* (Oxford: Clarendon Press).

Matthew, H. C. G. (1990) (ed.) *The Gladstone Diaries, vol. 10, 1881–83* (Oxford: Clarendon Press).

Montgomery Hyde, H. (1973) *Baldwin: the Unexpected Prime Minister* (London: Hart Davis, MacGibbon).

Morgan, K. O. (1974) *Lloyd George* (London: Weidenfeld and Nicolson).

Morgan, K. O. (1978) '1902–1924', in D. Butler (ed.), *Coalitions in British Politics* (London: Macmillan).

Pimlott, B. (1986) (ed.) *The Political Diary of Hugh Dalton: 1918–40, 1945–60* (London: Jonathan Cape & LSE).

Pimlott, B. (1992) *Harold Wilson* (London: HarperCollins).

Ramm, A. (1952) (ed.) *The Political Correspondence of Mr. Gladstone and Lord Granville 1868–1871* (London: Royal Historical Society).

Stephen, M. D. (1964) 'Gladstone's Ecclesiastical Patronage, 1868–1874', *Historical Studies, Australia and New Zealand*, 11/42.

Sykes, Sir Frederick (1942) *From Many Angles: an Autobiography* (London: Harrap).

Thomas, I. (1936) *Gladstone of Hawarden* (London: Murray).

Turner, J. A. (1977) 'The Formation of Lloyd George's "Garden Suburb": "Fabian-like Milnerite Penetration"?', *Historical Journal*, 20, 165–84.

Turner, J. (1980) *Lloyd George's Secretariat* (Cambridge: Cambridge University Press).

Urban, G. (1996) *Diplomacy and Disillusion at the Court of Margaret Thatcher: an Insider's View* (London: I. B. Tauris).

Waterhouse, N. (1942) *Private and Official* (London: Jonathan Cape).

West, A. (1899) *Recollections, 1832 to 1886*, vol. I (London: Smith, Elder).

Wilson, H. (1976) *The Governance of Britain* (London: Weidenfeld and Nicolson, and Michael Joseph).

Wilson, H. (1977) *A Prime Minister on Prime Ministers* (London: Weidenfeld and Nicolson, and Michael Joseph).

Williams, M. (1972) *Inside Number 10* (London: Weidenfeld and Nicolson).

Williams, M. (1975) *Inside Number 10*, rev. edn (London: New English Library).

5
The Conservatives, New Labour and Whitehall: a Biographical Examination of the Political Flexibility of the Mandarin Cadre

David Richards

> *It is not easy nowadays to remember anything so contrary to all appearances as that officials are the servants of the public; and the official must try not to foster the illusion that it is the other way round.*
>
> Ernest Gowers, *Plain Words* (1948)

Labour's Inheritance

It is now some time since the new Labour government took office. In that time, both the new set of Labour ministers and the ranks of the senior Civil Service have been keen to emphasize that the 'seamless web of Government' has been maintained (see Theakston, 1998; Hattersley, 1998; Jones, 1998). Of course, it is in the interests of the core executive to maintain the outer façade that all aspects of constitutional propriety have been upheld during the period of transition.

Since April 1997, we have witnessed the retirement of Robin Butler as Head of the Civil Service, having carried out his promise to 'oversee' Labour into office and his replacement by the mercurial Richard Wilson from the Home Office. Indeed, apart from a number of teething problems surrounding Labour's desire to bring in a greater number of departmental special advisers than was previously the norm, and clashes with Millbank Tower over the replacement of Whitehall Press Officers with Labour's 'own people' (see Norton-Taylor and MacAskill, 1997; Pollard, 1997; Cameron, 1998; White, 1998), the only apparent

carbuncle in the new evolving relationship between the Labour government and their mandarins can be found in the Department of
Environment, Transport and the Regions, where the Deputy Prime
Minister insists on referring to his Permanent Secretary simply as 'Hum-
phrey'.[1]

More seriously, the outward appearance of harmony among the political elites can, in some ways, mask important questions concerning the
cultural change in Whitehall during the 1980s and 1990s, the longevity
of the Conservatives in office and the effect this has on mind-sets, or
what Peter Hennessy refers to as 'thought colonization' (Richards 1997,
p. 240). Since April 1997, it is clear Labour's desire has been to consolidate their first electoral victory in 18 years and ensure that they are
returned for a second term. As such, I would argue considerable continuity with the Major administration exists in many policy areas: on
the economic front, Labour have been cautious, most noticeably, by
accepting Conservative spending targets for the first two years; they
have had a Home Secretary who, though very different in style to his
Conservative predecessor, has, on the basis of the December 1997
'Crime and Disorder Bill', continued with a similar law and order
agenda; whilst, ironically, in the area of social welfare, the introduction
of the Green Paper *New Ambitions for our Country – a New Contract for
Welfare* has seen an explicit attempt by a Labour government to build
on the reforms of the previous Secretary of State for Social Security,
Peter Lilley, and abandon some of the commitments to Beveridge; on
Northern Ireland, there has been rapid and successful movement
towards securing a peaceful and, possibly, lasting settlement, but this
has been achieved through bipartisan consensus between Labour and
the Conservatives (as is normally the case when dealing with Northern
Ireland).

Indeed, one of the few areas in which New Labour has displayed what
may be considered a radical break from the past, which distinguishes it
from its Conservative predecessors, has been in the area of constitutional reform. In particular, this can be seen in the proposed plans for
devolution of power, not only to Scotland and Wales, but also to new
regional, English assemblies, as well as reform of the House of Lords and
the Commons and the introduction of a new Freedom of Information
Act. On this evidence, one may argue, it is unsurprising that Labour's
accommodation with its inherited mandarins has been anything but
cosy, for they have broadly engaged in policies which can be located
within the neo-liberal paradigm of their Conservative predecessors (see
Crouch, 1997; Hay, 1997; Kavanagh, 1997).

But what if New Labour, having consolidated its position in government, (similar to the way in which the Conservatives consolidated power between 1979 and 1983) wished to attach itself to a more radical agenda, one which broke with the present neo-liberal consensus? Would the existing relationship with their senior officials remain as comfortable or, alternatively, would the mandarin elite, wishing to protect the presently entrenched neo-liberal consensus, try to undermine them? Here, parallels can be drawn with the Bancroft/Wass generation of senior mandarins. Although initially relieved that a government had been elected with a reasonably clear set of policy goals, subsequently these mandarins found themselves unwilling to turn their backs on the post-war, Keynesian consensus. Thus, after 1979 some became alienated from their political masters and out of kilter with the Conservative government's overall political strategy. A similar scenario, though not clearly discernible at this stage in the electoral cycle (but the same could have been said in 1979), leads one to question just how politically flexible are the mandarin cadre which Labour inherited in 1997?

A Conservative Effect on the Mandarinate?

In a recent piece of research (Richards, 1997), I examined the effects of 18 years of Conservative administration on the senior personnel serving at the highest tiers in Whitehall. In particular, I was interested in exploring the notion that the active interest Margaret Thatcher displayed in the appointment of senior officials and, subsequently, the increase, under Major, of outsiders to the ranks of the mandarinate, in any way politicized the Civil Service – an institution which, at least constitutionally, still clings to the notion of being neutral and impartial. My research was based on three main sources: a quantitative analysis of civil servant appointments and promotions throughout the 1980s and 1990s; secondary information drawn from commentaries by academics and journalists; and qualitative data taken both from the numerous memoirs and biographies of ministers who served under Margaret Thatcher and John Major and, more significantly, from a series of interviews I conducted with both contemporary and retired senior civil servants.

The evidence drawn from the quantitative and qualitative analysis led me to conclude that both Thatcher and Major had a tangible but contrasting effect on the senior Civil Service. In the Thatcher case, she displayed a more active interest than her predecessors in promotions and appointments to the most senior levels in Whitehall. She influenced the appointment of a number of officials to the highest grades in Whitehall and, in so doing, personalized the procedures. She intervened as part of a broader project to foster a new culture in the senior Civil Service, one in which officials spent more time dealing with the efficient management and implementation of government business, at the expense of the policy advice function. While Prime Minister, Mrs Thatcher was attracted to individuals who displayed enthusiasm and a proactive approach to the implementation of her government's policies. It was these types, often those who had spent a period of time working at the centre of Whitehall, who 'caught her eye'.[2] In so doing, they greatly enhanced their promotional prospects. This, I argue, was the main thrust of a 'Thatcher effect' on the higher Civil Service.

Under John Major, my analysis led me to conclude that, at least in relation to the appointments procedure, he was willing to adopt a more consensual approach. When the Cabinet Secretary presents the Prime Minister with a short-list, in order of preference, of two or three names for a vacancy to one of the highest two grades in Whitehall, Major seldom, if ever, rejected the prime candidate (see also Seldon 1997, p. 739). On the rare occasion when this did occur, he certainly had no need to go beyond the remaining names on the list. Thus, following an earlier epoch in which proactivity and personalization had become the key words to describe the Thatcher approach towards the appointment of the mandarinate, under Major there was a marked reversion back to a more traditional, passive and constitutionally propitious style. However, this does not necessarily imply that, in the 1990s, there was a similar reversal to a more 'traditional' type permanent secretary. Two notable occurrences arose during the Major era: the first was a partial 'fall-out' with the Thatcher generation of appointees – Peter Kemp (Cabinet Office – sacked), Clive Whitmore (Home Office – resigned) and Geoffrey Holland (Education – resigned), all over clashes with ministers in the Major Cabinet; the second was a clear increase in the number of 'outsiders' appointed to the Senior Civil Service. The most celebrated appointment of this type was that of Michael Bichard as Permanent Secretary at Employment.

In this chapter I wish to present a series of vignettes which depict various categories of senior civil servants affected by 18 years of Conservative administration. I will adopt a thematic approach, looking firstly at the Thatcher administration and, then subsequently at the Major generation of mandarins. It is hoped that such an approach will provide some insight into the cultural change the personnel of Whitehall underwent between 1979 and 1997. Consequently, it is hoped, this will provide some indication of the political flexibility of the present generation of senior personnel serving the Labour government.

Thatcher's People – 'We can do Business Together'

> *Our doubts are traitors,*
> *And make us lose the good we oft might win,*
> *By fearing to attempt*

> Margaret Thatcher (1993, p. 106), citing William Shakespeare's *Measure for Measure* in her memoirs

The individuals I have identified as having been affected by Margaret Thatcher's personalization of the appointments procedure are each different, but nevertheless they fit relatively comfortably into a number of broad, general categories. These categories are neither absolute, nor are they mutually exclusive. The categories are:

- those I regard as *'managerially-oriented, can-doers'*;
- those consistently accused of being *'overtly political'*;
- those disillusioned with the Civil Service, having been *black-balled*;
- those more traditional Deputy Secretaries who, during the Thatcher era, fitted uncomfortably with the newly emerging generation of managerially-oriented, senior civil servants and, as such, never reached the levels they may have done in another Whitehall era, i.e. the *'also-rans'*;
- *the traditionalists* who, despite rather than because of the Thatcher era, still scaled the heights of their profession, remaining there until retirement. This final category is important because it indicates that the Thatcher effect was far from universal; it was often the case that civil servants took a traditional Whitehall path to the top.

Managerially-Oriented, Can-Doers

The officials in this category are those who displayed what Margaret Thatcher would regard as efficient management techniques and were also able policy implementors. They were positive types, who, when presented with a government policy to be implemented, would look for the most effective means of executing that policy, rather than identifying any potential implementation problems (Richards, 1997). They were the type of individuals who, at an early stage in their career, would have spent time at the centre in Whitehall. Whilst there, they attracted and impressed Margaret Thatcher and, later, through her intervention, their careers blossomed. This does not mean to suggest that the individuals in this category would not have made it to Permanent Secretary in another Whitehall era, but that their careers flourished more rapidly during the 1980s. The two individuals I have selected, as representatives of this group, both possess the characteristics referred to above, but they differ in that one was a Whitehall 'lifer', while the other was appointed from outside the Civil Service.

In 1983, the elevation of Peter Middleton to the post of Permanent Secretary in the Treasury arose through the controversial intervention by Margaret Thatcher in the appointments procedure to ensure the appointment of 'her man'. The late Tony Rawlinson had been the Second Permanent Secretary in the Treasury since 1977. Although he was not regarded as the strongest candidate for the post vacated by the retiring Douglas Wass (see Hennessy, 1989, p. 629), it was generally seen as an insult in Whitehall circles to promote Middleton over Rawlinson's head.

Certainly, Middleton possessed qualities of both high intellectual ability and managerial effectiveness and, as such, at Margaret Thatcher's behest, he received the top post in the Treasury. Anthony Howard (*The Times*, 22.12.1992) described Middleton's appointment as 'adventurous leap-frogging'. Hennessy (1989, p. 634) argued that, if SASC had got its own way, then either Brian Hayes or David Hancock would have received the top post at the Treasury. As it was, Middleton, an avowed monetarist who had been responsible for implementing the Conservative government's medium-term financial strategy, was preferred. Middleton's appointment was clearly not overtly political. It was his ability as an effective manager and administrator and his well-documented monetarist views, which helped explain why he caught the eye of Margaret Thatcher. In an interview, Middleton commented:

> I accept I was young for the post, but I think it is quite a good age for a job like the Treasury. I would ideally have liked to have stayed a little less long than I did. I think eight years is a long time, but I got into a rather confused period at the end: Nigel Lawson resigned; then John Major was appointed Prime Minister; then Norman Lamont came in. I had to see both the Chancellors into their job. (Middleton interviewed 16.11.94)

Other officials I interviewed had some pronounced views on Middleton's appointment. One accepted that Middleton leap-frogged over four or five of his colleagues, but strongly refuted the notion that he was a straightforward 'Thatcher man'. However, if Middleton was not overtly political, he was certainly a positive-type official, as Charles Powell noted: 'One or two stood out as being energetic, possibly abrasive, action-oriented, Peter Middleton being one very clear case'. (Powell interviewed 16.11.94).

Middleton enjoyed Margaret Thatcher's patronage in his accelerated rise to the top. There is little doubt he would have made it to Permanent Secretary under a Labour administration, but the speed of his graduation through the Whitehall ranks owed much to Margaret Thatcher's attraction to his aptitude for carrying out the tasks asked of him, despite any potential obstacles; and his open embracing of monetarism.

There were few occasions in which Margaret Thatcher intervened to ensure the appointment of an individual from outside of the Civil Service. However, in 1982 Robin Ibbs returned to ICI and was replaced, as Head of the Central Policy Review Staff (CPRS), by John Sparrow, a Morgan Grenfell employee. As Sparrow noted in an interview, there were interesting circumstances surrounding his outside appointment to the CPRS: 'On this occasion, Robert Armstrong and Clive Whitmore saw me. They asked me if I would take over as Head of the CPRS. I didn't actually see the Prime Minister on that occasion, until after I had been appointed. However, I would be extremely naive to think she was unaware of what was going on' (Sparrow interviewed 15.11.94).

Sparrow observed that his background had been in the City and he accepted that prior to his appointment, Margaret Thatcher 'knew me and to some extent trusted me'.[3] He then commented that one of Margaret Thatcher's characteristics was her considerable personal loyalty: 'I think the fact that I knew her and had worked well with her, helped. I assume that she had formed the impression that I was of at least average intelligence because if she formed the contrary impression, however much she liked me, I don't think she would have wanted me to be Head of the CPRS' (Sparrow interviewed 15.11.94).

Sparrow then went on to argue that he never saw, nor felt that his appointment could, in any way be construed as political, at least not in the overt sense. However, he did address the issue as to whether it was his economic orientation that had attracted the eye of Margaret Thatcher:

I have never described myself as a monetarist. I don't belong to any particular school of thought. What I couldn't do and I don't think I could ever do is possess the ability to be a member of the Treasury and oppose, for example, road programmes because they cost money and then get promoted to the Department of Transport and promote road programmes. (Sparrow interviewed 15.11.94)

Mrs Thatcher very much regarded Sparrow as a positive-type individual and his outside appointment was a conciliatory gesture to the CPRS, offering it a final chance to salvage itself. Ironically, despite the Sparrow appointment and the undoubted warmth of his relationship with Margaret Thatcher, he was not able to save the CPRS from abolition. However, the Sparrow case does provide an interesting study of one of the few outsiders appointed by Margaret Thatcher as a 'managerially-oriented, can-doer'.

The Overtly Political

This category reflects the many accusations in both political and media circles of overt politicization in the Civil Service. I uncovered no such evidence of this during the Thatcher years; that is, there was no substantiated proof that, at any stage, Mrs Thatcher intervened in the appointments procedure to appoint or promote individuals on the basis of their being sympathetic to the Conservative Party. Of course, this is not to imply that Conservative Party sympathizers were not appointed to the highest grades in Whitehall during the 1980s. However, Mrs Thatcher did not include, in her criteria for assessing civil servants for a post, the individual's political outlook. Nevertheless, a subset of 'overt politicization' can be created: those individuals who, having already secured their appointment to the highest grades, became politicized through too close an association with the Thatcher government. The two case studies I have selected as representative of this category are both individuals who, throughout the 1980s, experienced a high media profile. This is hardly surprising; given that media coverage was, in part, responsible for their being associated with politicization.

One of the most (in)famous senior civil servants of the 1980s was Margaret Thatcher's Chief Press Secretary, Bernard Ingham. Although he only rose to Deputy Secretary status and, even then, belatedly, the Ingham case is enthralling and his promotion certainly came about as a result of Margaret Thatcher's active involvement in the appointments procedure. This despite Ingham's previous association with the Labour Party: in the 1950s and 1960s he was a Labour Party member. Indeed, in May 1965, he stood as a Labour Party candidate in the local council elections in Leeds. His appointment to Chief Press Secretary, after the briefest of meetings with Mrs Thatcher, and the subsequent accusations of politicization are a central part of the controversy which surrounded his Whitehall career.

Ingham worked as press secretary for the entire duration of the Thatcher administration. Despite attempts by both Robert Armstrong and, later, Robin Butler to prise Ingham away from the Press Office and back into the Whitehall mainstream, he steadfastly refused their overtures. Partly due to the longevity of the time he spent in this one post, his Whitehall career will almost inevitably be tarnished by accusations that he became politicized during the Thatcher years. Indeed, in an interview he accepted that he probably did become too closely associated with Mrs Thatcher:

> I think in a sense you could say I did because I was there for eleven years. But my job was to support her. Robert Armstrong tried to move me to become Head of the Central Office of Information and I was profoundly unenthusiastic. I had been there long enough in Armstrong's view. I think it was a mistake to stay for eleven years. I got a lot of clobbering as a consequence. (Ingham interviewed 22.12.95)

I asked Ingham if his position became untenable after Margaret Thatcher's downfall in November 1990:

> When she said she was going, I said I was going as well. I saw my way out, because it was becoming increasingly burdensome. If she had stayed, I would have found it very difficult. I had reached the age of sixty. But when she went, I thought that was a natural break, I could then go. Departing from No. 10, with Mrs. Thatcher still there, would have been very hard for me. You form a bond after eleven years. (Ingham interviewed 22.12.95)

Ingham accepted he had become too closely associated with Margaret Thatcher and, therefore, had no choice but to leave when she did.

He also addressed the notion as to whether or not he had ever been guilty of interpreting what he thought were the musings of his Prime Minister, rather than only relaying to the media her explicitly stated views. As an example, I asked him about the case of the 1984 discussion of the free floating of sterling, in which Nigel Lawson claimed that Ingham's unsubstantiated comments produced a run on the pound (see Young, 1989, p. 546):

What happened there was that I told the truth. What I was saying was that you are not going to throw good money after bad, because you can't buck the market. What I didn't say and what I couldn't say and what I ought to have said, was that we ought to put up interest rates. *The Observer* reached the conclusion that that is what would have to be done, because that day the Treasury had been too timid in putting them up by only 1 per cent. They should have put them up decisively and we wouldn't have had a problem. That was the real problem and, once again, this is what happens to press secretaries. They sometimes make mistakes, because they are coping with a problem that overwhelms them.

Obviously, Ingham had difficulty distinguishing the thin line between being the mouthpiece of the government (through the lobby system) and being an impartial, neutral civil servant. Undoubtedly, there were incidents where Ingham overstepped the line, the Westland Affair probably being the most notable, and where his actions were blatantly political. Thus, it was Ingham's length of tenure in office, combined with a series of high profile political blunders in which he lost sight of his role as an impartial government official, which justified his being labelled a politicized bureaucrat.

It is difficult to examine the case of Ingham, without also reviewing the career of Charles Powell. These two names have become almost synonymous with each other. Following his appointment as Private Secretary advising Margaret Thatcher on foreign and defence affairs, Powell did not enjoy the same initial degree of access to the Prime Minister which Ingham experienced. However, in the last years of the Thatcher government, Powell undoubtedly established himself as one of her closest confidants.

Harris (1990, pp. 180–1) argues that the Ingham–Powell relationship was one of the most powerful forces at the heart of government in the 1980s, despite the fact that, nominally, they were only Deputy Secretaries. Like Ingham, Powell often lost sight of his responsibilities as an impartial government official. In an interview with *The Times* in June 1994, he outlined where he felt his public responsibility lay: 'At Number 10 you have such a small staff, the Prime Minister has got to feel that you are on his or her side. You have got to cut departmental ties. Your loyalty has to be to the Prime Minister.' It is also a clear indicator of the primacy of Powell's commitment to the Prime Minister he served. Here, the implications are clear: if conflict arose between the Prime Minister and the government (as embodied in a collectively responsible Cabinet), Powell regarded his sole loyalty as being to the Prime Minister and not the Cabinet or, more broadly, the public in general. In an interview I questioned Powell on the principles of loyalty within government. His priorities were clear:

> I think it is quite simply a question of loyalty while someone is serving in a Private Office, particularly No. 10. It should never be seen that someone seconded from another department to No. 10 is there as that department's spy or agent. You cannot work the system like that. The Prime Minister has virtually no staff; every Cabinet Minister has thousands of Civil Servants at his beck and call, producing papers. No. 10 has got about ten people in the whole building, actually doing anything serious. While you are there, your loyalty is to No. 10, to the Prime Minister of the day, and I think that is extremely important. (Powell interviewed 16.11.95)

In addressing the issue of whether or not he had become too closely identifiable with the Thatcher government, Powell replied:

> I suppose you scratch me on the whole, you get conservative, with a small 'c', rather than socialist views. But equally if you stay that long as Private Secretary, you do become clearly identified with somebody, in the eyes of the system, the Civil Service, with Parliament and the press. That frankly was one of the reasons why I decided to leave the Government service. I actually thought it was not fair on the rest of the public service to confront them with the dilemma of my return as somebody who was tainted or identified with a political party and a person who had been in power. (Powell interviewed 16.11.95)

One can have some sympathy with Powell's argument that both he and Ingham were the product of a unique set of circumstances; serving in specialized Whitehall posts, during an administration whose longevity in the twentieth century will not be surpassed. However, many would argue that the most substantive evidence that Ingham and Powell became overtly politicized, was the fact that both left Whitehall almost immediately after Mrs Thatcher's downfall in November 1990. They both carried too much political baggage to try to start afresh under a new government, be it Conservative or Labour. The cases of both Powell and Ingham were inextricably linked. Their appointments were secured through the patronage of Margaret Thatcher and, while in office, both politicized themselves (or, at least, allowed themselves to become politicized). It would also appear that both lost sight of the fact they were officially employed as public servants and not as key actors in an alternative Thatcher 'kitchen' Cabinet.

Disillusionment by the Black-balled

The clearest affirmation of Margaret Thatcher's active intervention in the appointments procedure does not necessarily appear in the 'managerially-oriented, can-doers' category. Instead, I would argue, it occurs among the group of individuals who, for a variety of reasons, were informed that, while Margaret Thatcher remained Prime Minister their chances of further promotion were negligible – the black-balled. It is not surprising that individuals in this category provided the strongest corroborative evidence of a Thatcher effect, given the fact that they were alienated from Whitehall in the 1980s and, as such, tended to harbour a degree of disappointment and resentment towards their former employers.

The most notorious case is that of Donald Derx, an official whose career at the Department of Employment was effectively terminated by Margaret Thatcher. In their memoirs, Prior (1986) and Clark (1993) both deal with the Derx affair, while Hennessy (1989) provides the details. Therefore, in this section, I wish to examine two similar but less infamous cases of black-balling, those of William Ryrie and John Steele. The common strand between all three was that, during initial contact, they clashed with Margaret Thatcher. In so doing, they each caught her eye, but in a negative, not positive, sense. What is interesting about these three cases, was that no attempt was made in Whitehall circles to conceal the Prime Minister's disapproval. The respective Cabinet Secretaries confirmed to each individual that, while Mrs Thatcher remained in office, their chances of further promotion were effectively non-existent. Not surprisingly, all three opted to leave and each went on to a successful career elsewhere: Derx left in 1986 to take up a Directorship at Glaxo Holdings plc; Steele moved on to an auspicious career in Brussels, as Director General of Transport for the EC and a consultant for Prisma Transport Consultants; and Ryrie left to become Executive Vice-president and Chief Executive of the International Finance Corporation at the World Bank.

When Ryrie left Whitehall in 1984, he did so as Permanent Secretary at the Overseas Development Agency, one of the more peripheral Whitehall departments. Hennessy (1989, p. 191) said of Ryrie: 'He was an Assistant Secretary in the Treasury who rose to lead his own, Overseas Development department, and might well have headed the Treasury if Keynesianism had not acquired the status of heresy, at ministerial level at least, by the early 1980s.'

Ryrie displayed the type of credentials which, in a previous Whitehall era, might have led him to one of the great permanent secretaryships. However, the Thatcher government was not renowned for its receptiveness to demand-side apologists. I asked Ryrie if he was disappointed at the treatment he had received:

> I am not disappointed that I didn't become a full Permanent Secretary, because only in those last two or three years before leaving, did I really understand something that I think most of my colleagues had understood long before; the role of a top official is purely an advisory role. You are not really expected to be a leader, you are not expected to take charge, especially in the Treasury where there is very little management function. The role of the Treasury official is to advise ministers who take all the decisions. (Ryrie interviewed 19.6.95)

Ryrie went on to recollect his clashes with Margaret Thatcher and outline the circumstances surrounding his premature departure from Whitehall:

> I remember one about steel in which I think I said some things that she didn't approve of and the Head of the Civil Service called me in and just said, to my absolute amazement: 'Bill, the Prime Minister would like you to take the position of Comptroller and Auditor General'. I nearly fell off my chair. Of course, the meaning of saying 'would you be Comptroller and Auditor General' was clear, she didn't want to give me further promotion. I was being kicked upstairs and something didn't fit with my personality. I was told that she had said that she was not prepared to see me made a full Permanent Secretary and therefore I took it for granted that SASC could not put my name forward. There is no doubt at all, in these questions of Mrs Thatcher's relationships with the senior Civil Service and with her own political colleagues, that personal preferences played a considerable part. (Ryrie interviewed 19.6.95)

The Ryrie interview confirmed that Margaret Thatcher was prepared to make clear to her Cabinet Secretary (as the Chairman of SASC) which individuals she was not willing to consider for promotion. This is primary evidence that she actively interfered in the appointments procedure, in order to foster a new culture which encouraged implementation, rather than emphasis on officials questioning the broader remit of government policy.

The John Steele example is further evidence of this, as one official highlighted in an interview:

> The case of John Steele, who was a Deputy Secretary in the Department of Trade and Industry. He was very well thought of and was again expected to be a Permanent Secretary. He went to a meeting with Keith Joseph, on something to do with steel. Margaret Thatcher asked a question which he didn't answer, as he wasn't sure on the detail and she basically said: 'never let me see that man again'. So, it was suggested to John that he went to Brussels.

This evidence has serious longer-term implications for Whitehall. The cases of Derx, Steele and Ryrie indicate that Mrs Thatcher intervened to ensure that certain individuals did not reach the apex of Whitehall. In addition, through her Cabinet Secretary, she actively encouraged these officials to leave the Civil Service and seek a career elsewhere. The ramifications of such actions are grave: Mrs Thatcher unwittingly(?) reduced the range of individuals from whom her successor could draw, whilst also restricting the broad range of intellectual types in Whitehall. Her actions were self-seeking; a means to an end, which in a long-term, broader context smacked of myopia.

The Also Rans

This category includes officials who, though competent Deputy Secretaries, were not able to adjust to the changes in the Civil Service introduced in the Thatcher era: in particular, the increasing emphasis on managing and administering departments, at the expense of the policy function. As such, they were rejected as serious contenders for a Permanent Secretaryship. There are two representative cases I have selected from this category, whose anonymity, for obvious reasons, remains protected: one was an official in the Department of Energy and the other served in the DTI. Both were university graduates from Oxbridge and each entered the Civil Service at the outset of their professional careers and remained there for over thirty years. I do not wish to suggest they were individuals who, in a different era in Whitehall, would inevitably have become Permanent Secretaries. However, they represent a more traditional type of civil servant who led respectable careers, yet, when nearing the pinnacle of their vocation, discovered that their more traditional approach to a civil servant's job was out of step with the newly fashioned Whitehall trends of the 1980s emphasizing management over policy advice.

The first official spent nearly all his professional life in the Civil Service. After spells in the Treasury (the centre) and a number of other Whitehall departments, he was appointed to a senior grade in the Department of Energy. He remained a servant in that department for seven years, before, prematurely, turning his back on Whitehall. When interviewing this official, I asked him whether he had become disillusioned with the newly emerging Whitehall of the 1980s and had, therefore, decided to leave, or if he was simply seeking horizons elsewhere?:

> It was a mixture of both. I was in my early fifties when I left. Now for one reason or another and much to one's own surprise, you find yourself at some stage, near the top of the pile and people say: 'you know the next job coming is Permanent Secretary'. If you had asked me earlier what my chosen career pattern would have been, I would have liked to have been Permanent Secretary for two years and then gone out to industry. But undoubtedly the Civil Service changed, and changed greatly. Of the years I was there, the first 15 were splendid. Progressively though, I thought the role of the senior civil servant was getting less interesting. One's impact on policy was getting less and it was getting a much more frustrating job.

This official is a classic example of the traditional type of civil servant who scaled the Whitehall ladder, excelled in the role of policy adviser to his minister, but who did not wish or was not able to immerse himself in the administrative/management function. This became apparent when I asked him to compare the Civil Service he joined in the 1950s to the one which evolved during the 1980s:

> That it has changed I have no doubt. That it has changed dramatically, I think it has. In my own personal view, it has changed for the worse and this will be regretted, but that could be an old man growing older. In the early 1950s and 1960s, they would talk about bright young people going into the Civil Service. They never talk about that nowadays. The managerial line is the one now taken. In a way it is a reflection of how society has changed. If you look at recruitment, at one time, the Civil Service did prefer intellectuals. Now some of those were outstanding and they would be brilliantly analytical, but they could not run an agency. Now, I think ministers are in danger

of losing some of the great independent thought and advice they used to receive.

Although not a Conservative sympathizer, as a professional civil servant this official maintained he would have been prepared to work willingly with the Conservative government throughout the 1980s. However, it was obvious during the interview that he had become alienated by the changing role of the senior civil servant under Mrs Thatcher – in particular, the explicit shift, encouraged by the Thatcher governments, away from the traditional policy-making/advisory function towards a much more managerial approach, based on 'efficiently' administering a department. Alienation bred resentment and this, coupled with the fact that he found he was becoming increasingly marginalized in his own department, meant that the returns, in terms of job satisfaction, were diminishing. In such an environment, it became increasingly apparent that further opportunities for promotion were limited and so, when the chance presented itself, this official opted out.

The second case runs along parallel lines to the Energy official. This official was an individual who, in another era, had the potential to become a Permanent Secretary. However, in the 1980s he found himself, as a high-ranking DTI official, in an environment which had vastly changed from the one he had joined thirty years earlier. The increased pressure on senior officials to engage in management and administration to the detriment of policy advice was a cultural change he opposed. He therefore opted to leave, accepting that, as things stood, he would not become a Permanent Secretary. This official joined the Board of Trade in the 1950s. He followed the path of a typical 'Whitehall high-flyer' of his generation, spending the next three decades working in a variety of departments. However, despite almost reaching the hierarchical peak of Whitehall, he left early, believing that under Margaret Thatcher's government he could no longer work as an impartial, neutral, civil servant. Asked about the final stages of his Whitehall career and his increasing sense of alienation from the institution he had joined in the 1950s, he replied: 'I certainly would not have been comfortable working with the Thatcher Government. I was offered a job at ____, which I accepted, as I was increasingly disenchanted with being a civil servant. I would have felt miserable serving throughout the eighties'.

I then asked whether, after the first few months of the Thatcher administration, it had become obvious that he was not going to be appointed to a Permanent Secretaryship. 'I don't think I would have made it to Permanent Secretary', he said. 'I think the reason for it is the top civil servants, the Bancrofts of this world, didn't think I was "sound". The reason why I think this, is because my minister informed me that that was the case. Likewise, I didn't have a lot of respect for the minister I was working for.'

This official differed from the Energy official in that he predicted that the newly elected government, led by Mrs Thatcher, would put an immense strain on his own approach to being a professional, senior civil servant, and so he decided to leave early. He also appreciated that his capacity to climb a grade higher to Permanent Secretary was severely constrained by changing attitudes in the Civil Service. Thus, the official opted to go, rather than become side-lined in the new regime.

This category, like the black-balled category, suggests worrying, longer-term implications for the Civil Service. Both the Energy and DTI officials had become unhappy with an institution visibly different to the one they joined three decades earlier. Realizing their limited chance of progressing in such an environment, they voted with their feet and opted to leave.

Traditionalists who Made the Grade

This final category contrasts directly with the previous one: here, I present two cases of individuals who followed a traditional Whitehall career path, did not display the more fashionable traits associated with the newly emerging mandarinate of the 1980s, yet nevertheless achieved Permanent Secretary status. This is an important category in two respects. First, it highlights the fact that an outstanding, yet traditional, civil servant could still scale the organization's hierarchical ladder during the 1980s. Second, it demonstrates that the Thatcher effect, while crucial, was not universal.

The first of the two cases in this category is that of Michael Quinlan, who in 1983 was appointed Permanent Secretary in the Department of Employment and, five years later, became the Permanent Secretary in the Ministry of Defence. Ironically, his appointment to Employment was viewed, at the time, as having been at the expense of Donald Derx.

The bulk of Quinlan's career was in the Ministry of Defence and it was while serving as a Deputy Secretary in that Department that it is believed he caught the attention of Mrs Thatcher. However, it is hard to see Quinlan as an official who displayed proactive, managerially-oriented tendencies. He was a cerebral-type figure, devoted to analysing and criticizing government policy, rather than rushing head-long into various implementation options. As such, one would assume his character was not the sort which normally attracted the attention of Margaret Thatcher. Yet, as Charles Powell commented: 'There were some very reflective senior civil servants appointed by Margaret Thatcher. The excellent Permanent Secretary at Defence, Michael Quinlan, was an archetypal intellectual, being a great writer on nuclear weapons and so on. He was entirely the opposite of a can-doer and not an action man at all' (Powell interviewed 16.11.94).

It was Sir Frank Cooper, Quinlan's predecessor at the Ministry of Defence, who explained why, despite Quinlan's character, Mrs Thatcher believed him to be the best individual for that particular post:

> She certainly, initially, was very dubious about Michael Quinlan, but she did, particularly after his arguments on Cruise and Pershing missiles, come to greatly respect his intellect and his quiet way of arguing and, of course, his total commitment to the nuclear deterrent. She thought that he was a very clever chap and you need clever people thinking about these kinds of issues. I think she did respect him, because he is not naturally the kind of person she would take to. (Cooper interviewed 20.12.94)

Quinlan's appointment is an example of rationality triumphing over personal characteristics. Mrs Thatcher would possibly have preferred a more proactive type of official to be appointed to the post of Permanent Secretary at the Ministry of Defence, if a suitable one had been available. Thus, although initially she frowned on Quinlan's more reserved, dispassionate approach to his work, he was still the one outstanding candidate for the job.

Similarly, Angus Fraser was not the type of individual who, in most circumstances, would have attracted the admiration of Margaret Thatcher. Despite this, in 1983, Fraser was promoted to Permanent Secretary in HM Customs and Excise from Deputy Secretary in the Management and Personnel Office. Having entered Customs and Excise in 1953, as an Assistant Principal, Fraser's career followed what can only be described as a traditional path through the various ranks of Whitehall. He was never regarded as one of the new breed of 1980s Permanent Secretary which the Thatcher effect nurtured. John Cassels said of Fraser:

> Certainly the Civil Service Department used to attract people like Angus Fraser, who were brought in from other departments. He is an interesting case because he was not beloved, I guess, of Mrs

Thatcher and still made it to the top. Obviously, there were some people in the Civil Service who she did not think well of and yet still made it to the top. I think that perhaps might have been, and in my view deservedly so, the case of Angus Fraser. (Cassels interviewed 20.12.94)

Despite Fraser's more pondersome, less 'can-do' approach to his work and a reputation for allocating an unusually large proportion of time to the consideration of the viability of government policy, he still managed to reach the grade of Permanent Secretary. Indeed, his reputation in that post grew to such an extent that, in 1988, following Robin Ibbs' return to the private sector, Fraser was appointed his successor as Adviser to the Prime Minister on Efficiency and Effectiveness in Government. He had developed into one of Mrs Thatcher's closest advisers, without shedding a critical approach to government policy, and also despite some obvious personal differences between the two. Clive Priestley commented on Fraser's second promotion: 'When it came to the succession of Robin Ibbs as adviser, she appointed Angus Fraser, who was serving as a Chairman of the Customs and Excise Board. This showed how open her mind could be on some appointments. She could sometimes be influenced less by thinking about categories, than her experience of individuals' (Priestley interviewed 14.11.94).

What the cases of both Quinlan and Fraser highlight is that, in appointments to Grades 1 and 2, both of which required the approval of Mrs Thatcher, the final decision would, in the majority of cases, have been based on SASC's assessment of the most suitable individual available. The Prime Minister simply gave her approval to the preferred candidate on the SASC short-list. However, this was not the case if the appointment involved was to a post which Margaret Thatcher felt of strategic importance, or where an individual appeared (or in some cases did not appear) on the SASC short-list about whom she held strong views. Those views may have been either positive or negative and were often the result of the briefest of encounters with a particular individual. Either way, in such cases, Mrs Thatcher's impression had a direct bearing on the outcome of the final appointment. However, Quinlan and Fraser provide examples of individuals who were the outstanding choice for senior ranking posts in Whitehall and who had not crossed swords with the Prime Minister. This despite the fact that neither possessed some of the more fashionable traits associated with the mandarinate of the 1980s.

Major's People – the Blue and the Grey

In a community where public services have failed to keep abreast of private consumption things are different. Here, in an atmosphere of private opulence and public squalor, the private goods have full sway.

J. K. Galbraith, *The Affluent Society* (1958)

In November 1990, John Major replaced Margaret Thatcher as both Leader of the Conservative Party and Prime Minister. Major surprised a number of Whitehall watchers by not only picking up the mantle of transforming the Civil Service bequeathed him by the Thatcher government, but also by dramatically increasing the pace of reform. By the 1997 election year, one had witnessed the rapid expansion of the anti-statist, New Public Management programme through the proliferation of Next Steps agencies, the increasing contracting-out (or privatization) of government business and, finally, the introduction of the Citizen's Charter. This last initiative has been regarded by many (including Major), as his government's 'big idea'.

John Major's approach to senior appointments was far less interventionist than that of his predecessor. He certainly took an interest in the top promotions system, but rarely queried the suitability of the candidates being offered him for appointment. As one official put it: 'Although I was not privy to the private conversations between John Major and Robin Butler (the Cabinet Secretary and Chairman of SASC), it was quite clear to the remaining members of SASC that our recommendations were, in general, being adhered to'.

Yet, a fundamental change in top appointments occurred in the Major era: there was a sharp rise in the number of outsiders introduced to the highest ranks in Whitehall. Of course, this is mainly a corollary of the partial opening up, in the 1990s, of senior Whitehall posts to outside competition. However, a second, and perhaps more disquieting, trend has seen both the resignation and sacking of senior ranking officials. In my view, this reflects the failure of a number of the Thatcher generation of mandarinate appointees to endear themselves to the Major generation of ministers. As Barberis (1995, p. 217) observed: 'The hue of Thatcherism seems to have gotten into the timber of Whitehall. It has coloured the roles of permanent secretaries and their relationships with ministers under the Major Government.'

Outsiders find a New Home in Whitehall

As Robin Butler noted when giving evidence to the TCSC in November 1993: 'Eight out of the present 35 Permanent Secretaries were appointed from outside' (Treasury and Civil Service Committee: 1994, vol. II p. 51). The main factor accounting for this change has been the tentative moves towards the open advertisement of Civil Service vacancies.

The most notable of these outside appointments and the one I wish to dwell on is that of Michael Bichard. As of June 1998, he is the only Chief Executive of a Next Steps Agency to have been appointed to a Permanent Secretaryship. However, his case may provide some interesting pointers for the future. Bichard's earlier career was spent working as Chief Executive, firstly with Brent Borough Council and, subsequently, Gloucestershire County Council. In 1990, he was appointed Chief Executive of the Social Security Benefits Agency under the new, open, arrangements for selection. In March 1995, following another open competition, he was appointed Permanent Secretary in the Department of Employment, becoming the first chief executive from a Next Steps Agency to cross the divide into the traditional mandarinate. Appointed at the age of 48, he remains one of the youngest Permanent Secretaries in the Civil Service. The Whitehall correspondent for *The Times*, Nigel Henderson, wrote of Bichard's initial appointment: 'The appointment is being seen as something of a breakthrough. Some have even described Mr Bichard as "an outsider", Whitehall-speak for anyone who has been a civil servant for less than a decade and who has work experience outside the governmental machinery' (*The Times*, 6.3.95). More surprisingly, in Autumn 1995, following a major upset in the Whitehall promotion stakes, Bichard beat Tim Lankester, a career civil servant, to the top job following the amalgamation of the two departments of Employment and Education. Even in the 1980s, when a departmental merger occurred, the permanent secretaries affected would always be accommodated within the Whitehall community. However, prior to the departmental merger, Lankester was informed by the Cabinet Secretary that he would have to openly compete alongside Bichard for the one available permanent secretaryship. He declined to do so.[4]

With the Bichard case, it is unclear whether the appointment of a Chief Executive to the ranks of the mandarinate is a one-off, or whether his case ushers in a new, less predictable, pattern for appointments to the highest grades in Whitehall. Moreover, Bichard is important because the Rubicon between Permanent Secretary and Chief Executive has now been crossed. This raises three issues: first, how well-equipped is a trained administrator to successfully work in what may prove an alien and highly-charged political environment?; second, is it possible for an outsider, not educated in the principles which shape and guide a senior mandarin and encapsulated in the notion of a 'public sector ethos', to distinguish between the public and private good?; third, there is the potential that outside appointees, often on short-term contracts, may be chosen on the basis of a similar ideological outlook to the incumbent government.

Fall-out from the Thatcher Appointees

The second area of controversy surrounding the Major era and senior appointments concerns a number of highly public 'fall-outs' which occurred between the senior mandarins appointed by Margaret Thatcher and the Cabinet Ministers appointed by Major.

The most notorious incident was the 1992 sacking of Peter Kemp by William Waldegrave, then Minister at the Office of Public Service and Science. The event had a whole section devoted to it in the 'Summary and Recommendations' section of the TCSC 1993–4 Report (Treasury and Civil Service Committee: 1994, vol. 1, pp. cvi–cvii). The official gloss the Report gave the sacking, emphasized that Kemp had been an individual with the necessary qualities to launch Next Steps, but that, once the programme was up and running, a different individual, with a contrasting range of qualities, was required to consolidate the progress already made. Of course, official versions rarely reflect the reality of an event. In 1996, I quizzed Kemp about the details surrounding his departure and, while, he still remained puzzled, he thought there might have been two sets of reasons:

> The first reason was basically that I fell out personally with William Waldegrave. He had come from big departments – the Department of Health was his most recent – and he wanted big department style. And, up to a point, he was right; the OPSS, as it became, was a slightly bigger department than the old OMCS. It was not unreasonable to suggest that different skills might be needed, though we were scarcely given the chance to test this. But I believe that there was more to it than just that. Perhaps Waldegrave did not enjoy having something of a star on his staff. And the second reason may have been because I had my own views about how we should go forward with reforms, such as the market testing exercise – something which in itself I thoroughly approved of – which were not apparently

attractive to people like Peter Levene who was in charge of the thing or to Waldegrave himself. Neither of them ever really understood the Civil Service. Which ever way up it was, Waldegrave did not want me, and was not prepared to let us both try harder to get on; and when that happens it is right and proper that it is the official and not the minister who has to depart. The difficult bit that followed on from this was that contrary to what has happened to other people on previous occasions of this nature, no attempt at all seemed to be made to find me another job, so I had to leave. (Kemp interviewed 16.4.96)

Historically, in the few isolated cases when a Permanent Secretary could no longer work with his minister, he was normally transferred to another department. There was the occasion, in November 1981, when Ian Bancroft was effectively sacked from the Civil Service, following the abolition of the Civil Service Department. It was true that Bancroft and Margaret Thatcher did not regularly see eye-to-eye. However, a compromise was sought and he was able to end his career in Whitehall with dignity intact. The Kemp affair differed because there was no obvious attempt at conciliation. The government formally accepted that they were sacking Kemp. As Theakston (1995, p. 136) points out, what was even more surprising to outsiders was that 'Whitehall's elite did not close ranks to protect him'. However, as the Kemp interview highlights, this was no ordinary clash of personality between a minister and his official, as it also involved Peter Levene, another senior mandarin. Hence, the elite failed to step in and resolve what eventually became a very public falling out. Something had to give; in this case it was Kemp, the 'unconventional' figure, who had always been considered, even by his own staff, an outsider.[5]

The importance of the sacking was that, for first time, the government signalled to its higher civil servants that they no longer enjoyed security of tenure. Kemp felt his undignified departure from Whitehall sent out worrying signals concerning the future security of tenure for an increasingly demoralized mandarinate: 'It was quite a precedent. Previously, people had bent over backwards to keep Permanent Secretaries in jobs. The echoes go on; it has been written that my precedent would enable a future Labour government to sack top advisers' (Kemp interviewed 16.4.96). This is a key point: Kemp's dismissal does have wider implications for the Civil Service. It could be the precursor for further sackings of the Conservative generation of senior civil servants by a Blair government dissatisfied with their inheritance. Although, after one year, this has so far not be the case – both the new government and their senior Whitehall officials have, publicly at least, been keen to stress the cordial working relationship which exists. Yet, this does not preclude a Cabinet Minister or Blair himself, at some point further into the lifetime of this present government, using the Kemp precedent to force the removal of an official he or she has found to be less than cooperative. If this were the case, then two of the fundamental Northcote–Trevelyan principles on which the Civil Service was founded, permanence and impartiality, would come under further stress.

Since Kemp's ignominious departure, there have been no further public sackings of senior civil servants of the Thatcher generation. However, in November 1993, Geoffrey Holland, the Permanent Secretary in the Department for Education, resigned from the service. Afterwards, claims were made (which were denied by his department) that John Patten, his Education Secretary, had stopped talking to him. This was followed, in May 1994, by Clive Whitmore announcing that he was prematurely leaving his post as Permanent-under-Secretary in the Home Office for a job in the private sector. The *Observer* (6.5.94) reported that: 'Sir Clive Whitmore has made it clear in private that he is dismayed by the low standard of political competence displayed both by Mr Howard [his Minister] and the Government as a whole. He has contrasted ministers' performances with the defter touch of senior ministers during the Thatcher heyday.' In a recent series of interviews I conducted with many senior Home Office officials who worked alongside Howard and Whitmore, most willingly testified to the extent to which relations between the two had broken down.[6]

Since these two resignations, and the Lankester affair, there has been no additional political fall-out. However, what these cases indicate is that the 'Thatcher effect', coupled to the reforms which Whitehall underwent during 18 years of Conservative administration, in particular during the Major era, has created serious ramifications for the new Labour government.

Conclusion: Political Passivity of a New Mandarin Cadre

The ideal civil servants should always be colourless, odourless and tasteless.
Roger Peyrefitte, *Diplomatic Diversions* (1953)

At the outset of this chapter I posed the question: how politically flexible are the mandarin cadre which Labour inherited in 1997? What I hope to have illustrated through the series of vignettes which have depicted the various categories of senior civil servants affected by 18 years of Conservative administration, is that the mandarin class of today is different to that of its predecessors in 1979. It would not be misrepresentative to portray the present senior Whitehall cadre as less policy-orientated than yesteryear. Their job remit has increasingly placed greater emphasis on managing and administrating their departments, at the expense of time spent on the actual detail of policy formulation. Indeed, as I observe elsewhere: 'At the senior levels in Whitehall, the greatest change has been a shift from policy-making . . . to a focus on efficiency and costs of service delivery . . . The consequence of this shift in the role of officials from policy formulators and advisers to efficient managers involved in cost delivery is profound' (Richards, 1997, pp. 235–7).

Thus, in answer to the question, it is ironic to note that 18 years of Conservative administration have led to a senior Civil Service which, one could argue, is more politically passive. By that, I mean that their primary concern is for the efficient and economic running of the machinery of government and not the prospective consequences of the overall direction in which government policy maybe heading. Thus, they are (probably unwittingly) more politically flexible than previous generations of the mandarin class.

Indeed, one could project that if, during a possible second term in office, the present Labour government did attempt to break free from the existing neo-liberal consensus, then the minds of the mandarins would be more concentrated on the minutiae of achieving this break, in conjunction with the cost-effectiveness of the projected expenditure involved, than in questioning the broader ramifications of striking out in a new, maybe radical direction.

Whether or not these changes in the culture of senior Whitehall personnel are good or bad is contingent on one's own political disposition, but also whether one believes bureaucrats exist to simply run the machinery of government for their political masters/mistresses, or, more broadly, to question in which direction the whole cabal is heading. However, what is certain is that the Wass/Bancroft generation of mandarins displayed much greater resistance to radical change after 1979 than their present counterparts are ever likely to do. Perhaps the above words of Roger Peyrefitte finally ring true!

Notes

1. Private information.
2. By the centre of Whitehall, I refer to the Cabinet Office, the Prime Minister's Office and the Treasury. For more information on a centre effect, see Richards (1997, pp. 163–77).

3. Sparrow had been an unpaid consultant for Mrs Thatcher in the 1970s on matters concerning the City.
4. Lankester had already, at an earlier stage in his career, surrounded himself in controversy. Whilst Permanent Secretary in the Overseas Development Agency, he sent a minute to the Public Accounts Committee expressing his belief that the government's offer of a well-publicized grant to Malaysia, for the building of the Pergau Dam, was a misguided use of public money. As Foster and Plowden (1996, p. 232) rather severely concluded of the whole Lankester affair: 'His [Lankester's] view was upheld by the Public Accounts Committee. However innocent the circumstances leading to his departure may have been, it was impossible for many not to draw the moral that, however justified, a permanent secretary who writes such a minute censuring ministerial behaviour will be caught up with in the end.'
5. For more details on the Kemp sacking see Kavanagh and Seldon's (1994) *The Major Effect*, pp. 67–8.
6. Private information.

References

Barberis, P. (1996) *The Elite of the Elite* (Aldershot: Dartmouth).
Cameron, S. (1998) 'The Gentlemen in Whitehall Knows Best', *The Times*, 27.1.98.
Clark, A. (1993) *Diaries* (London: Weidenfeld and Nicolson).
Crouch, C. (1997) 'The Terms of the Neo-Liberal Consensus', *Political Quarterly*, 68/4.
Foster, C. and Plowden, F. (1996) *The State Under Stress* (Buckingham: Open University Press).
Harris, R. (1990) *Good and Faithful Servant* (London: Faber and Faber).
Hattersley, R. (1998) 'He has the Power but None of the Glory', *Observer*, 18.1.98.
Hay, C. (1997) 'Blaijorism: Towards a One-Vision Polity', *Political Quarterly*, 68/4.
Hennessy, P. (1989) *Whitehall* (London: Fontana).
Jones, M. (1998) 'Keeper of the Skeleton Closet', *Observer*, 4.1.98.
Kavanagh, D. (1997) *The Re-Ordering of British Politics* (Oxford: Oxford University Press).
Kavanagh, D. and Seldon, A. (eds) (1994) *The Major Effect* (London: Macmillan).
Norton-Taylor, R. and MacAskill, E. (1997) 'Whitehall Blocks Blair over Favourite Aide's Role', *Guardian*, 3.6.97.
Pollard, S. (1997) 'How Blair's Fixers are Creating a Whitehall Revolution', *Evening Standard*, 3.6.97.
Prior, J. (1986) *A Balance of Power* (London: Hamish Hamilton).
Richards, D. (1997) *The Civil Service Under the Conservatives 1979–97: Whitehall's Political Poodles?* (Brighton: Sussex Academic Press).
Seldon, A. (1997) *Major: a Political Life* (London: Weidenfeld and Nicolson).
Thatcher, M. (1993) *Margaret Thatcher: the Downing Street Years* (London: Harper-Collins).
Theakston, K. (1995) *The Civil Service Since 1945* (Oxford: Blackwell).
Theakston, K. (1998) 'New Labour, New Whitehall?', *Public Policy and Administration*, 13/1.

Treasury and Civil Service Committee (1994) *The Role of the Civil Service: Fifth Report, Session 1993–94* (London: HMSO).
White, M. (1998) 'Hacks at the Helm', *Guardian*, 21.5.98.
Young, H. (1989) *One of Us* (London: Macmillan).

6
Chief Executives and Leadership in a Local Authority: a Fundamental Antithesis

Kester Isaac-Henry

Introduction[1]

This chapter explores the role of chief executives of the Birmingham City Council between 1973 and 1997 as a means of throwing some light on managerial leadership in public sector authorities. In so doing it examines

- the attempt by chief executives to introduce a more corporate style to the management of the City;
- the relationship between the chief executives and the political leaders;
- the relationship between the chief executive and officers of the authority:
- the powers of chief executives and their influences on policies to evaluate their role as leaders in Birmingham.

The research for this chapter is based on interviews with the five persons who have held the post of chief executives in Birmingham since its inception in 1973 as well as one former officer who has been a major player in the City for the last quarter of a century. In addition, with permission, I have had access to two videos of interviews between two political leaders of the Council and their chief executive and have used documents from the official archives of Birmingham City Council.

Some provisos must be made in relation to the methodology. First it must be accepted that the interviewees might put the most favourable interpretations on actions and events affecting them. Second, a lack of balance might accrue from the absence of other views and perspectives. In defence of this latter point, it should be noted that the interviews undertaken form the first part of a wider study of leadership in the City which will involve interviewing other players from both the political and the private sectors.

Development of Chief Executive

In 1967 the Maud Committee argued that to obtain coherence, corporateness and direction in local government, there must be leadership on both the political and the administrative/management side (Maud Report, 1967). It thus proposed that town and county clerks, who traditionally were first amongst equals on the administrative side of their authorities, should be formally recognized as head of the paid service, should have dominion over other officers and should be the main channel of responsibility between councillors and officers.

By 1974, at the start of the restructured system of local government, these proposals began to bear fruit. The Bains Working Party set up in 1972 to advise the new local authorities on their management structures and practices, built on the foundation of Maud and emphasized the need for a corporate approach to managing local government. Such an approach would be facilitated by the introduction of a Policy and Resources Committee with the task of setting priorities and objectives. Unity on the officers' side would be achieved by the existence of a management team, headed by a chief executive having a superior status over all other officers (Bains, 1972, pp. 38–51). When the new authorities began operating in 1974 almost all of them appointed chief executives.

The enormous changes in local government in recent years have had major implications for the developing role of chief executives. Both the Widdicombe Committee (1986) and the Audit Commission (1989) were of the view that the role ought to be nationally defined. The Widdicombe Report argued that the role needed to be enhanced, clarified and formalized, while the Audit Commission suggested that chief executives should be the local authority's source of continuity and agent of change (p. 8). Yet, as Clarke and Stewart observed (1991), since the chief executive is in charge of no specific functions or services, the role he plays has to be described and set by relationships. The Society of Local Authorities Chief Executives (SOLACE) also rejected the idea of a nationally defined role, arguing that the job performed varies according to the size of the Authority; the management structure inherited; the members' structure and the way they perceive their role; the existing style and culture of the organisation; the locality and geography of the area; the attitude, strength and experience of the Council Leader; the degree of homogeneity of the controlling Group and the extent to which political control can vary. (Solace, 1992, p. 7)

Chief Executives and the Concept of Leadership

In 1989 the Audit Commission argued that 'local government needs leadership in the next few years to restore a sense of direction. A strong chief executive can provide much of the new leadership and direction if he or she is allowed to do so' (Audit Commission, 1989, p. 1). In stressing the need for 'leadership' the Commission was merely echoing a theme, which by the 1990s, had become conventional wisdom in management theory, namely that in a rapidly changing and turbulent environment, organizational effectiveness can no longer depend on effective management alone. Salvation must come from leadership.

In seeking to differentiate between the two concepts of management and leadership, theorists maintain that management is coping with complexity by planning, organizing, budgeting and staffing. Leadership, on the other hand, is more crucially concerned with managing change, which involves motivating and inspiring people, creating a vision and pointing the direction in which the organization should go (Kotter, 1992). A distinction is made between transactional and transformational leaders.

> transactional managers make only minor adjustments in the organisation's mission, structure, and human resource management, transformational leaders not only make changes in these three areas but they also evoke fundamental changes in the basic political and cultural systems of the organisation. (Tichy and Ulrich, 1984, p. 59)

In the 1990s effectiveness of organizations is said to depend on the transformational (heroic) leader who

- possesses enormous power, derived from his/her charisma, to alter organizations;
- through creating, expressing and communicating a vision, can command such commitment from employees as to change the values

and assumptions of organizations and indeed transform the organization itself;
- is not afraid to abandon the most sacred of traditions in order to find
innovative ways of doing things. (Terry, 1995, pp. 42–3)

Hence, for example, the suggestion that role of the chief executives in
local government should include 'practical leadership, vision, setting
the style [for the organization] and changing the culture' (Sabin, 1989).

Not all theories on management lead to the transformational leader
as the solution to effective management. Paul Bates, for example, argues
that in large and complex organizations there are too many unknowns,
countervailing forces, demands on ingenuity and too many things to
get done, for one person to bear the palm alone. Culture change (and
this is the essence of managing change) demands a multi-dimensional
process of leadership since culture is itself a multi-dimensional phe-
nomenon. Change cannot be accomplished by one person since 'culture is socially created, socially maintained and socially transformed.
The image of the leader or a striking figure on a rearing white horse cry-
ing "follow me" is rather an unfortunate one.' The reason for this is that
those who seek change 'must learn to be good followers as well as good
leaders' (Bates, 1994, p. 239). Leadership is a collective enterprise. This
is a view shared by Pettigrew *et al.* (1992 p. 20) in evaluating change in
the National Health Service. They argue that the task of managing
change was more fragmentary and incremental than is portrayed by
concept of the 'heroic' manager. 'Moving to bold action could be costly,
and instead the prior need was found to be building a climate for
change.'

There is a widely held view that the chief executive should play the
crucial role in the development of organizational culture, in creating
the vision and in pointing the direction in which the authority should
go (Audit Commission, 1989; Asquith, 1994, pp. 67–8). But such a role
raises a number of issues. First, if the role of the chief executive is to be
that stated above, what role is then left for the elected member? Is not
politics about values, missions and direction, or is there a difference
between organizational values and policy values?

Second, the concept of chief executive in local government is equated
with that of the private sector counterpart. In the case of local government, it must always be acknowledged that leadership also comes from
the political side and that the relationship between chief executives and
political leaders is absolutely crucial to the former's role, effectiveness
and success. It is the recognition of the power of the politicians and the

legitimacy they bring to their role that is, in part, spurring the movement towards elected mayors which it is hoped will 'give municipal government a new sense of vigorous direction by formalising the position of chief executive and imbuing it with authority that comes uniquely from election' (Walker, 1991, p. 19).

The Birmingham Context

Birmingham is the largest local authority in Britain. If it is not unique as a city, it at least has a special place in the history of urban development (Newton, 1976, p. 1). In the last quarter of the nineteenth century, with the drive and foresight of Joseph Chamberlain and others, it set a pace in innovation, social improvements and local political leadership that transformed it and made it difficult for other urban areas to follow. Indeed it was said by some to be the 'best governed city in the world' (Briggs, 1952, p. 67). That confidence and drive was carried into the twentieth century when, in the heyday of fordism, it forged ahead to become, with its surrounding region, the industrial heartland of the United Kingdom. Based on manufacturing cars, engineering and allied industries (Bryson *et al.*, 1996, p. 156–67), even when other urban areas such as Glasgow, Liverpool and Manchester were being 'traumatised by manufacturing decline and loss of population in the 1960s and early 1970s Birmingham had continued to grow' (Loftman and Nevin, 1992, p. 10). But a future shock awaited.

By the mid-1980s the industrial heartland had become an industrial wasteland. The onset of post-fordism with its transformation of production processes, use of new technologies and increasing globalization had wreaked havoc on Birmingham and the West Midlands region, to the extent that between 1971 and 1993 there was a decline of 50 per cent in manufacturing employment. To add to the crisis, the Handsworth Riots of 1985 demonstrated that there was an important link between the industrial collapse and the decline in its social fabric. The riots were said to have dominated the social and political thinking of Birmingham during the 1980s and sapped some of its confidence.

The once 'best governed city' was coming dangerously close to becoming one of the worst governed, at least in Britain in terms of not being able to provide the services and environment to which it thought its citizens were entitled. If there was a time for leadership to be demonstrated it was then. It was recognized that returning to 'metal bashing' was not a solution. There was a need to encourage service-sector industries which could be facilitated by encouraging inward investment, attracting monies from Europe, working more closely with the private sector and forcefully promoting the City's image. The result was the development of what has come to be called the 'prestige projects', including, amongst others, the International Convention Centre, National Indoor Arena, Bingley Place Development, Hyatt Hotel and Symphony Hall. Between 1986 and 1992 it was reckoned that the city had spent £276 million on these projects (in addition to substantial sums from elsewhere).

Thus during the twenty years or so up to the middle of the 1990s, the city's major policy concern appeared to be that of economic expansion through the growth in the service sector, to meet the pressing problems faced. In this period, the political parties were broadly united in the cause of the regeneration of Birmingham as a business centre (Loftman and Nevin, 1992, p. 20).

Corporateness Versus Autonomy: the Fundamental Antithesis

In 1972 the Birmingham City Council adopted the Bains Report by setting up a Policy and Resources Committee to formulate objectives and policy priorities. It was, unusually then for local government, a one-party committee. In 1973 the first chief executive, Francis Amos, was appointed. He was made leader of the management team of senior officers advising the Policy and Resources Committee. His main task was to bring a more corporate and integrative approach to the management side of the authority by being responsible for the coordination and implementation of policies throughout the Council. So began the experiment of introducing corporate unity and leadership into the city council.

In managerial terms, in the last 24 years the city has been dominated by a fundamental antithesis between:

- a desire to move to a more corporate integrative approach to management, and
- a desire to maintain the very strong cultural independence of committees and departments.

All the chief executives who embraced a more integrated approach have faced resistance from both politicians and officers. The extent to which this conflict is yet to be resolved, may be gauged by the fact that the first chief executive, in 1973, set himself the objective of ensuring that policies 'of the different committees are complementary and consistent and that the implementation of programmes through departments are co-ordinated' (Amos, in Birmingham City Council, 1975). In 1997 the present incumbent, Michael Lyons, saw his most important task as that of shaping the organization to work more integratively and corporately.

It is within this tension, between integration and cooperation versus independence of action by committees and departments, that the chief executives' leadership and managerial roles, functions and relationships were (and are being) developed, practised and evaluated.

The Problem Aired

This tension came to a head in 1976 when Neville Bosworth, Conservative leader of the city council, repudiated the experiment in corporate management. He argued that the approach had brought no discernible improvement or economy to the management of the city. Chief officers were spending too much of their valuable time at interminable meetings when they should have been running their departments. His remedy was to return to the traditional structures and practices which had (in his opinion) served Birmingham for well over a hundred years and which were based on independent committees performing the functions allotted to them (Birmingham City Council, 1976).

The major criticisms of the 'traditional' structure was that it:

- bred over-independent and over-powerful chairmen and committees;
- encouraged departments to become autonomous and detached from others;
- lacked any body responsible for determining priorities and painting an across-the-board picture of the authority's work.

Bosworth, on the other hand, considered these to be the real strength in managing the city. He thus returned to an administrative structure where

- departmental boundaries would be sacrosanct;
- the primary responsibilities of chief offices were to their committees and not to the authority as a whole;
- interdepartmental and interdisciplinary communication were to be kept to the minimum. (Haynes, 1980, p. 185)

The Policy and Resources Committee was to be discontinued and what remained of its responsibility passed to a new committee – Finance and Priorities Committee. Meetings of the management team were to cease. The chief executive's main function was now to act as liaison between the City and external private and public organizations. He was effectively demoted. In June 1977 he was informed that the role of chief executive was now defunct and he was to seek employment elsewhere. The legacy of the Bosworth Report and the subsequent actions have had a profound effect on the style of management in Birmingham and demonstrate the difficulties facing those chief executives who see their role as managing in corporate style.

The Five Chief Executives

In the last 24 years up to 1997 the Birmingham city council has employed five chief executives. Although their backgrounds vary considerably, as can be seen from Table 6.1, none came from the private sector, all had had connections with local government before and none were women.

Francis Amos (1973–7), the first, was a town planner from Liverpool, who had worked for the London county council and for the Ministry of Housing and Local Government, where between 1959 and 1962 he was seconded as technical adviser to the Ethiopian government. *Bill Page* (1977–82)[2] was a 'local', born and educated in neighbouring West Bromwich. Between 1935 and 1949 (with a break during the war years) he worked for the West Bromwich authority and joined the Birmingham city council as an accountant in 1949. He rose to become Deputy Treasurer in 1966 and Treasurer in 1973. In 1977 he was asked to become the Council's Principal Adviser while still being its Treasurer. The title of chief executive was bestowed on him in 1980.

Tom Caulcott (1982–8) had won a scholarship to Cambridge in the early 1950s, where he switched from his intended discipline of history to law, obtained a first class degree, passed the civil service examination to the Administrative Class and worked in that service for over 30 years. In his capacity as civil servant he had worked with two Chancellors of the Exchequer and in 1964 became principal private secretary to George Brown in the then newly formed Department of Economic Affairs. His main contact with local government came as Principal Financial Officer at the Department of the Environment (1974), where he was involved with local government grant negotiations and, in that capacity, was in constant touch with leading members and officers of local authorities.

Table 6.1 Background of Birmingham chief executives

Name	Date of birth	Chief Exec. Birmingham	Education	Qualifications	Work organization	Position
Francis Amos	1924	1973–7	Dulwich College	Registered Architect (1953)	Harlow New Town D.C. (1951)	Assistant Architect
					London County Council (1953–8)	Planning Offcier
			School of Regional Planning	Chartered Town Planner (1956)	Min. of Housing & Local Govt. (1958–63)	Planning Officer (Technical Adviser to Ethiopian Govt.)
			LSE (1956)	B.Sc. Sociology	Liverpool City (1962–6)	Divisional Planning Officer
					(1966–73)	City Planning Officer
William Page	1918	1977–82	Local College	Accountant (1948)	West Bromwich District Council (1935–49)	Treasurer's Dept.
					Birmingham City Council (1949–66)	Accountant
					(1966–73)	Deputy Treasurer
					(1973–7)	Treasurer
					(1977–80)	Principal Adviser & Treasurer
					(1980–2)	Chief Executive
Thomas Caulcott	1927	1982–8	Cambridge University	Law (1st class)	Civil Service	Administrative Class
					(1955)	Private Sec. to Chancellors of the Exchequer
					(1964–5)	Ass. Sec. to Sec. of State, DEA

Name	Born		Institution	Qualification	Position	Role
Roger Taylor	1944				(1967–9)	Ass. Sec. to Min. of H. & Local Govt.
					(1976–82)	Principal Finance Officer: DOE
		1988–94	Birmingham University	Law	Staffordshire CC	Legal Clerk
					Cheshire CC Lindsay (Lincs)	Ass. Solicitor
					Northampton	Deputy County Clerk
					Manchester City Council (1979–85)	Deputy Town Clerk & Chief Exec.
					(1985–8)	Town Clerk & Chief Exec.
Michael Lyons	1949	1994–present	Middlesex Polytechnic London	BA Soc. Sci.		Street Trader (1970–2)
				M.Sc. (Econ)	Crookes-Aneshan (1971–2)	Brand Manager
					Northampton Univ. (1970–2)	Lecturer/researcher
					West Midlands CC (1975–8)	Senior Research Officer
					(1978–82)	Principal Economist
					(1982–5)	Deputy Director/Director of Econ. Dev.
					Birmingham City Council (1980–3)	Councillor
					Wolverhampton (1985–90)	Chief Exec.
					Nottinghamshire (1990–4)	Chief Exec.

He was ambitious to become a Permanent Secretary, but by 1976, realizing that the path to that post was blocked, he moved to the Association of Metropolitan Authorities as Secretary.

Roger Taylor is the only one of the five who fitted the career pattern and experience of a former town or county clerk. Having obtained a law degree at Birmingham University he joined Staffordshire County Council, obtained his articles, and in 1971 joined Cheshire County Council as an assistant solicitor. While there he was impressed by the charismatic chief executive, John Boynton. After working for both Lincolnshire and Northamptonshire in 1979 he joined the Manchester City Council as Deputy Town Clerk. In 1985 he became its Town Clerk and Chief Executive, a job which he held until 1988 when he joined Birmingham.

Michael Lyons held the post of chief executive in two other authorities (Wolverhampton and Nottinghamshire) before coming to Birmingham. He was a chief executive by the age of 36. His main experience in local government before becoming a chief executive in Wolverhampton was his work in the economic development section of the (now defunct) West Midlands County Council (1975–85), rising in ten years to become Director of Economic Development. Having served as a member of the City Council (1980–3) he is, so far as can be ascertained, the only person to become chief executive of the authority for which he had served as a councillor.

Management Styles[3]

Francis Amos was appointed to implement corporate management on the officers' side of the council. From the beginning he faced enormous obstacles in attempting to achieve that objective. Birmingham was structured on the basis of a rampant individualism of departments and committees. In trying to bring senior officers together in a management team, he found that many of them had never before met each other. This demonstrated the depth of fragmentation and lack of corporateness which existed in the management of the city at time. In management team meetings there was a very noticeable reluctance on the part of departmental heads to discuss any matter which was perceived to be 'trespassing' on the ambit of another department.

The relationship between officers and the chairs of committees also added to Amos's problems. He found that chairpersons on Birmingham city council were excessively powerful in relation to their officers and were deeply and openly involved in operational matters relating to the departments for which they were responsible. Each chairperson possessed an office and a secretary and often sent for chief and other officers to 'issue instructions'. Given such a situation, not surprisingly, even senior officers were reluctant to discuss matters relating to their departments without prior approval from their chairpersons.

Amos was also caught up in the political crossfire between disgruntled committee chairpersons and their leaders as well as between the majority party and the opposition. Some committee chairpersons, not being members of the Policy and Resources Committee, felt left out in the cold and bitterly resented it. In addition, even those powerful committee chairpersons feared loss of power if, through a corporate approach and a management team, officers were now to be responsible to the Policy and Resources Committee and not to them. Furthermore the Conservative opposition abhorred the 'non-democratic anachronism' of the one-party Policy and Resources Committee and viewed the institution of a chief executive as part of the whole discredited system.

When the Conservatives became the majority group in May 1976 Amos was effectively isolated, his advice neither valued nor sought. In June 1976 the Policy and Resources Committee was reconstituted as a two-party Finance and Priorities Committee. In November 1976 came the Bosworth Report, published without consulting Amos and effectively ending the corporate management experiment in Birmingham, at least for the time being. The role of chief executive was to be discontinued. Amos was now to chair an advisory panel consisting of the Treasurer, City Solicitor and City Personnel which would 'meet from time to time, at irregular, and I hope, fairly infrequent intervals, to discuss matters of mutual concern' to the city council (Birmingham City Council, 1976).

In March 1977 Amos was 'sacked' on the grounds that the reforms of the management experiment were to be discontinued. Amos's failure was very largely due to the fact that the gap between the objective of corporate management and the traditional culture of management in the city was too great to be bridged at that time. Although the leader of the council, Clive Wilkinson, was sympathetic to the corporate approach, this was not true for the majority of members and officers (Haynes, 1980, pp. 167–96). This presented insurmountable obstacles to attempting any kind of (administrative) leadership, and so failure was in-built.

Bill Page, appointed as the Principal Adviser of the Council kept his position as City Treasurer. That he held these two very important positions simultaneously, indicates the relative lack of importance given to the concept of 'leadership' on the officers' side. He and others saw his role as that of soothing the frazzled nerves of the council (both members and officers) after the upheaval caused by the corporate experiment. His style was not so much to lead as to let others get on with their jobs.

He had no sympathy with the concept of a 'chief executive' as portrayed by Bains. For one thing, it increased the layer of management (with the development of chief officers and other teams). For another, it did not fit in with the workings and experiences of local government officers in Birmingham. 'Everybody ought to have a [departmental] function and the chief executive, who appeared to have none was trying to do other people's jobs.'

Bill Page's management style was certainly on a firmer footing than Amos's. He was a 'local'. He had the advantage of being a long-serving officer in the city, and as such had worked with both major political parties when they were in the majority. He did not seek to be a leader in the sense of a chief executive. As one of his colleagues put it: 'Page was a safe pair of hands. He was not a corporate freak. He let everyone get on with their job. He was essentially carrying on the Treasury work and was back [*sic*] pre Bains. There was a loose rein. Corporate performance was not stressed.'

Head-hunted as chief executive at the beginning of 1982 by the leader of the city council, Tom Caulcott was surprised to find the extent to which managerial 'feudalism' existing in the council. Committees and their accompanying departments acted like 'robber barons', putting up strong walls around their functions and responsibilities and defending them vigorously. He did not, however, espouse a corporate style. He had had over 30 years' experience in the civil service which, up to the 1980s, despite the Fulton Report, was not famed for being a hotbed of corporate leanings. He interpreted corporate management as 'everybody interfering in everybody else's business'. He was a passionate believer in line management where managers get on with their jobs of managing their section of council's work. He considered activities and processes such as regular meetings of management teams as wrong in practice and in principle.

Nevertheless, as a chief executive, whose role it was to ensure that council policies were properly and effectively administered, he realized that he must be in a position to know what was going on in the authority. In short, he saw his role as one of a coordinating agent, 'pulling things together'. His way of doing this was to create a (small) 'Management Effectiveness Unit' whose purpose was to probe policy areas of departments from time to time and to monitor and investigate areas and practices as directed or, in some cases, as seen fit. In many ways the Management Effectiveness Unit was analogous to the Programme Analysis Review (PAR) introduced into the Civil Service in 1970 as a mechanism for regulating, monitoring and coordinating departmental programmes. The unit did not meet with universal acclaim but it did not provoke the adverse reaction of the corporate experiment of the early 1970s. Caulcott had resisted any temptation to make full-scale restructuring of the city's administrative set-up. Indeed, as he argued, the organizational structure of the local authority 'wasn't really much different when I left from when I came'.

New Breed Chief Executives

The latter part of the 1980s saw the installation of what might be termed the newer younger breed of chief executives in Birmingham (Isaac-Henry and Painter, 1991). Roger Taylor was chief executive and Town Clerk of Manchester city council at the age of 40 before he came to Birmingham. Michael Lyons was chief executive for Wolverhampton borough council at the age of 36 and had become chief executive of Nottinghamshire (1990–3) coming to Birmingham. Both had a corporate outlook. They both saw their main task as that of reshaping the organization in Birmingham, which they believed lacked a naturally corporate culture.

Within a year of his taking office Taylor had put forward a bold plan for radically restructuring the management side of the authority. Convinced that the authority should behave in a more integrated manner, he argued that there 'is at present no capacity to provide as a matter of course clear concise advice on how the Leadership of the council should respond to impending legislation, or administrative changes or opportunities which do not readily fall into departments' (Birmingham City Council, 1988). He proposed a central organization under his control which, *inter alia*, would review and coordinate council policies, monitor performance and develop a strategic approach to the management of the council. He merged the three non-financial central departments, the personnel, legal and chief executive departments, to form a central department under his control but run by four executive directors, with a senior executive director responsible for developing a long-term strategy concerned with how the authority was to be run. These executive directors together with the Treasurer would form the central management team. His own role he clearly defined to include

- monitoring and reviewing performance;
- coordinating council policy and activity;
- thinking ahead about the role that the City and council services are to perform for the next five to twenty years.

These proposals put the chief executive at the heart of the city's management process. The expectation was that he would be apprised of and involved in all the important decisions to be made in the authority. He would also be responsible for drawing up a strategic plan to 'provide a bridge between rapidly moving external changes and the overall direction the Council should take'. The introduction of performance appraisal gave him the opportunity to set targets and objectives which matched the overall strategy of the city. Although the political side was not involved in the restructuring, the hope was that the changed structure and the strategy framework would force the political groups to discuss both the direction and policies of the council, in preference to the normally incremental and sometimes secretive ways in which decisions were made.

As one might expect, there was enormous opposition to such a radical plan, especially from some senior officers as well as some members. At one time the leadership of the majority party seemed likely to reject it. It was only 'after rows and battles' that the leader backed the new chief executive and it was approved. Unfortunately for the changes proposed, the majority of politicians did not seem to understand or accept it.

Roger Taylor attempted to bring a more corporate approach to the city. In the years before he left in 1993, a great deal of effort was spent setting out the strategic framework and priorities of the city. His efforts won praise from the Audit Commission, which stated that the 'City can be proud of the way it has documented its strategic objectives and priorities. They are clear, concise, visionary and provide a framework for communicating a sense of purpose down through the organisation' (Birmingham Strategy Document, 1992).

The machinery for a corporate structure was in place before Roger Taylor left in 1993. His successor, Michael Lyons, gave him much credit for attempting to manage the authority on a more corporate style. Yet by the middle of the 1990s attempts to implement such a style seemed to have run out of steam, demonstrating that it is easier to change structures of organizations than the hearts and minds of people.

Despite Taylor's effort, Michael Lyons, yet again, sees his main task as that of creating a corporate style in the city: 'My overriding objective is to promote a greater cohesion in the life and work of the City Council and I believe that in turn can make a significant contribution to greater cohesion in the life of the City as a whole' (Birmingham City Council, 1996). Once again a strategy has been drawn up to achieve this corporate cohesion by setting out what should be the key values of the council and by modifying the structure of the central organization left by Taylor. Lyons is acutely aware that 'no matter how much work you do with the officers you are not going to get anywhere unless the politicians act more corporately'. He thinks any attempt to impose a corporate style would prove counter-productive. His preference is to build on this highly devolved system, and develop mechanisms which help committees and chairpersons to share. To this end he has initiated the 'One Organisation Programme', thereby throwing his weight behind cross-departmental work and collaboration as one means of effecting change towards a more corporate style. In addition to this and perhaps more importantly, he has persuaded the political side of the council to develop a Coordinating Forum (consisting of all committee chairpersons, senior members of the Labour Group and officers with an interest in what is being discussed) which meets monthly.

The attempt to move from an individualistic and fragmented management approach to a more corporate integrative one has, to a large extent, dominated the managerial scene in Birmingham for the last 25 years. Despite attempts to effect change, the culture of very powerful individuals and departments ploughing their own managerial furrow still exists. Nevertheless the present climate seems more favourably disposed to change than hitherto. One reason for this was that over the years the Conservative government's agenda paradoxically fragmented local government functions while at the same time creating pressures for local authorities to operate on a more coordinated basis. The pressures on finance, for example, are forcing authorities to prioritize and to make hard decisions concerning the whole authority. It could be argued, too, that the political climate has changed to the extent that ordinary council members are less willing to be led and are demanding a more participative and open process where polices are brought out into the open (Elcock, 1995, p. 552). In addition, the present leadership of the majority Labour party seems to possess the political will to effect such a change. The debate, which led up to a change of leadership in 1994 and resulted in Theresa Stewart being installed as leader, was partly based on a dissatisfaction with the traditional political management of the city, with what was regarded by some in the Labour party as a non-consultative style which created a need for a more disciplined, integrative approach to managing the City's problems. Theresa Stewart herself has argued that in the past, departments were too competitive, decision-making too secretive and relationships too antagonistic to enable the city to deliver the best service to its customers (video interview, 1995).

Political Relations

Although the chief executive is officially adviser to the council, the political reality is that the crucial relationship is between the leader of the majority party and himself. Given the experience of the five chief executives, it is a relationship which is determined by personalities, methods by which political parties operate, the political complexion of the council and, it would seem from recent history, by the likelihood of a change of majority on the council.

Over the past 23 years that relationship has become stronger, more intense, more personal and less formal. There are many reasons for this. First, as Caulcott has argued, 'there developed, from the 1970s on, a class of full-time councillors who, if their party was in power, and particularly if they became chairman of a committee, became full-time managers. This class of full-time executive member began to resemble the Minister in central government. They had personal offices in the town hall, and secretaries working for them. They treated the officers of the authority as answering only to them, rather than the authority as a whole' (Caulcott, 1996, p. 44). This was certainly the situation in Birmingham. Thus the leaders who are in reality full-time members, are in constant, almost daily, touch with the chief executive, creating an opportunity to develop closer links.

Second, despite the claims made in some quarters for a radical and transformational role for chief executives, in Birmingham at any rate, it has been admitted that hardly anything can be achieved on the managerial side of the authority without backing from members. As one chief executive explains, endorsement by the politicians will signal acceptance to officials and vice versa. It is a view borne out by the observations of Frances Taylor, who, having studied a recent attempt by Michael Lyons to encourage cross-departmental workings, concluded that: 'The evidence suggests that it is vital either to have or obtain political support in the sense of elected members leading or being involved in some way in the work. Without this senior managers are less likely to release staff for the [cross-departmental] work and officers themselves may not prioritise the task involved' (Taylor, 1996, 40).

Being close to the leader provides opportunities to convince him/her of the efficacy of decisions and help to get political support for administrative actions. In any case a close and harmonious relationship with the leader 'who can deliver a group'[4] enhances enormously the status and power of the chief executive in relation to his officers. As one chief executive put it, being close to the leader and being the first to be informed of policy issues and the one to communicate these to other officers is like 'Moses descending from the mount with the tablet of stone'. It gives the chief executive added status and power.

The advantage to the leader of this close relationship is that a trustworthy chief executive is someone with whom embryonic policy issues can be discussed with a view to implementation, while crises can be anticipated and dealt with and all sorts of ideas can be tried out on a confidential basis. The chief executives in Birmingham add the role of political adviser to their job.

Such a close relationship has not always existed. Amos saw his role more in the true constitutional sense, as one of being responsible for advising the whole council as well as maintaining frequent contact with the opposition. The reality was that little contact took place between him and the opposition since the latter was opposed to the corporate management which he symbolized. Indeed when the Conservatives came to power in 1976 he had no relationship with the leaders at all. They hardly communicated and he knew little of their plans.

Bill Page's position *vis-à-vis* the political leaders was very much in the mould of the traditional town clerk. His meetings with the leaders were formal. There was no sense in which the relationship was a tightly knit one. It was not desired nor was it sought. It must be remembered, too, that for much of the time Page's major role and power base was that of Treasurer. His main concern was to deal with the whole council as its principal adviser and not exclusively with the majority party.

Tom Caulcott operated as chief executive under three different leaders. He was appointed by the Labour leader, Clive Wilkinson, at the beginning of 1982. The Conservative group won control in May of that year. Two years later the Labour group regained the majority with a new leader, Dick Knowles. Again his relationship with all the leaders was perhaps more formal than those with later chief executives seem to be, although he states that the relations with all of them were good and cordial.

There is little doubt of the closeness of relations between leader and new breed of chief executives. In the case of Roger Taylor the relationship was also to a large extent exclusive, in the sense that he was almost the sole channel of communication between leadership of the majority party and the officer core. Michael Lyons' relationship with the leader, Theresa Stewart, although close, appears not to be as exclusive as that between Taylor and Knowles. Stewart meets and discusses matters with other chief officers, especially those responsible for education and finance. But exclusivity has its advantages for chief executives as mentioned above. It brings a certain status and lessens the chances of 'wires being crossed'.

There are also side-effects to too close a relationship with the leader. Opposition parties are traditionally suspicious of chief executives who are chosen by or work for the majority party,[5] a suspicion which often translates itself into hostility when the opposition becomes the majority. Francis Amos is convinced that his treatment by the Conservatives in 1976 and 1977 was due partly to his having worked for a Labour administration. In Conservatives' eyes he had become a 'Labour spy'. Again, although Tom Caulcott was appointed in 1982 by a Labour administration which lost office two months later, when Labour regained power two years later a number of the Labour group distrusted the chief executive because he had worked for the 'Tories'. The closer one gets to a leader the more distrustful the opposition will become, and this adversely affects relationships when that opposition becomes the majority.

A chief executive closeness to the leader also runs the risks of alienating members of the leader's political group. In the Labour party in particular there are traditional tensions and conflicts between factions. Too close a relationship can result in the chief executive being too intimately identified with policies of one faction as opposed to another. It might also arouse the jealousy of group members. As is frequently pointed out, Birmingham traditionally boasts strong leaders and politicians who become powerful chairs of committees. The fact that the appointed officer is having far more contact with the leader than a chairman or other important members of the group, and might at the same time be influencing 'policies', can be anathema to some.

What this means for the chief executive is that even if a new leader takes over from within the same party, his position might still be in danger. He himself may feel that he has been so close to the policies and action that he could not work with another.

Relationships with Officers

The management and leadership of the officers within the authority is the responsibility of the chief executive, as head of the paid service. Yet effectiveness of leadership depends on the relationships that the chief executive forms and develops rather than on any defined role. It is influenced by the culture of the organization, the personalities involved and the circumstances existing at any one time.

The concept of power is an important factor in the chief executive–officer relationship. It was noted above that in Birmingham power was not in the hands of one or two persons but was shared around the authority. Apart from powerful leaders and chairpersons, there are officers who, by the position they hold (such as the Treasurer) or by the backing they obtain from politicians, gain heightened status within the authority. There is the implication that by the time a chief executive comes to hold office there is not much power left for them. They would seem to be at quite a disadvantage coming into a new local authority. They have no professional role from which to operate and 'each holder of the office has to recreate it according to his or her own concepts in a struggle with rapidly changing demands from within and outside the authority' (Norton, 1991, p. 90). Additionally, they usually inherit a team of officers they have not chosen. There are, of course, exceptional cases. In Kent County Council, for example, Paul Sabin, the chief executive, in 1990 presided over a chief officers' group which contained only two of the thirteen chief officers he inherited four years earlier. Normally, powers to hire and fire are not usually within the grasp of chief executives (Norton, 1991, p. 92).

The natural reaction to this situation is for the chief executive to build a power base, suggesting that the effectiveness of relationships with the other officers necessitates developing a position of strength. In the case of Amos he arrived in his position 'bereft' of power. His attempt to work through a management team and with other officers failed simply because these officers were anxious about their own positions and status and were resentful and distrustful of the attempted change of management style. He did attempt to build a power base, with the development of an intelligence unit, but it was small and did not begin to match the more generous resources possessed by other chief officers. Importantly he lacked the backing of the leadership. Bill Page, on the other hand, held an enviable position in terms of power. He was one of 'them'. As principal adviser to council he did not threaten power positions any more than he did as the City Treasurer. In fact his role was to remove such threats after Amos had departed. He had a powerful base had he chosen to use it. Importantly in his case, he was the finance officer of the authority at the same time as being its principal officer. He also had a direct line into the administration and he had the backing of the leader.

Caulcott found, on his arrival in Birmingham, a 'disembodied' chief executive office with no departmental support except the three secretaries used by the outgoing chief executive. His first important change was to recreate the Chief Executive's department and put all the general work of running the council in it, including the work of the committee clerks, the provision of services to members and, importantly, the press and publicity functions. He then attempted to build a power base mainly through having a cadre of personal staff and the development of the Management Effectiveness Unit – a project team – responsible to him. They were his eyes and ears 'as well as your trouble shooters and your right hand men [*sic*] who go out and do things'. He also developed a policy of talking to, and getting advice from, second and third tier officers rather than always interacting with chief officers. Such action, on his part, did not always endear him to senior officers in the authority.

Roger Taylor and Michael Lyons, having been a chief executive before coming to Birmingham, had the advantages of being fairly well known and of having experience in that role. Nevertheless every chief executive has to prove him/herself before being taken seriously by other officers. The restructuring of the managerial side by Taylor, apart from improving the management of the authority, was also meant to give him a powerful platform in relation to other officers. Coincidentally, the restructuring resulted in the modification and rearrangement of power relations between other officers. At the same time the close and almost exclusive relationship with the leader added to his status and power.

Although Michael Lyons does not consider power to be the main factor in managing effectively, he is undoubtedly in the managerial driving seat of the local authority. He emphasized that for the chief executive to work effectively with chief officers, he must have the demonstrable support of the political side. The effectiveness of a relationship is not to gained by threatening the use of power. A chief executive, he suggests, has to demonstrate management skills and ability and must 'over time establish a reputation for being impartial but not colourless. Unless you are seen to be somebody who actually does have strong views, then you are not going to offer anything. But you have to be seen to be not in anyone's pocket.'

Chief Executives: Influences on Policies

Leaders are of course expected to influence policies, but as observed above, there are in local government two types of leaders, the political and the managerial. Inevitably, any question concerning effectiveness of chief executives and leadership touches on the influence such offi-cers have on local authorities' policies. This at once involves us in debate with a long pedigree – namely whether policy can clearly be separated from implementation and can strictly be allocated between officers and members. In the 1940s and 1950s the prevailing view was that such a distinction and separation existed. By the 1960s, this view was increas-ingly being discredited, and in local government the influential Maud and Bains reports rejected it. Bains, for example, pleaded that: 'for local government to have any chance of achieving a corporate approach to its affairs, members and officers must both recognise that neither can regard any area of the authority's work as exclusively theirs' (Bains, 1972, p. 8). In the 1990s there seems to be a swing back to the concept of strict distinction between 'policy and administration' with the cent-ral government using this as a basis for some of its policies, in areas such as compulsory competitive tendering and Next Step agencies. The intention here is not to revisit that argument[6] but briefly to consider the extent to which chief executives can lead or influence polices other than by way of giving policy advice to leaders and members.

In his path-breaking book on decision-making in Birmingham, *Second City Politics*, Kenneth Newton observed that assessing the influence of the 'bureaucrat' on policy is fraught with difficulties, since 'getting any quantity of hard evidence is like trying to get blood from red tape' (Newton, 1976, p. 146). Politicians, he argued, are unlikely to admit that they are led by their officers, while the latter are not likely to boast publicly of having trespassed in a forbidden area. This difficulty defeated Newton's attempt to give a definitive assessment of the 'dictatorship of the bureaucrat'. None the less, he did vouchsafe 'that much of the cur-rent literature on officer–member relations over-emphasizes the power of officers and under-emphasizes that of member' (p. 164).

Certainly on this issue, the chief executives interviewed tended to be politically correct, none taking responsibility for initiating major council policies, although they did claim their share of influence and effective implementation. The impression gained is that Birmingham is definitely politically led and politicians are extremely jealous of their policy-making powers and responsibilities. They are most suspicious of officers trying to lead them. On the other hand there is general agreement that councillors frequently involve themselves with management issues. There is tacit understanding that politicians are not only concerned about what things are done but also about how things are done. Councillors have an interest in how the council is structured and managed since this affects political power positions and policies. For example, the very political decision to decentralize services to neighbourhood offices in the 1980s, dictated how the council was to be structured organizationally, with smaller units needed for more direct contact with 'customers'.

What then were the chief executives' attitude towards policy-making? Amos argued that his attempt to influence policy came from the intelligence unit, which was meant to provide economic, demographic and other types of information which he hoped would be used by the council. Bill Page had no doubt that the policy area was taboo for officers and that his role was to implement council policies. Tom Caulcott also took a similar view. For instance, he had little doubt 'that the politicians wanted to try and get Birmingham back on its feet after the disaster of recession of the early 1980s, and that the way, they thought, was somehow to do economic development. I personally thought they were right, but even if I hadn't thought they were right that was my job and I carried them out.' Nevertheless, a proactive chief executive is not without influence on policy. Caulcott's role in the regeneration of the city in the latter part of the 1980s is considered by observers to be crucial. By 1982 the city was in the depths of economic decline with its manufacturing base fast crumbling. It was at this stage that a strategy of regenerating the city by developing service industries emerged. Starting perhaps with the Aston Science Park, regeneration blossomed into a number of prestige projects. Observers argue that the continued development and sustenance of the project owed a great deal to Caulcott, who, it has been said, was:

- adept at obtaining funds from Whitehall (his civil service background considered a factor) and from Europe;
- not afraid to take the initiative in giving advice to politicians about which projects were to be supported;
- ensured that the regeneration strategy was not only a political but an administrative priority;
- ensured that projects were properly managed.

Chief executives differed in their views as to whether policy and administration could each be encompassed by strict boundaries. Roger Taylor argued that the reason for his success as chief executive in Birmingham lay in the very clear view both he and his leader had of the boundaries of their respective roles (although he had to manage with a split Labour group). Dick Knowles, the leader, was the professional politician managing the political side of the council's work, while he (Taylor) was the 'professional' managing the official side. Neither trespassed on the other's territory. This he suggested was the basis for a construct-ive and fruitful relationship between leader and chief executive. This was not a view shared by the other chief executives. Michael Lyons, for example, although strongly of the opinion that policy should be the preserve of the politicians, admitted there were times when matters were not that clear-cut. In such cases a proper and constantly open channel of communication between the two sides was essential.

In Birmingham, leaders do not employ political advisers, relying on the chief executives for advice and information. This means that chief executives have to be extremely politically sensitive about matters such as the views of the opposition party on any issue, how policy proposals are likely to be received by the various sections or factions in the major-ity party, the timing of proposals, and so on. They must be able to pick up the political nuances and relay these to the leader and help policies to be developed in such a way as to avoid (or lessen the strength of) political storms. In so doing it would appear difficult for them at times not to trespass in the political arena.

As with Newton, the jury is still out on any definitive assessment on chief executives' influence on policy matters. From the interviews, it would appear that the extent of officers' influence on policy areas depends on the political culture of the city and on the personalities and situations involved, but that the culture in Birmingham is one of very strong political leadership.

The Chief Executive and Leadership in Birmingham

A fundamental antithesis has dominated the management arena in the city of Birmingham in the last quarter of a century. The question, as well as the problem, is how can the need for a more corporate integrat-ive style of management in an authority facing enormous problems and changes, be reconciled with a culture which displays 'the characteristics of one most conducive to the successful operation of a highly differenti-ated, bureaucratic organisation' (Haynes, 1980, p. 187). The answer might well be that they cannot be reconciled and that in the word of the popular song 'somehow somewhere something got to give'.

There is a sense in which chief executives, in attempting this more integrative approach to management, are tilting at windmills when they seek to change the culture of the officials whilst leaving intact the strong culture of independent committees. These are not two different cultures, one for officers and one for members. It is the same culture spread across the two parts of the organization. Strong Committee chairs control departments and control officers in Birmingham. The separateness of committees is reflected in the separateness and independence of officers. Increasingly, the later chief executives were coming to the conclusion that to change the managerial structure to a more corporate one, the political structure also had to be changed. One chief executive observed that 'Birmingham would be better managed if the controlling group acted cohesively, which it never does. And it will be better managed if we should get right the subsidiarity issue about what decisions should be taken at the nucleus and at the heart the organization and which should be taken on a more devolved basis. It is a debate with which we are plagued and one which we are now trying to address informally.' In seeking effectively to change the managerial side of the council, change on the political side must also be sought. Here chief executives are on less firm ground, if indeed they are on any ground at all. Another cultural problem faced is that for managerial and administrative actions or policies to carry any weight with local authority staff, they must be endorsed openly by members.

So it would seem the conflict goes on; and Caulcott (1996, p. 56) gives very little comfort to reforming chief executives when he argues that for all the attempts to move local government towards a more corporate approach to its management, the basic departmentalism, reinforced by the committee structure, remains.

Leadership and the Vision

As I mentioned in the introduction, there is now a distinction being made between management and leadership. The latter concept is said to be related to having a mission (concerned with the 'overall purpose of the organization, its scope and boundaries') and having vision (of what the organization should be like if it is to achieve its full potential), as well as a possession of skills to communicate effectively and convince people in the organization (Asquith, 1994, pp. 77–9). The Audit Commission thinks that this is the role which chief executives should be playing, arguing that the chief executive should be 'both the authority's centre of continuity and its agent of change'. Asquith suggests that the chief executive should have the pivotal role in implementing fundamental and cultural change (1994, p. 68). Lest it be forgotten, however, there is an alternative and, some would say, more important leadership coming from the political side, and that cultural change would be, and is seen as, the responsibility of the elected members.

In Birmingham it would appear that effective managerial leadership is very closely allied to that of political leadership – so much so that the two can hardly be separated. As Lyons acknowledged in 1996, 'I have already begun to tackle the problem within the officer structure, but it needs to be recognised that the issue [of cohesiveness] does have implications for resolving some of the big issues and, indeed, the political processes within Birmingham' (Birmingham City Council, 1996).

What then did these chief executives think they contributed to leading Birmingham city council? Amos did not consider himself a leader. In his view he was not allowed to be. Resented by officers and many members (more through the position he held than any fault of his own), he could not point the authority in any direction. Even after the introduction of a Policy and Resources Committee in 1973, the authority continued to display the characteristics of separateness. Although he had a view about building coherence into the administration, he lacked what leaders need: followers.

Bill Page did not see himself providing a vision for the authority. That was role of the politicians and vested particularly in the leadership of the majority party. Nevertheless, he thought he gave a lead, by:

- providing the right atmosphere in which chief officers could get on with their jobs;
- giving the whole administration a sense of pride in what it was doing;
- ensuring that the politicians have faith in the administration.

But it was difficult to chart the way these leadership objectives were achieved and demonstrated.

Caulcott believed that there is very little difference between management and leadership, except that perhaps leadership is management practised on a grander scale and in a larger arena. Although he thought management should have a vision as to 'where you are going and a passion about getting there', his concern was not so much to influence what the political leaders were doing as to ensure their wishes were carried out. Neither did he attempt to direct the whole of the organization but, as noted above, his objective was that of coordination. Effective leadership was achieving the will of, and the objectives set by, the council. Yet, in his case, to accept such a view without qualification would result in the underplaying of his role as chief executive. As mentioned above, he played a crucial role in the strategy of regenerating the city, especially in the development of the so-called 'prestige projects'. In addition he is generally regarded as instrumental in persuading the city council to develop the Arts by subsidizing the City of Birmingham Symphony Orchestra generously, by the building of Symphony Hall, and by arranging the transfer of the Sadlers Wells Ballet to Birmingham (as the Royal Ballet). Thus most observers saw him as leader because he got things done and argued his case on an intellectual basis rather than ever falling back on status. His position was greatly helped by the fact that he, as well as both (Labour and Conservative) leaders, were very much in favour of trying to recover the wealth-generating activities of the city.

If being a leader involves the attempt to change the whole organization and to manage that change then Roger Taylor comes closest to being one after 1974. He clearly had a view as to how the organization was to be managed. He certainly attempted to change the structure to achieve greater unity of policy and purpose. He and his executive directors were to be the power-house of the administration. At the same time he attempted to articulate values for the organization, stressing 'quality, choice, access and equity'. He had a vision of the city being the very best governed one in the country and one providing a dramatically enhanced quality of life for all its citizens, while becoming a major European City (Birmingham City Council, 1992). But in order for change to be effective, the values and behaviour of people within the organization have to change. The evidence, for example, is that despite Taylor's efforts, the traditional values remained, especially as far as the councillors were concerned. On the other hand, Caulcott (who had not attempted to change the organizational structure) could be considered as a leader since, as Pettigrew suggests, in managing change there is a crucial role not only for continuity but also for stability (Pettigrew *et al.*, 1992, p. 278).

Michael Lyons may be considered in the same mould as Roger Taylor. Brought to Birmingham as a tried and successful chief executive he is fully in agreement with the Taylor approach. He sees himself as someone who has his feet on the ground by having a department of his own and as one who runs a complex organization and gets things done. On the other hand, as a leader, he charts a direction and encourages people to follow. In this mould the experiment in 'Forward Framework' and the 'One Organization Programme' is a good example of leading by attempting to change the values and culture of the organization, not by directing and cajoling, but by communication, involvement and persuasion. He argues that as a chief executive, one has to get the right balance between leading and management since both are important in their own right.

Transformational Leadership

In Birmingham, given the reputational powers of the political leaders, can chief executives become transformational leaders? The answer may lie in two parts. In the first, there are a number of chief executives who are considered to be (or have been) transformational leaders because they have reputedly radically reshaped their organizations. It is argued that in these organisations, not only are structures and processes radically differently from before, but also the style and values have changed. In this transformational category of leadership are to be found chief executives such as Michael Bichard, formerly of Gloucestershire County Council and now Permanent Secretary at the Department for Education and Employment, Robert Hughes (Kirklees Metropolitan Council), Paul Sabin (Kent County Council) and indeed Roger Taylor and Michael Lyons (Isaac-Henry and Painter, 1991; Asquith, 1994).

As the second part of the answer, it can be argued that in these examples of transformational leadership, the real transformers are the politicians who have had the vision of where the authority should be going and the power to see that it goes in the desired direction. They quite often need to bring the managerial side into line by appointing chief executives who are skilled in communicating the vision and have the ability to implement the process. So as one chief executive suggests, wherever there is a transformational chief executive one should ask who has appointed him/her, and in the answer one will find the real leader. Ian Halliday, in assessing the conditions of change in Kent County Council, indicated that the role of the politicians in directing change was particularly great where in the mid-1980s 'a new Conservative leadership embarked on a programme of organisational and managerial reform which has ramifications throughout the County Council and set KCC in the vanguard of local change' (Halliday, 1991, p. 442). Again in Kirklees Metropolitan Council, with its reputation for forging ahead in management development and change, John Hartman has been seen as the inspiration for a transformational approach to leadership in that authority. One facet of this was to appoint a chief executive (Robert Hughes) to translate the mission and vision into reality (Walker, 1991, p. 19).

This does not detract from the importance of the chief executive, who must not only possess the ability, skill and personality to lead but must also share the vision. It appears that it is the combination and synthesis of the two roles (political leader and chief executive) which make for transformational leadership in local government. Nor must we assume that the chief executive is the only leader on the managerial side in the authority. Michael Lyons, for example, eschews the idea that effective leadership is singular. He believes that it is collective, not in the sense of a democratic or consensus leadership, but that it is multi-dimensional and that an effective authority will have transformational leaders in many of its areas. A good example of this is the employment of Tim Brighouse (with a national reputation in the field of education) to be the director of education in Birmingham. That service had taken a critical battering in the 1990s for being neglected (sacrificed on the altar of prestige projects) and for being to some extent substandard. There was a need for the city to regain its reputation for educational excellence. Hence it set out deliberately to attract a very high-profile figure to lead and transform the service. Yet at the same time both he and the chief executive have to work together effectively.

Conclusion

This chapter has taken a brief look at the role of chief executives in the management of Birmingham city council from 1974. It has suggested that the major concern for three of the five chief executives was how to move the management of the authority from a disaggregated, fragmented or even at times federal type of management, to one which was more corporate and unitary. The implication was that it was only when this condition was satisfied could a chief executive give effective leadership to the council. The first attempt to do so, under the flag of corporate management and planning, foundered on the rock of Birmingham's tradition of 'differentiated' management style. Page and Caulcott did not attempt to resurrect that corporate style nor was it their chosen one. The 'new breed' officers, seeking for a more corporate style, began again to push at the door of traditional management in Birmingham. It could be argued that the door has opened somewhat. Taylor's corporate agenda did have some effect (although the evidence so far is that it has not yet worked through the culture of the organization). One of the major reasons for the door being ajar is that the political side has begun to see the need for such an approach. By 1986 the leader of the council, Sir Dick Knowles, instituted the 'monastic weekend', where leading members and officers meet to discuss policies and priorities. He began to change the process. Before this it was said that a 'good chairman' could button-hole a leader and get things changed. Now once policies have been decided by a group of the leading politicians, it is difficult for one or two people to get them changed.

Birmingham, by its size and variety of communities, naturally develops tensions which are reflected in the political and the managerial processes. At the same time there is hardly a leader in the last thirty years or so who has not been a recognizable figure nationally. Chairpersons are themselves powerful figures too. There is, said one chief executive, a well-developed notion in the city of 'executive members' and a very strong feeling that things are under their control, even some things which ought to be in the realms of officer responsibilities. Thus there are sometimes tensions, too, between chief executives and members. Hence it is a difficult authority to manage and lead.

One of the major problems faced in attempting to evaluate leadership of a chief executive in Birmingham (and perhaps local authorities in general) is the difficulty of separating the political from the administrative. But even if such a distinction were clear, the fact remains that many of the most important developments in the administrative/management areas need political consent and support. This has meant, as Elcock has argued, that 'the leading political and administrative figures of a local authority must work so closely together and the distinction between the political and administrative roles can become so blurred, until on occasion they become virtually indistinguishable from one another' (Elcock, 1995, p. 552).

Birmingham has a reputation for leadership and for getting things done. Its transformation from facing the abyss in the mid-1980s to (although not yet out of the woods) being a rising European star is constantly being admired. For example, Francis Amos, the first chief executive, who perhaps might have been least expected to admire the city given his earlier treatment, has in 1996 'really been impressed at the way they've turned the City around. I think Birmingham has always been an achiever and I always ask myself whether it is an achiever because it is so self-centred and always individualistic or is that a necessary requirement to being an achiever.' Much the same has been said by others and, despite the Audit Commission's fondness for proposing more powers for chief executives, some of these officers are themselves cautious about assuming them, as far as Birmingham is concerned. They believe that much of the vitality and risk-taking in Birmingham comes from the politicians 'being visionary and being bloody stubborn'. What makes Birmingham an exciting place is that many of its achievements are based on bold visions by politicians with good, bold officers following them.

However, the system of leadership might well be changed in the near future as the bandwagon for the introduction of elected mayors roles on. As London moves towards such a system, the pressure for cities such as Birmingham to follow suit will be almost irresistible. Not surprisingly, given contemporary thinking on leadership, the mayor is expected to play the 'transactional' role: 'A powerful mayor will be an effective voice for the community, an effective counter balance to the power of Westminster and Whitehall, an effective facilitator who brings together all the stakeholders we need ... [he/she] will excite public interests ... help to raise public turnout, focus people on local rather than national issues [and] rekindle enthusiasm for local government' (*The Guardian*, 1997). Such a system will create new kinds of politicians and chief officers not only in Birmingham but also in local government generally.

Acknowledgements

The author is indebted to Francis Amos, Tom Caulcott, Michael Lyons, Bill Page, Graham Shaylor and Roger Taylor, all of whom, though very busy people, created time for the interviews.

Notes

1. Where quotes are made without acknowledgement of the specific source they relate to interviews with one of the five persons in the case studies. For reasons of sensitivity and prudence the author refrains, in some cases, from giving the name of the source, although in others it will be obvious.
2. Bill Page held the title of Principal Adviser to the Council and City Treasurer up to 1980. In that year the title of Chief Executive was bestowed on him. For this research I have examined his role from 1976.
3. Reference to corporate approach or corporate management relates more to the attempt to manage the authority as an integrated, coordinated unit rather than to the corporate planning approach favoured by the Bains Working Party.
4. The ability to obtain political party group agreement on particular issues.
5. Although it must be noted that for the past twelve years the Labour Party has been in power, and in 1997 held 87 of the 117 seats on the city council.
6. For an in-depth and up-to-date discussion on this theme, refer to Stewart (1996).

References

Audit Commission (1989), *More Equal than others: the Chief Executive in Local Government* (London: HMSO).

Asquith, A. (1994), *Change Management in Local Government: Strategic Change Agents and Organisational Ownership*, Ph.D. thesis, University of Central England.

Bains, M. (1972), *The New Local Authorities: Management and Structure* (London: HMSO).

Bates, P. (1994), *Strategies for Cultural Change* (Oxford: Butterworth/Heinemann).

Beecham, Sir J. (1996), Leadership in Local Government, *Public Policy and Administration*, 11 (3), 43–50.

Birmingham City Council (1975), *Corporate Working in Birmingham, Report of the Chief Executive to the Management Team*.

Birmingham City Council (1976), *Report of Councillor Neville Bosworth to the Finance and Priorities (Ad Hoc) Committee: a Revised System of Management and the Officer Structure*.

Birmingham City Council (1988), *Chief Executive Report on the Future Function of the Central Services of the Council* (Part 4).

Birmingham City Council (1992), *Birmingham Strategy*.

Birmingham City Council (1995), *The Future Organisation and Management of the Birmingham City Council*.

Birmingham City Council (1996), *The Future Organisation and Management of the Birmingham City Council*.

Boynton, J. (1985), *Job at the Top: the Chief Executive in Local Government* (Harlow: Longman).

Briggs, A. (1952), *History of Birmingham*, vol. 2 (London: Oxford University Press).

Bryson, J., Daniels, P. and Henry, D. (1996), From Widgets to Where?: the Birmingham Economy in the 1990s, in *Managing a Conurbation: Birmingham and its Region*, eds A. J. Gerrard and T. R. Slater (Warwickshire: Brewin Books).

Caulcott, T. (1996), *Management and the Politics of Power: Central and Local Government Compared* (London: LGC Communications).

Clarke, M. and Stewart, J. (1991), *The Role of the Chief Executive* (Luton: Local Government Management Board).

Elcock, H. (1995), Leading People: Some Issues of Local Government Leadership in Britain and America, *Local Government Studies*, 21 (4), 546–67.

The Guardian (Margaret Hodge) (1997), 10 March, p. 15.

Haynes, R. (1980), *Organisation Theory and Local Government* (London: Allen & Unwin).

Halliday, I. (1991), The Conditions of Local Change: Kent County Council since Reorganisation, *Public Administration*, 69 (4), 441–57.

Isaac-Henry, K. and Painter, C. (1991), The Management Challenge in Local Government: Emerging Trends, *Local Government Studies*, 17 (3), 69–89.

Kotter, J. P. (1992), What Leaders Really Do, *Harvard Business Review*, 70, 103–11.

Loftman, P. and Nevin, B. (1992), *Urban Regeneration and Social Equity: the Case of Birmingham 1986–1992*, Research Paper no. 8, University of Central England, Birmingham.

Loftman, P. and Nevin, B. (1996), Prestige Urban Regeneration Projects: Socioeconomic Impacts, in *Managing a Conurbation: Birmingham and its Region*, eds A. J. Gerrard and T. R. Slater (Warwickshire: Brewin Books).

The Maud Report (1967), *Report on the Committee on the Management of Local Government* (London: HMSO).

Morphet, J. (1993), *The Role of Chief Executive in Local Government* (Harlow: Longman).

Newton, K. (1976), *Second City Politics* (Oxford: Clarendon Press).

Norton, A. (1991), *The Role of Chief Executive in British Local Government* (Birmingham: INLOGOV).

Pettigrew, A., Ferlie, E. and McKee, L. (1992), *Shaping Strategic Change* (London: Sage).

Sabin, P. (1989), *The Role of the Chief Executive and the Management of County Councils – a Personal View* (Conference Paper).

SOLACE (1992), Chief Executives' Development Survey, LGMB, London.

SOLACE and the Local Government Management Board (1992), *Chief Executives' Development (for Effectiveness)*, SOLACE, London.

Stewart, J. (1996), A Dogma of Our Times – the Separation of Policy-making and Implementation, *Public Money and Management*, 16 (3), 33–40.

Taylor, F (1996), Toward More Effective Cross-Departmental Working, *Local Government Policy-Making*, 23 (3), 37–47.

Terry, L. (1995) *Leadership in Public Bureaucracies – the Administrative Conservator* (London: Sage).

Titchy, N. and Ulrich, D. (1984), The Leadership Challenge – a Call for the Transformational Leader, *Sloan Management Review*, Fall, 59–68.

Walker, D. (1991) Economist, Ambassador and Wheeler Dealer, *Local Government Chronicle*, Jan., 19–21.

Widdicombe Committee (1986), *The Report of the Committee of Inquiry into Local Authority Business*, Cmnd 997 (London: HMSO).

7
Lord Cockfield: a European Commissioner as a Political Entrepreneur

Christopher Lord

Arthur (Lord) Cockfield was one of the unlikeliest political entrepreneurs of recent times. Described in Hugo Young's biography of Margaret Thatcher as 'eccentric, apolitical and unelected' (Young, 1989, p. 301), he was more of a policy enthusiast than a politician. His qualifications for national and European office included an improbable combination of jobs in industry, quangoes, the civil service and voluntary associations. But not once did he ever hold an elected public position. He had been Chairman of Boots the chemists, an Inland Revenue Commissioner, Chair of the Price Commission and even President of the Statistical Society. He had sat on the Council of the Confederation of British Industry and on the National Economic Development Council. In so far as he can be said to have had a 'political career', it did not begin until he was 62 when he became a junior Treasury Minister in the 1979 Conservative government. It did not take off until he was 65, when he was brought into the Cabinet as Trade Secretary, probably for no better reason than to 'keep a seat warm' until Thatcher was better placed to shape her team as she wanted. And it did not reach its brief apogee until he was appointed, at the age of 68, for what was to turn out as a single four-year term (1985–9) as one of Britain's two European Commissioners. At the time, some even regarded his appointment as a deliberate insult to 'Brussels' and there was some talk of a legal challenge on the grounds that a peer was caught by the Treaty rule that members of national parliaments could not serve as European Commissioners. Two things are, however, certain. First, Thatcher expected Cockfield to be 'her man' in the Commission. Geoffrey Howe recalls: 'Margaret looked for someone entirely after her own heart – for "one of us" in the familiar phrase' (Howe, 1994, p. 405). Second, Cockfield had served neither of the two apprenticeships that are generally considered essential preparation for membership of the Commission. It was not immediately obvious that he had either the brute skills at domestic politics that come from a lifetime fighting elections, wheeler-dealing in political parties or handling Cabinet and interdepartmental disputes, or the smooth silky talents at intergovernmental bargaining that come from long service in international organizations or frequent exposure to negotiations. During his fourteen months as Secretary of State for Trade, he had, by his own admission, only attended one meeting of the relevant Council of Ministers (Cockfield, 1994, p. 22).

Yet, as Internal Market Commissioner, Cockfield was to put a distinctive personal stamp on the Single Market Initiative that was to emerge as the 'policy core' of the present European Union. While playing down more grandiose claims that it 'marked the critical turning point between stagnation and dynamism', Helen Wallace and Alasdair Young have remarked, 'the Single Market has drawn other European countries towards EU membership and changed the context in which many other policies are shaped' (H. Wallace and A. Young, in Wallace and Wallace, 1996, p. 126). By the time Cockfield arrived in Brussels, the decision to make the Single Market a priority for the 1985–9 Commission had already been taken in a round of consultations between Jacques Delors and the Heads of Government. In his first tour of the national capitals, the incoming Commission President supposedly offered four options for a relaunch of a largely stagnant and fractious European Community: 'institutional reform, monetary union, closer co-operation in defence and economic revival based on completion of the internal market' (Grant, 1994, p. 66). The first was Delors' own preferred alternative but the last commanded the most consensus. However, Cockfield seems at least to have had a hand in the decision to lay down a deadline of 31 December 1992 for the completion of the market; and he can also be credited with persuading Delors to adopt the potentially high-risk strategy of framing a full Single Market programme in advance, rather than allowing it to emerge piecemeal: 'it was essential that we had a properly structured programme covering all the vital elements of the Internal Market. It was no good proceeding as previous Commissions had done . . . by picking out subjects that happened to catch the eye of particular member states. *It had to be the lot*' (Cockfield, 1994, p. 29).

In the brief interval between the Brussels (March 1985) and Milan (June 1985) meetings of the European Council, Cockfield and Delors

managed to produce a massively detailed – yet elegantly shaped – programme of no fewer than 279 measures that they considered necessary
to the operation of a 'frontier free Europe'. This was, moreover, presented
at a Commission press conference two weeks before the Milan summit,
as might befit a body that considers itself to be an independent cataly-
ser of *public* interest in European initiatives, rather than a mere secretariat for private and secretive intergovernmental proceedings. At a risk
of some superficiality, the Single Market White Paper was an interesting
blend of EC and British traditions of policy entrepreneurship. Its rapid
preparation and very public announcement in a manner designed to
shape the agenda and lock governments into consideration of something definite was reminiscent of Jean Monnet's preparation of the
Schuman Plan in May 1950. Yet, the Schuman Plan had originally only
run to a hundred lines. For all its Cartesianism, the White Paper format,
which Cockfield later characterized as 'setting out a philosophy followed by a programme in detail . . . every single proposal having its own
time schedule', was a British import to Community usage (Cockfield,
1994, p. 32).

II

Membership of the European Commission provides a distinctive context for the exercise of political leadership. At one level, there are few
political institutions whose mission is more explicitly linked to entrepreneurship. The role of the Commission is most developed in relation
to the innovationary aspects of governance, as opposed to decision-
making and implementation. The whole of the EU's political system is
constructed around the rule that is for the Commission to propose and
the Council to decide (with such separation of power as exists at the EU
level following this principle, rather than classic distinctions between
executive and legislature). Those who designed the EU's institutions
expected the Commission to construct Europe from within, cultivate
'spill-overs' from one initiative to another, and earn its passage as an
embryonic government for the new Community. The prospects for
integration were seen to depend as much on the capacity of the Commission to 'supply' useful ideas as on the 'demand' of governments and
non-state actors for policies that might usefully be made at the European level (Haas, 1958; Lindberg and Scheingold, 1970; Tranholm-
Mikkelsen, 1991). Less sympathetic perspectives – such as rational
choice approaches – would likewise predict that once a supranational
tier of governance was in being, it would be permanently on the prowl

for opportunities for policy entrepreneurship; though they, of course, would give more weight to the 'private utility functions' of office-holders seeking to expand the bureaucratic influence of their own institution, rather than any public utility to be gained by making policy at a new transnational level (Vibert, 1994). Either way, policy solutions would tend to chase economic and social problems, as much as the other way round (Peters in Richardson, 1996, p. 70).

Yet, the Commission's right of initiative is both contested and constrained. Slender administrative resources mean that it is a long way from being a self-sufficient political entrepreneur with a capacity to gather all the information necessary for meaningful decision-making. Tight financial resources (with a budget of only 1.26 per cent of EU GNP, most of which is committed in advance to policies that have already been established) limit its ability to use the power of the purse to oil its coalition-building or compensate losers from innovation. Even those with an optimistic view of the political autonomy of the Commission, point to what is problematic in the notion that a body can have the power of agenda-setting without those of decision and implementation. For, unless these are all of a piece, there is a danger that the Commission will tend to rouse expectations that it cannot meet, as well as insulate itself from the normal 'feedback loops' in policy-making. Above all, the Commission is painfully aware that it lacks its own direct source of political legitimacy. This frequently puts it on the defensive in its relationships with the member states and compels it to channel its political entrepreneurship into areas that can be portrayed as 'technical' rather than 'political': to wait either for a clear mandate from the member states or, failing that, for an overwhelming consensus amongst public opinion and non-governmental actors for change.

In this connection, Thomas Christiansen points to the central contradiction between a body that is at once supposed to be intensely political by 'stirring up change' – with all that means for dividing actors into 'winners and losers' – and to function as a source of impartial administration (Christiansen in Richardson, 1996). After all, the effective use of its administrative powers – and especially those that concern the supervision of implementation – will often require the cooperation of the very same actors who feel aggrieved by the manner in which the Commission has exercised its powers of innovation. Under these circumstances, the monopoly right of the Commission to make new proposals for Union policies exists more clearly in law than in political practice (Nugent, 1994) . The Commission often follows and anticipates, rather than leads, the political preferences of others. And in a sure sign of its limited self-sufficiency, it frequently prefers to promote the interpenetration – even fusion (Wessels, 1992) – of supranational and intergovernmental processes to insisting on its institutional integrity. This makes it hard to disentangle the relative contributions of the following to any single act of political leadership: the six-monthly meetings of heads of government in the European Council; individual member states who frequently make proposals in the form of single or joint papers; the permanent representatives of the member states (COREPER) who are often used by the Commission as a sounding board for new initiatives (Hayes-Renshawe and Wallace, 1997); non-governmental actors who increasingly lobby both the Commission and member governments and whose influence is especially important in specialist areas of policy-making (Mazey and Richardson, 1993); and, of course, the Commission itself.

The notion that an individual Commissioner such as Lord Cockfield might make a difference is even more problematic. The Commission operates according to a strict principle of collegiality in which all policy has to be adopted on a majority vote of all Commissioners – 14 in the first months of Cockfield's term and 17 after Spanish and Portuguese accession in 1986 – and no individual has the final say in the handling of his or her own portfolio. Given that it is also a transnational bureaucracy fragmented into fiefdoms colonized by particular nationalities and personalities, without clear command structures and a tendency towards all-consuming turf battles (Schink, 1992; Egeberg, 1995), the Commission has a notoriously quicksilver character in which it is often hard to trace the origins of an idea or to link actions to outcomes with the predictability implied by the notion of political leadership. In the absence of clear hierarchies and plausible administrative demarcations, two opposing schools of thought have emerged as to the preconditions for successful policy initiation within the Commission. The first suggests that an inspirational or ruthless Commission President can turn confusion to his own advantage by substituting personalized authority for the direction that cannot be achieved through structures. As George Ross has put it, 'Unless Commission resources could be mobilised to produce proposals, argument and momentum few results would be possible. Manufacturing such things inside the Berlaymont involved "presidentialising" the College...Delors was the key' (Ross, 1995, pp. 231–2). The contrasting view is that the Commission only achieves cohesion where socially defined policy networks or 'epistemic communities' (shared values, commitments and cause–effect assumptions) emerge to unite individuals into coherent action. These allow effective coordination to be achieved across otherwise unworkable administrative structures (Heclo, 1978, pp. 103–4). However, neither of these two approaches – Presidentialism nor consensus – suggests that single Commissioners are very important in promoting change.

III

Given everything that is so problematic in the notion of Commission rights of initiative, the emergence of the Single Market is often explained in a manner that leaves little room for political leadership. One school of thought has accounted for it in terms of the 'convergent domestic political interests' of the principal member governments (Keohane and Hoffman, 1991; Moravcsik, 1993). The British government was apparently eager to 'export Thatcherism' and secure its domestic revolution by embedding it in the international trading regime that most affected the UK's immediate economic environment. In the run up to the 1986 elections to the National Assembly, Mitterrand was looking for a high-profile European initiative that would paper over the failure of the domestic programme on which he had himself secured the French Presidency in 1981. Kohl needed an external economic stimulus to hold together his fractious three-way CDU–CSU–FDP coalition and remove the prediction that continued membership of the government would lead to unacceptable levels of electoral punishment. A 'foreign policy success' would also help him consolidate his shaky personal authority in a context in which he was not widely regarded as the most obvious politician from the three governing parties to hold the Chancellorship (*Financial Times*, 11 June 1985).

A second view is that the Single Market programme was the more or less inevitable product of pressures from the international system. West Europe was faced with the exhaustion of the 'national champion strategy' by which each government had attempted to foster its own producers. Political discourse at the time was obsessed with 'competitiveness', 'Eurosclerosis', the wasteful fragmentation of markets, and the notion that Europe was caught in a pincer movement between American and Japanese technology on the one hand and low-cost production from newly industrializing countries on the other. The OECD warned that Europe was being driven towards more 'downstream production', and at least one indigenous multinational – Phillips – made the remarkable claim that it was considering relocation to another continent. As one piece of contemporary press comment put it the weekend after Cockfield issued his White Paper:

Dazzled by the brisk euphoria of the US economic advance and the relentless industrial advance of Japan, Europe has been wondering why it has been left out of the party ... many industrialists blame Europe's missed opportunities on its patchwork of national markets ... in most countries, the pace of innovation is controlled by self-regulatory monopolies ... national champion strategies have produced companies more geared to winning favours than winning markets ... their international competitiveness depends upon being sheltered from the full rigours of competition at home. The leaders of Europe's protected industries now acknowledge that they are living on borrowed time. (*Financial Times*, 17 June 1985)

Already burdened with competitiveness problems, EC countries also interpreted a spate of US–Japanese bilateral trade deals as an attempt by the two economic leaders to stitch up the international trading system between themselves. European countries needed a Single Market initiative as a source of negotiating leverage and cohesion, and they needed to get it under way before the opening of a new round of GATT talks for which the Reagan Administration was pressing. Against this background, corporate interests organized to promote a major regime change in market regulation. In 1983, 25 of the EC's largest multinationals formed themselves into the European Round Table of Industrialists (Cowles, 1995). With the Single Market programme and the Single Act, the European political system adjusted to these shifting producer interests.

A third view is that the Single Market programme had long been maturing within the EC's institutional framework and that all Cockfield had to do was to uncork some fine vintages that had already been laid down by his predecessors. Desmond Dinan remarks that Cockfield was able to put such an 'extensive compilation together in record time' because most of the items that made up the White Paper already lay around the Commission in draft form (Dinan, 1994, p. 139). Of vital importance to the simplification of the Single Market was a series of pre-1985 developments that allowed the Commission to soften its regulatory touch and improve the prospects of consent and compliance. The perfection of the 'directive' as a legislative instrument allowed the EC to limit itself to stipulating goals or a broad range of acceptable solutions, while member states were free to decide details and methods of implementation for themselves. Since the 1970s, both the drafting and implementation of regulations had been in the hands of three-way consultative committees, made up of the Commission, member governments and private addressees of EC law. By the mid-1980s, the member states were already practising an informal moratorium on new national regulations so that common standards could emerge as new products replaced old ones. Above all, the European Court of Justice had established the all-important simplifying principle of 'mutual recognition' in the *Cassis De Dijon* case of 1979. From now on, products that met standards in any one member country would be acceptable anywhere in the Community. This meant the EC could abandon the impossible task of harmonizing all regulations and concentrate on a minority of cases where regulatory negligence by one member state could pose unacceptable risks to others.

More broadly, the Single Market programme can be seen as a spillover from the original Common Market that had been put in place between 1957 and 1970. The removal of tariffs had only encouraged the proliferation of non-tariff barriers and the member states were now confronted with a choice between abandoning the original goal of market integration or Europeanizing the myriad features of domestic policy-making with a capacity to distort trade and investment: state aids, rules for public procurement, product standards and so on (Pelkmans and Winters, 1988). Moreover, it was arguably necessary for the member states to go through the frustration of repeated policy failure before they were ready to accept the two institutional preconditions for the enactment of Cockfield's programme: first, that the Commission's right to use its power of initiative with boldness and creativity should be acknowledged (as it had been in the days of Walter Hallstein before De Gaulle's empty chair policy of 1965–6); and, second, that member states qualify their veto rights and consent to the Single Market being passed by majority vote. This was a vital rule change that unblocked the Council, freed governments from domestic veto groups and greatly expanded the Commission's power of initiative, now that it did not have to worry about every possible objection from each of the 12 member states. By mid-1985, even the British government was proposing an elaborate 'gentleman's agreement' to allow the Single Market to be passed by majority voting (though it was less keen on writing this into the Treaty!). As George Ross has put it, 'Something extraordinary happened in the mid-1980s. The context around Community institutions began to change, the willingness of member states to contemplate European solutions to their problems increased and, most importantly, the European Commission came alive to assert its claim as the proposition force' (Ross, 1995, p. 26).

IV

Yet even a 'political opportunity structure' as promising as that described in the last section left room for Cockficld to place a distinctive personal stamp on the programme. The obvious shortcoming of accounts that stress systemic pressures making for some new European initiative, is that they fail to explain why pride of place should have been taken by the Single Market programmes as defined by Cockfield: why this emerged as it did and when it did, not to mention with the sustainability that was to carry it to completion in almost unamended form. Closer inspection of the historical record shows that the Cockfield White Paper faced some tough competition for dominant place on the political agenda that it eventually secured. Delors' personal preference for monetary over market integration had not entirely disappeared as late as April 1985, when the Commission President gave evidence to a hearing of the Foreign Affairs Committee of the US Senate. Indeed, a commitment to Monetary Union was to appear in the Single European Act itself (December 1985), and it could conceivably have become more salient under three conditions: first, if it had engaged more directly with current US-led initiatives to push the advanced industrial countries towards more 'managed' exchange rates; second, if the connection between 'one market' and a 'single money' had been made more quickly; and third, if France and Germany had been more prepared in the mid-1980s to take the risk of leaving Britain out of the next phase of European integration. Another possibility is that the EC might have been relaunched around a proposal for a tighter and more comprehensive collaboration in the development of new technologies. Several technology projects were under discussion in 1985, including the RACE programme to promote compatibility between European telecommunications industries, European space cooperation, the European joint fighter aircraft, and what were to become the Eureka and Esprit programmes to promote networking between producers and researchers in different EC countries. In addition, the West Europeans had to find some response to Reagan's invitation to participate in the research side of the Star Wars project. They were also under pressure to cut the costs that duplication of technological development and procurement imposed on their own defence budgets. A final possibility is that in place of a credible Community-wide initiative of the kind launched by Cockfield, the EC countries could have edged towards greater cooperation through a series of bilateral agreements. For example, France and Italy announced four bilateral agreements including the relaxation of border controls the same week that Cockfield unveiled his own White Paper (*Financial Times*, 17 June 1985).

One of the problems with the 'domestic political convergence hypothesis' is that it is by no means clear that it did suit all Heads of Government to have Cockfield's initiative capture the political agenda in the way it did. Mitterrand's political entourage was apparently worried that 'in this decisive moment in European history, the liberal conceptions of Bonn and London had come together to the detriment of the Franco-German couple... what emerged was only a modest result in relation to French ambitions... it was more of a Europe of free exchange than one of grand harmonisation political, economic and social' (Favier and Martin-Roland, 1991). Meanwhile, a typical comment from the serious press of the time was that 'there is something in the White Paper to make every government shudder. There will have to be a quantum leap in each government's acceptance of standards applied by others... governments will have to lose a great deal of freedom in the way in which they raise indirect taxes... Britain has a historic preference for border controls as a means of maintaining internal security... France and Italy will worry about the free trade bias of the document' (*Financial Times* leader, 17 June 1985).

Another difficulty is that of explaining why Cockfield's programme was implemented almost in its entirety over the next seven years (with enlargements and elaborations but very few subtractions from the original scheme). In all, 264 of the original 279 measures would be enacted by the end of 1992 (HMSO, 1993). Of two answers that are often given, one suggests that the rule change on the Council to QMV was more important in holding the programme together than Commission guidance, and the other that the Commission sustained the programme through stealth as much as honest and open political leadership. However, the first argument confuses the direction of causation. For, the British government only changed its position on writing majority voting into the Treaty *after* the publication of Cockfield's White Paper made it clear that there was an attractive and credible opportunity to create a Single Market that could be lost without a rule change. In other words, the act of Commission leadership came first. The 'stealth argument', on the other hand, is simply wrong. Members of Delors' Cabinet would later talk about the 'Russian doll strategy' whereby governments would keep on finding that there was a further and unexpected doll inside the last that would need to be opened if they were to keep the Single Market on the road. But in the case of the Cockfield White Paper the approach to political leadership was one of almost reckless frankness in which the costs, risks and spillover implication were put up front. Cockfield told the press conference 'they [the governments] have asked for it; they have got it', and as the *Financial Times* leader on the subject put it:

> there is a real danger that the Commission's vision has been portrayed too honestly, and that governments will challenge the basic premise that frontier controls have to be removed ... Cockfield has rightly exploded the fallacy that it is possible to enjoy the benefit of a Single Market of 320 million people without concessions to national sovereignty ... the White Paper shows that the internal market offers no painless way to develop the Community. (*Financial Times*, 17 June 1985)

V

If we dismiss the views that Cockfield's role was marginal or based on stealth, his example allows us to illustrate the importance of individual European Commissioners to two very different approaches to political leadership. The one portrays the initiatory powers of the Commission as being very important but limited, none the less, to the efficient realization of state interests. In other words, the Commission is the 'agent' and the Council is the 'principal' (Marks *et al.*, 1996, p. 356). The other suggests that it is a far more political – rather than technical – actor. Through the exercise of its leadership role it actively shapes the political preferences of governments (Risse-Kappen, 1996); it 'breaks up existing equilibria' and provokes realignments (Majone in Richardson, 1996, p. 272, discussing Riker, 1986, p. 64); and it changes the balance of political forces by mobilizing new actors into the political arena, particularly sub-national ones. By any one of these means, it can dramatically shift the constraints on policy change without expending considerable resources.

The core of the argument that Cockfield's role was important but limited to the realization of a given set of state preferences is that governments were only prepared to acquiesce in an independent source of initiative because this lowered the bargaining and other transaction costs attached to goals they wanted to attain anyway. To see why these savings may have been considerable we need, first, to observe that the White Paper was an enormous package deal of 283 measures. If there was something in it for everyone, there were also costs and risks for all governments. The British and Irish governments (which, uniquely, had zero rating for VAT that covered up to half of goods sold) felt that indirect tax harmonization was politically 'too hot to handle' (Lawson, 1992, pp. 895–8); most governments apart from the British were deeply concerned about the implications for banking supervision of applying the principle of mutual recognition to financial services; almost everyone was worried about the removal of frontier controls; and, of course, a genuine Single Market with constraints on state aids always had the potential to trigger a painful period of corporate restructuring and transitional unemployment (Jacquemin and Sapir, 1991). Governments would no longer be able to adjust the costs and risks of market regulation to the rhythms of the electoral cycle. Yet, in spite of these difficulties, the programme was widely acknowledged to be coherent, feasible and likely, in the round, to leave all member states better off. The obvious question was whether they would have been able to reach such a solution by negotiating each item 'bottom up' between themselves. As Cockfield was himself to put it, 'under the terms of the Treaty, the Commission has the sole right of initiative. The reason is simple: if all member states had the right to institute legislation, the result would be total confusion with everyone proposing what suited them with scant regard to what suited others or the Community as a whole' (Cockfield, 1994, p. 98).

Various related arguments show how an independent source of political leadership can help governments move closer to their 'pareto frontier'. All of these were present to some degree in the case of Cockfield's Single Market initiative. First, time and information are precious resources, and, in any case, governments are not well placed to gather it together in a global impact assessment at European, as opposed to national, level. Second, many mutually profitable agreements may fail to be struck because there is a lack of mutual trust in the absence of an independent enforcement mechanism. Asymmetries of information and lack of simultaneous performance will provide opportunities for deception and cheating (Keohane, 1994). Third, policy programmes may involve governments in incomplete contracting. Where they are only able to go some of the way towards specifying an agreement in advance, they may find it convenient to delegate powers to an impartial agency to 'fill in the detail' (Williamson, 1985). Fourth, one reason why governments may find it difficult to negotiate something like the Single Market initiative 'piecemeal' and from the 'bottom up' is that they are often precluded from coherent trade-offs by domestic 'political capture' in particular policy sectors. Where, on the other hand, they are confronted by a completely defined package of supranational origin, they may gain greater autonomy from domestic constraints. They are better placed to play 'winners' off against 'losers', if the preferences of the latter are prevented from becoming too salient in the policy process before the former can see what they have to gain from an initiative. Fifth, any movement towards a pareto-efficient solution will always involve a mixture between 'creating value' (enlarging the cake) and 'claiming value' (slicing the cake). Very often negotiations that should have succeeded break down because the parties get so heated about distributional conflicts that they lose sight of their common interest in cooperation (Sebenius, 1992). An independent agency can lessen problems such as these by just stipulating what it considers to be a fair solution. Put technically, governments may find it easier to reach pareto efficiency frontiers where they do not have to argue about which of an infinite number of possible points on the frontier (each with its own distributional implications) they are going to aim at.

This last point would explain why Cockfield's solution proved a durable one: although each government disliked individual items in the package, it knew that any movement away from the 'Cockfield equilibrium' could be unstable, because it would re-open an endless stream of distributional conflicts that would prevent the Single Market meeting its already tight target for completion by 1992. As for the other points, the Cockfield initiative clearly did provide heads of government with a valuable economy of time that allowed them to concentrate on other things. A study of the European Councils of June and December 1985 shows that they were primarily concerned with an overall 'systems transformation' of the Community's institutional structures and arrangements for foreign policy cooperation. Following the publication of the Cockfield White Paper, the Single Market was largely assumed to have been a done deal, so long as the other components of a Treaty change could be put together. The importance of 'incomplete contracting' can be seen in Cockfield's repeated use of the mandate his programme had received from the Heads of Government in the European Council to support the passage of particular directives and unblock Councils of lesser ministers: 'the public endorsement by the European Council on this and subsequent occasions was not only valuable in public relations terms but of the utmost value in dealing with the Council of Ministers. It enabled me to argue that the principle had been decided by their Heads of Government and their concern was not to decide the principle but to deal with the legislation that implemented the principle' (Cockfield, 1994, p. 100). Meanwhile, governments, for their part, were quick to use the Single Market programme to increase their autonomy from domestic actors. For Socialist governments in France and Spain, in particular, it was to be an important political resource in loosening constraints of parties and interest groups on the marketization of domestic policies, while the UK government was able to use the prize of market integration to negotiate the only trouble-free passage of Treaty legislation to strengthen EC jurisdiction in the 25 years of British membership to date. However, it would be a mistake to assume that the benefits of supranational entrepreneurship described in this paragraph were there for the taking. Many are only available to Commissioners with a reputation for independence. As his appointment evoked De Gaulle's image of Britain sending 'chevaux de Troie' into the centre of Community – and he wanted to promote a programme that could so easily have been portrayed as an assault on the 'European model' of mixed economies and social consensus – Cockfield was initially regarded with suspicion. In his own memoirs, Geoffrey Howe suggests that Cockfield's 'inherent integrity of personality' and loyalty to whatever institution he was asked to serve eventually impressed itself on other governments and members of the Commission (Howe, 1994, p. 405). From the point of view of easing his policy entrepreneurship with a reputation for independence and impartiality it was, however, also useful that Cockfield fell out so quickly with his original sponsor. He shrewdly judged that the one person he did not need to please to secure the passage of the Single Market programme was Thatcher. His own reappointment to a second term after 1989 would be another matter.

A still more ambitious account of the Commission's leadership – that it actively shapes the likes and dislikes of governments, rather than just provides the technology for their fulfilment – assumes that governments approach European negotiations with only an inchoate and partially formed set of political preferences. This might follow from a variety of factors: the 'bounded rationality' of decision-makers under conditions of great uncertainty and complexity; the game structure of the EU as a field of strategic interaction in which no one party can calculate what is in its own interests until it knows more about the preferences and likely behaviour of others (Sandholtz, 1996); and norms of EU negotiation that require governments to justify points of view and leave some room for mutual learning and persuasion, rather than approach negotiations from inflexible positions (Richardson, in Richardson, 1996). Bounded rationality in turn means that creative agenda-setting – or the ability to frame the social and political construction of an issue – will often be as important to its overall determination as the decision to consider it at all (Peters in Richardson, 1996). There is, once again, evidence of all these conditions in the case of the Single Market initiative. Several of the governments seem to have been remarkably imprecise in their thinking until the programme was well under way. Cockfield reveals that when Delors visited London in October 1984 even the British government, which supposedly saw the Internal Market as a priority, only gave it seven lines in a nine-page briefing (Cockfield, 1994, pp. 37–8). Lord Young recalls 'being surprised' when he became Trade and Industry Secretary in June 1987 to discover that 'we were the lead Department' on the Single Market initiative (Lord Young, 1990, p. 241). On the other hand, Cockfield was aware that, by moving quickly, he could decisively shape the way others conceptualized the Single Market project. Perhaps a little immodestly, he remarks in his book, 'it was the sheer speed with which I produced the White Paper that allowed "the tide" to be taken at the flood' (Cockfield, 1994, p. 54). And by publishing the White Paper two weeks before the European Council he hoped to 'give heads of Government sufficient time to read the document and appreciate the immense importance of the opportunity being opened up. But it did not give their officials enough time to pick it to pieces' (Cockfield, 1994, p. 49).

Apart from directly changing the political preferences of member governments, the Commission may change outcomes by introducing new actors to the game in a manner that constrains existing players and alters the identity of winning coalitions. The argument that the Commission is tightly constrained by the structure of intergovernmental preferences is a good deal less convincing when it is recalled that each of those governments is – in turn – a complex, non-unitary actor, whose bureaucracy consists of several departments with non-identical views of the national interest and whose political leadership is a coalition of political parties or at least of individuals with conflicting ambitions and values (Sandholtz, 1996). In forming a coalition for change, the Commission is, therefore, by no means constrained to treat each member state as an entity and may, instead, form alliances with particular ministries and political tendencies within governments. It may go even further and form alliances with non-governmental actors (Marks *et al.*, 1996). This will be especially important in matters of economic governance, where governments have their own resource dependencies or cooperative relationships with leading companies.

There is little evidence that tactics such as these were a conscious aspect of Cockfield's policy entrepreneurship. As seen above, several major corporate actors were already agitating for the Single Market and did not, therefore, need to be mobilized into the European arena to lend extra support to Cockfield's initiative. However, a transformation to the Commission's advantage of relationships with non-governmental actors, and particular sections of governments, rapidly became an important dimension of the Single Market programme. The sectoral Council of Ministers concerned with the Internal Market programme gelled as a 'policy network', as Cockfield's White Paper provided a focal point for a convergence of analysis and commitment. It helped that the ministers and departments responsible for its enactment rapidly gained a stake in its success, for the whole enterprise raised their status and power within their own governments. Meanwhile Cockfield's success in establishing 1992 as the deadline and the White Paper as a definite agenda roused public expectations. It also ensured that it was the Commission that set the measure of any backsliding or policy failure from which the popularity and governing credibility of individual governments would not be immune. Finally, Cockfield's approach intensified the mobilization of economic interests into the European arena, beyond anything that had helped produce the programme in the first place. The passage of what was to turn out to be more than 500 Single Market measures required a far more systematic institutionalization of consultation mechanisms that reached beyond those large multinational organizations that had previously cared to organize themselves at the European level (Wallace and Young, in Wallace and Wallace, 1996). Meanwhile the Treaty changes that owed so much to the enticement of Cockfield's White Paper transformed the logic of lobbying to the Commission's advantage. Now that regulations could be determined by majority voting it would no longer be sufficient for economic interests to concentrate their efforts on single governments in the hope that these might veto unwelcome decisions. They also had to ensure that favourable proposals emerged from the Commission in the first place (Panebianco, in Bell and Lord, 1997). Through mechanisms such as these, the Commission built up its own 'client relationships' with sub-national economic actors (Wallace and Young, in Wallace and Wallace, 1996). It also transformed the game by offering these actors a choice of political arenas and a competition of regulatory regimes (European and domestic), where national decision-making had previously held a monopoly (Sandholtz, 1996).

VI

However, the success of Cockfield's policy initiative depended as much upon establishing a dominant position within the Commission as on reasserting the leadership potential of the institution itself. As we have seen, the ability of Commissioners to make coherent policy is usually reduced by the fragmentary character of the Commission. It is difficult to arrange portfolios so that each Commissioner has clear control of any one policy area and the right to command all the administrative resources necessary to get things done. Cockfield softened this difficulty by making a remarkable 'land-grab' in the carve-up of responsibilities that takes place at the beginning of each new Commission. He persuaded Delors to give him 'not only the internal market portfolio (the most important part of DG III)...but also financial institutions and company taxation (the major part of DG XV)...the Customs Union and Indirect Taxation (subsequently DG XXI):...it was, I said, impossible for me, if I was to do the job properly and quickly, to be put in the position of having to argue with other Commissioners and officials' (Cockfield, 1994, p. 30). In addition to making a move that must have further reduced the prospects that all his colleagues would receive meaningful responsibilities, Cockfield resisted the formation of explicit policy linkages between his programme and those proposed by other Commissioners (Cockfield, 1994, p. 46). Rather than alter the design of the Single Market, he preferred to pre-empt colleagues and lock them into success of his own initiative. The decision to 'gain early mover advantage' by announcing the Single Market programme so publicly in the lifetime of the new Commission meant that colleagues had little choice but to support an initiative that was publicly associated with prospects for the overall revival of their institution. Other Commissioners were reduced to shaping their hopes for progress in their own policy areas around spillovers from the Single Market initiative. However, if he was not particularly solicitous of his colleagues themselves, Cockfield was careful to work two vital networks that he correctly perceived to be the real vertebrae of the College of Commissioners: those of the Secretary General and the *Chefs de Cabinets* (heads of Commissioners' personal offices). This was vital because the principle of shared responsibility for all policy areas in the College of Commissioners only works through the briefings Commissioners receive from their *Cabinets*. Indeed, a matter will not even go to the full College if the weekly meetings of the *Chefs de Cabinets* feel confident to pass it as an 'A point'.

A perception that he was emerging as an 'over-mighty subject' could, none the less, have fatally compromised Cockfield's powers of initiative by provoking conflict with Delors. The relationship with Delors was an indispensable political resource for the successful completion of the

Single Market. The Commission President is the sole personal link with the European Council and key heads of government (the Delors–Kohl–Mitterrand axis was of legendary importance); he structures the agenda for meetings of the College which need to pass proposals by a simple majority before they can be presented to the Council; and, in the case of Delors, the President's personal *Cabinet* emerged as a cross between 'think-tank' and 'hit squad' at the centre of the Commission. In fact, the two men were shrewd enough to form an axis in which they effectively pooled their political resources. Some observers even suggested that subsequent Delors Commissions (1989–93 and 1993–5) were less successful than the first because there was nothing to match the rapport between Cockfield and Delors (Grant, 1994). Contrary to predictions that they were an 'odd couple' fated to clashes of personality and ideology, the two men were remarkably compatible. Like Cockfield, Delors had spent a lifetime indulging his enthusiasm for policy-making, while doing his best to avoid party and electoral politics. He had only ever been elected to the European Parliament (1979–81) and his attachment to the Parti Socialiste had not been of sufficient fervour to prevent service as *Chef de Cabinet* to a Gaullist prime minister (1969–72). If, moreover, these two men of mutually sympathetic political biographies came together in the 1985–9 Commission, their appointments were, by a further irony, the joint product of the same guardedness towards supranational political leadership. For both men owed their positions to Thatcher (who had vetoed Claude Cheysson in favour of Delors).

References

Bell, D. and Lord, C. (eds) (1997), *Transnational Political Parties and the EU: Democratisation and Integration* (Aldershot, Dartmouth).

Cockfield, Lord (1994), *The European Union: Creating the Single Market* (London, Wiley, Chancery Law).

Cowles, M. Green (1995), 'Setting the Agenda for a New Europe: the ERT and EC 1992', *Journal of Common Market Studies*, 33, no. 4, pp. 501–26.

Dinan, D. (1994), *Ever Closer Union* (London, Macmillan).

Egeberg, M. (1995), 'Organisation and Nationality in the European Commission Services', *ECPR Joint Workshops*, Bordeaux.

Favier, P. and Martin-Roland, M. (1991), *La Decenne Mitterrand 2: Les Epreuves 1984–1988* (Paris, Seuil).

Grant, C. (1994), *Delors: Inside the House that Jacques Built* (London, Nicholas Brealey).

Haas, E. (1958), *The Uniting of Europe* (Stanford, Stanford University Press).

Hayes-Renshaw, F. and Wallace, H. (1997), *The Council of Ministers* (London, Macmillan).

Heclo, H. (1978), 'Issue Networks and the Executive Establishment', in King, A. (ed.), *The New American Political System* (Washington DC, American Enterprise Institute).

HMSO, *Developments in the European Community January 1993 to July 1993* (London).

Howe, G. (1994), *Conflict of Loyalty* (London, Macmillan).

Jacquemin, A. and Sapir, A. (eds) (1991), *The European Internal Market: Trade and Competition* (Oxford, Oxford University Press).

Keohane, R. (1994), *After Hegemony: Cooperation and Discord in the World Political Economy* (Princeton, Princeton University Press).

Keohane, R. and Hoffman, S. (eds) (1991), *The New European Community: Decision-Making and Institutional Change* (Boulder, Colo., Westview).

Lawson, N. (1992), *The View from No. 11: Memoirs of a Tory Radical* (London, Bantam).

Lindberg, L. and Scheingold, S. (1970), *Europe's Would-Be Polity: Patterns of Change in the European Community* (Englewood Cliffs, NJ, Prentice-Hall).

Marks, G. Hooghe, L. and Blank, K. (1996), 'European Integration from the 1980s: State-Centric vs Multi-Level Governance', *Journal of Common Market Studies*, 34, no. 3, pp. 341–78.

Mazey, S. and Richardson, J. (1993), *Lobbying in the European Community* (Oxford, Oxford University Press).

Moravcsik, A. (1993), 'Preferences and Power in the European Community: a Liberal Intergovernmentalist Approach', *Journal of Common Market Studies*, 31, no. 3, pp. 473–524.

Nugent, N. (1994), *The Government and Politics of the European Union* (London, Macmillan).

Pelkmans, J. and Winters, L. (1988), *Europe's Domestic Market* (London, Royal Institute for International Affairs).

Richardson, J. (ed.) (1996), *European Union: Power and Policy-making* (London, Routledge).

Riker, W. (1986), *The Art of Political Manipulation* (New Haven, Yale University Press).

Risse-Kappen, T. (1996), 'Exploring the Nature of the Beast: International Relations Theory and Comparative Policy Analysis Meet the European Union', *Journal of Common Market Studies*, 31, no. 4, pp. 53–80.

Ross, G. (1995), *Jacques Delors and European Integration* (Cambridge, Polity).

Sandholtz, W. (1996), 'Membership Matters: Limits of the Functional Approach to European Institutions', *Journal of Common Market Studies*, 34, no. 3, pp. 403–29.

Schink, G. (1992), *Kompetenzerweiterung in Handlungsystem der Europaischen Gemeinschaft: Eigendynamik und policy-entrepeneure* (European University Institute Ph.D. thesis).

Sebenius, J. (1992), 'Challenging Conventional Explanations of International Co-operation: Negotiation Analysis and the Case of Epistemic Communities', *International Organisation*, 46, no. 1, pp. 323–65.

Tranholm-Mikkelsen, J. (1991), 'Neofunctionalism: Obstinate or Obsolete? A Reappraisal in the Light of the New Dynamism of the EC', *Millennium*, 20, no. 1, pp. 1–22.

Vibert, F. (1994), 'The Future Role of the European Commission' (London, European Policy Forum).

Wallace, H. and Wallace, W. (eds) (1996), *Policy-Making in the European Union* (London, Oxford University Press).

Wessels, W. (1992), 'Staat und (westeuropaische) Integration: die Fusionsthese', *Politische Vierteljarhresschift*, Sonderheft 23/99, pp. 36–61.

Williamson, O. (1985), *The Economic Institutions of Capitalism* (New York, Free Press).

Young, H. (1989), *One of Us: a Biography of Margaret Thatcher* (London, Pan).

Young, Lord (1990), *The Enterprise Years: a Businessman in the Cabinet* (London, Headline).

8
Policy Entrepreneurship in Action: the Contribution to Health and Social Care Policy-making of Sir Roy Griffiths, 1982–92

Stephen Harrison and Gerald Wistow

Introduction

Ernest Roy Griffiths was born in Staffordshire in 1926, the son of a colliery overman. After grammar school, he worked as a 'Bevin boy' in a coal mine before winning an open scholarship to Keble College, Oxford, whence he graduated in law in 1948. He subsequently took a postgraduate law degree and qualified as a solicitor. After working for the National Coal Board, he joined the chemicals company Monsanto as legal adviser in 1956. He studied at Columbia Business School, New York and served as a Director of Monsanto (Europe) from 1964 to 1968, when he joined the Sainsbury chain of grocers as a Director, becoming Managing Director and Deputy Chairman in 1979. He was knighted in 1985 and retired from Sainsburys in 1988. During the decade 1982 to 1992, he wrote two major reports on public services, the first (published in 1983) on the management of the National Health Service (NHS), and the second (published in 1988) on community health and social care; for brevity, we refer to these hereafter as 'Griffiths I' and 'Griffiths II' respectively. Sir Roy Griffiths was subsequently an adviser in the Department of Health. He died in 1994.

Griffiths was an 'outsider' in Whitehall; he had no previous connections with the NHS social services, or other government departments beyond the routine dealings of Sainsbury with the Ministry of Agriculture, Fisheries and Food. Moreover, both his reports were radical in intent and contained a significant number of recommendations which were not immediately welcome to the government which had invited them. Yet both sets of recommendations were, after some delay, substantially implemented. We have told elsewhere the detailed story of how Griffiths came to be commissioned to write his reports, of the process he employed in doing so, and of how opposition to them was handled (Harrison, 1994; Wistow and Harrison, forthcoming). Here we address the character of Griffiths' 'policy entrepreneurship'. What follows is divided into four main sections. The first contains a brief discussion of recent literature on the characteristics of successful policy entrepreneurship. The second and third contain summary accounts of the stories of Griffiths I and II respectively, based on documentary evidence, interviews with contemporarily relevant actors, and to a lesser extent, on our own contemporary conversations with our subject. (All unattributed quotations are taken from our interview transcripts.) In the final section we summarize those aspects of the stories which connect with the policy entrepreneurship literature, and briefly discuss its relationship to contemporary concepts of leadership.

Policy Entrepreneurship

Griffiths was not simply a 'policy advocate' who made his recommendations and then departed from the scene; he saw his reports though to implementation against a good deal of opposition, and it seems appropriate therefore to examine his NHS work in terms of the literature of 'policy entrepreneurship', that is, as the mobilization of other actors in order to establish new policies, procedures or other organizational innovations in the public sector (Bardach, 1972; Lewis, 1980; Kingdon, 1984; Polsby, 1984; Marmor and Fellman, 1986; Doig and Hargrove, 1987; Oliver and Paul-Shaheen, 1997). It should be noted that successful entrepreneurship need not entail the invention of entirely new ideas, but may equally consist of applying old ideas in a new context. The term 'policy entrepreneur' has been applied to a number of rather different types of actor, mainly in the context of US public policy, and can include elected politicians, career civil servants, persons seconded into the administration as political appointees, or others (such as businesspersons and academics) who are never appointed to public office.

Ioannou (1992) notes that these different statuses may affect the *legitimacy* of entrepreneurial activity, and that policy entrepreneurship may be a more important means of securing policy innovation in a fragmented political system (such as the USA) than in an integrated one (such as the UK). Nevertheless, his extensive review of the literature has identified nine 'associated characteristics' of policy entrepreneurship; although these are not presented as a theory (and the author is anxious to avoid resurrecting a 'trait theory' of leadership), the implication is that they bear some sort of causal relationship to successful policy entrepreneurship. The characteristics may be grouped as follows.

Some are *personal* to successful entrepreneurs. First, many are in *some* sense 'outsiders'; irrespective of their formal relationship to the organization they are unlikely to be committed to established modes of operation, and even if they are formally members of the organization, they may be socially and intellectually isolated from colleagues. Second, they consistently display a number of characteristics which help them to overcome inertia in others, such as determination, zeal, self-confidence, optimism and energy; they are not 'cluttered by reality'. Third, they are risk-takers in the sense that they may have to bend the rules, thereby risking reputations and perhaps careers. Fourth, successful entrepreneurs tend to display 'uncommon rationality' (Doig and Hargrove, 1987, p. 11), based on a personal *Weltanshauung* (Kingdon, 1984, p. 93), whereby they are able to challenge existing paradigms and practices and to link their analysis to a larger political, social, economic or historical context.

Successful entrepreneurs tend to employ particular *behaviours and tactics* in pursuit of their objectives. First, they engage in what has been called 'pyramiding' to increase the political resources available to them; examples include proselytizing, forming alliances with sympathetic actors and groups and recruiting sympathizers to their staff. Second (and perhaps hard to distinguish from the above), they are mobilizers, motivators and catalysts of others. Third, they are opportunists in the sense of taking advantage of crises or policy vacuums. Fourth, they often seek to maximize their autonomy and discretion by exploiting their professional prestige and official status, adopting a cloak of disinterestedness and socializing staff into the entrepreneur's own views.

Finally, there is a *context*. Most policy entrepreneurs are critically dependent on legitimacy conferred upon them by political sponsors, and loss of such patronage is a common cause of failed entrepreneurship.

Griffiths I – General Management

The circumstances leading to the commissioning of the first Griffiths Report include both an attempt to deal with contemporary political criticism over government handling of the NHS, and a series of unsought consequences which led to a change in Griffiths' terms of reference and the production of a report which contained recommendations which were both radical and unexpected by the government (Harrison, 1994). The radical character of Griffiths I lay most obviously in its proposal to replace a distinctive style of NHS management which had developed over three decades with something resembling a commercial model of 'general management', including what were later termed chief executives.

There had been a long history of ill-focused discontent with NHS management. Partly as a result of the strength of the clinical professions (particularly medicine and nursing) NHS institutions had never been managed as unitary hierachies and were characterized by 'diplomatic management': 'a process concerned to facilitate, in as coordinated a fashion as possible, all the sub-groups within an organisation' (Harrison, 1988, p. 51). Although until 1974 some sections of the service had a single officer formally in charge (e.g. Medical Officers of Health for community services, Medical Superintendants in psychiatric hospitals), the more usual arrangement was an administrator for groups of hospitals, with the individual hospitals run by a triumvirate of chief nurse, senior physician and chief administrator. Although various official and quasi-official reports in the 1950s and 1960s had considered the possibility of a more unified hierarchy, including a chief executive (Harrison, 1988, ch. 2), the tendency towards management by collective was in the event reinforced and institutionalized in the 1974 reorganization of the service, which rejected the notion of a chief executive or general manager and introduced instead the notion of 'consensus decision-making' by multidisciplinary teams of formal equals. This was unpopular even with its exponents and gave rise to a good deal of criticism on numerous grounds (Harrison, 1982). Nevertheless, shortly after taking office in 1979 the new Conservative government published its consultation document *Patients First* (DHSS and Welsh Office, 1979), which rejected any fundamental change to this arrangement.

The formal announcement of what was to become the Griffiths I inquiry was made in October 1982 at what was recognized as probably the last Conservative Party conference before a general election. It was part of a government strategy to provide public reassurance in the wake of a leaked Central Policy Review Staff report on the possible replacement of the NHS with private insurance (Blackstone and Plowden, 1988), and to appease Select Committees, a number of backbench Conservative MPs and the Confederation of British Industry, all of whom had been trenchantly critical of the growing size of the NHS workforce.

Norman Fowler, Secretary of State for Social Services, closed the health debate with the statement that

> we want manpower directed at serving the patient, not at building new empires of paper and bureaucracy. Over the last twelve months I have set in hand ... a series of measures to ensure that we make better use of manpower. I want to make even faster progress, and with this in mind I intend to establish a small team, headed by people from private industry, to achieve it. Their job will not be to produce a lengthy report – there is no shortage of lengthy reports in the Health Service – but to help us produce results, not in years but in months. (Fowler, 1982, p. 12)

It took some time to determine the membership of the team, which consisted of Michael Bett, Board Member for Personnel of British Telecom, Sir Brian Bailey, already involved in the NHS as Chairman of a Regional Health Authority and with business interests in television, and Jim Blyth, Group Finance Director of United Biscuits. The Secretary to the Inquiry was Cliff Graham, an Assistant Secretary at the DHSS. It was not until December 1982, after all the others had been recruited, that Griffiths was offered its chair. He was initially reluctant, taking the view that the terms of reference were too restricted; his perspective was that to inquire into the 'manpower' of an overstaffed organization was to confine inquiry to a second-order problem. Rather, the first-order problem was 'a management problem, or general problem', and only if the proposed terms of reference for the Inquiry were modified to include this wider concern would he accept. Though 'taken aback' by the response, ministers agreed broader terms of reference for the Inquiry, reported to Parliament in February 1983 as 'to examine the ways in which resources are used and controlled inside the health service, so as to secure the best value for money and the best possible services for the patient [and] to identify what further management issues need pursuing for these important purposes' (DHSS, 1983, p. 2).

The Process of the Inquiry

The team did not perceive themselves to have been given any kind of political 'steer' towards a particular solution; indeed some senior DHSS civil servants regarded with some concern that they could not foresee the outcome. Two main lines pursued by the inquiry were as follows. First, members were involved in a programme of visits within the NHS. These were often performed by individuals (usually including Griffiths) and followed by relatively infrequent meetings at which ideas were pooled and Bailey's NHS experience used as a sounding board. The approach was later summed up by one of the team's support staff thus:

> The team decided they could not invite evidence formally. Instead they would be open to all advice, invitations and written evidence. . . . As time went on, they had to be more selective; for example, turning down invitations from local branches of national organisations. Otherwise we should have taken nine years, rather than nine months [*sic*]. (Barton, 1984, p. 41)

The approach adopted on visits was to listen to opinions offered rather than to ask specific questions. Early in the course of the inquiry the rumour had spread within the NHS that the creation of chief executives was a likely outcome (Sherman, 1983, p. 426), and many witnesses volunteered their opposition to this notion. A few, especially existing chairpersons, were more supportive. In general, the impression left upon team members by these visits was an absence of management and an excess of professional domination; this was variously described as 'a polo style of management' (i.e. with a hole in it, like the well-known confection), 'people banding together [in professions] in search of leadership', and 'top-level trade unionism in action rather than selfless devotion'.

Shortly after the Conservatives' re-election in June 1983, Griffiths had a meeting with NHS Regional Administrators at which the general manager notion was floated. The response was hostile, of which one consequence was a degree of public coyness on the topic by team members. In an interview in July 1983, Griffiths was paraphrased as saying:

> The Griffiths inquiry is not about instituting a tier of chief executives throughout the NHS or general managers or full time chairmen. It is about tracking down responsibility. While the NHS management inquiry set up earlier this year could end up recommending any of the numerous solutions already suggested by previous reports, it is at the moment still at the stage of asking questions rather than supplying answers. (Halpern, 1983, p. 832)

Yet the team *had* already made its mind up about general management, albeit perhaps subconsciously. Given the business backgrounds of three of them, 'we took this conclusion in with us'. The fourth member of the team 'came to acquiesce' on the basis of the visits: 'we drifted into the general manager assumption'. Another said, 'I was only rarely influenced by what witnesses thought'. As a member of the Inquiry staff subsequently put it, 'the team had been asked to advise from their own expert knowledge, so there was no need to try to justify their conclusions by claiming depths of knowledge' (Barton, 1984, pp. 41–2).

A second line of inquiry pursued by the team was to commission the NHS Management Advisory Service to conduct studies of the relationship between doctors and the management process at five NHS general hospitals. These were effected between May and July 1983. By its own account, the (unpublished) report 'set out generally negative observations on the management process' which reinforced a number of opinions that the inquiry team had already formed:

> Clinicians may view management as a service provided to them by someone else.... There is no obligation placed on the clinician to become engaged in any activity which might, however loosely, be described as management. The clinician's influence on the management process is, however, profound. He [*sic*] commits huge resource ... [and] ... influences management decisions over priorities for development or reallocation of funds and other resources, by forming a heavily influential lobby. (Management Advisory Service, 1983)

The team's progress report, a private document of only three pages, was considered by Cabinet in June 1983. The text of the main report was written, largely by Griffiths and Graham, during September. There had been no substantial dissent amongst the team, though some of its members would have liked to see *more* radical proposals, including the 'floating off' of the NHS from detailed ministerial accountability. What remained in the report was very much associated with Griffiths personally: 'Griffiths processed everything'. The team members fully expected their conclusions to be made public, but did not expect to be in any way responsible for implementing them. (Indeed, apart from a few presentational meetings, only Griffiths and Graham had any subsequent involvement.) Rather, they saw their task as policy advocacy: as one member put it, 'They [ministers] could take it or leave it.'

Although they recognized that general management was not likely to be immediately well-received by doctors, the British Medical Association (BMA) had actually been 'dispassionate' during the inquiry, having been reassured by Ministers that the proposals would not interfere with clinical freedom. Moreover, during the visits to hospitals 'Griffiths had the doctors eating out of his hand' by sympathizing with their views about poor management. It was not surprising, therefore, that the inquiry team were not overly apprehensive about the eventual medical reaction.

The team's report, which had been the subject of oral briefing but not a written draft within the Department, was sent to the Secretary of State on 6 October 1983 in the form of a 24-page letter signed by Griffiths. It began by emphasizing that it was not a report but rather a set of recommendations for action (as indeed had been the principle set out in Fowler's original speech). The first 7 pages set out the recommendations for action, whilst a further 15 pages contained background and some of the reasoning behind the recommendations. Although not very tightly structured, this section contained what can be seen as the four key elements of the inquiry team's diagnosis of NHS management.

Firstly, the team were concerned that individual overall management accountability could not be located:

it appears to us that consensus management can lead to 'lowest common denominator decisions' and to long delays in the management process. . . . the absolute need to get agreement overshadows the substance of the decision required. . . . In short, if Florence Nightingale were carrying her lamp through the corridors of the NHS today, she would almost certainly be searching for the people in charge. (NHS Management Inquiry, 1983, pp. 17, 22)

The second aspect of the team's diagnosis was that 'the machinery of implementation is generally weak' (p. 14).

there is no driving force seeking and accepting direct and personal responsibility for developing management plans, securing their implementation and monitoring actual achievements. . . . certain major initiatives are difficult to implement . . . [and] above all . . . lack of a general management process means that it is extremely difficult to achieve change . . . [A] more thrusting and committed style of management . . . is implicit in all our recommendations. (pp. 12, 19)

Third, the team drew attention to the lack of an orientation towards performance in the Service.

it lacks any real continuous evaluation of its performance . . . rarely are precise management objectives set; there is little measurement of health output; clinical evaluation of particular practices is by no means common and economic evaluation of these practices is extremely rare. (p. 10)

Finally, a lack of concern with the views of consumers of health services was identified:

Nor can the NHS display a ready assessment of the effectiveness with which it is meeting the needs and expectations of the people it serves ... Whether the NHS is meeting the needs of the patient, and the community, and can prove that it is doing so, is open to question. (p. 10)

The team's recommendations fell into four groups. First, changes within the DHSS were proposed: a Health Services Supervisory Board, chaired by the Secretary of State, to have strategic responsibility for the objectives and resources of the NHS, and (responsible to it) a full-time executive multi-professional NHS Management Board, chaired by a person who would in effect be the service's chief executive. Second, the appointment of general managers at each level of organization: regardless of discipline, such persons should have overall management responsibility for achieving the authority's objectives and were to have substantial freedom to design local organization structures. Functionally-based structures should be minimized and day-to-day decisions taken at hospital or similar level rather than above. Third, existing rudimentary systems of management by objectives should be extended and 'cost-improvement programmes' introduced to reduce costs without impairing services. Finally, clinical doctors should become involved in local management, primarily through the medium of workload-related 'management budgets'. The Report also urged that more attention be paid to patients' and community opinion, but made no substantive proposals for accomplishing this.

Response to the Report

In his speech to the Conservative Party conference in October 1983, Fowler made no reference to the Griffiths Report, though it was already known that he had received it (*Health and Social Service Journal*, 13 Oct. 1983, p. 1215). Much of the health debate at the Conference was occupied with attacks on NHS bureaucracy, though Fowler did provide some clues about Griffiths: 'too much administration and too little management': 'how can you talk of local devolution of responsibility if locally no-one knows who is in charge?' (p. 1244). Although Griffiths' report had the support of the Secretary of State and the Permanent Secretary, and had been approved at 'Number 10', it was two weeks later that the report was made public through a statement in the House of Commons:

> The Inquiry Team . . . say an enormous programme of management action is still needed. [They] found that at all levels in the National Health Service there is a lack of a clearly defined general management function. Responsibility is too rarely placed on one person. Although they would like to harness the best of the consensus management approach, they found that at present consensus management can lead to lowest common denominator decisions, and long delays in the management process. (Fowler, 1983a, p. 1)

Fowler went on to accept the inquiry's proposals in respect of the DHSS, and announced a period of consultation in respect of the other proposals after which it was hoped 'the general management function' could be implemented by April 1984. On 18 November, the formal period of consultation began; in a letter to chairpersons of health authorities, the Secretary of State sought views by 9 January 1984 on the general management function, and on the involvement of clinicians in the management process. The wording was reassuring in tone:

> I have it in mind to issue guidance early next year requiring [*sic*] Authorities to clarify the general management function by identifying a general manager . . . who would be drawn in most cases from amongst existing staff, to undertake the general management function for a defined period of 3–5 years. (Fowler, 1983b, pp. 1–2)

Those working in the NHS, however, were not reassured at the possible demise of consensus teams, but each profession took the view that if there had to be a general manager he or she should come from that group (*Hospital and Health Services Review*, March 1984, pp. 94–7; *Health and Social Service Journal*, 12 Jan. 1984, p. 37). In the event, a decision was taken by Fowler to extend the consultation period. The House of Commons Social Services Committee decided in December 1983 to make the Griffiths Report a topic of enquiry; oral hearings were held and a final report published on 15 March 1984 (Social Services Committee, 1984).

The BMA's view of the general manager proposals had hardened since the inquiry; the Chairman of its Council had written to the Secretary of

State in the following terms, which were also put in evidence to the Committee:

> It could be interpreted from the report that a somewhat autocratic 'executive' manager would be appointed with significant delegated powers, who would – in the interests of 'good management' – be able to make major decisions against the advice of the profession ... it should be clearly understood that the profession would neither accept nor cooperate with any such arrangement – particularly where the interests of patients are concerned ... (*British Medical Journal* 288, 14 Jan. 1984, p. 165)

This virtual declaration of independence was amplified at the subsequent oral hearing (Social Services Committee, 1984, p. 4). Critical, though not so trenchant, views were also expressed by the Royal Colleges of Nursing and Midwives and other nursing organizations (Social Services Committee, 1984, pp. 44–8). Not surprisingly, the Institute of Health Service Administrators was in favour of general management, and shortly afterwards renamed itself the Institute of Health Service *Management*. Yet in his own evidence to the Committee, Fowler was diffident:

> (Mr Meadowcroft) If you have a district or a unit where the evidence to you from them on consensus or unanimity is that they are happy with the way they are working, decisions to them appear to be reached quite adequately and effectively, are you going to insist that they conform to a uniform pattern and have to appoint a general manager?

> (Mr Fowler) ... we will have to consider as a result of the consultation. I cannot come to you and actually say we have made a decision on that point when we quite clearly have not. (Social Services Committee, 1984, p. 174)

This apparent change of view about general management did not pass without comment at the time: interviewed in February 1984 by the *Health and Social Service Journal*, Fowler made a virtue of his position, presenting it as open-mindedness, though still managing to sound diffident:

> HSSJ: You did indicate to the Select Committee that you had gone a little cold on the whole idea of the general manager ...

NF:... What I said to the Select Committee was basically this: that we're in the middle of considering the results of the many representations that have been made... (*Health and Social Service Journal*, 23 Feb. 1984, p. 221)

In its Report, published on 15 March 1984, the Social Services Committee welcomed the spirit of the Griffiths Report, but expressed the view, albeit obliquely, that the general management *process* did not require general manag*ers* (Social Services Committee, 1984, pp. vii–ix, xxiii–xxiv). In his immediate response, Fowler was still diffident: 'I welcome this report and would like to thank the Committee for working so quickly... I will study the report with great interest and make a formal response in the usual way' (DHSS, 1984a). At the press launch of their Report, however, the Committee were less oblique than their text had been: 'We don't go along with Griffiths, we don't go along with general managers' (Nicholas Winterton MP, quoted in *Health and Social Service Journal*, 22 March 1984, p. 338). The *Health and Social Service Journal* went on to comment that 'Mr Fowler's initial enthusiasm for Griffiths has, of course, progressively waned as he has had to face the political pressures that would result from full blooded implementation'. In the month following the Committee's Report, DHSS spokespersons continued to leave the general manager question open.

The Social Services Committee's Report was the subject of a poorly attended adjournment debate in the Commons on 4 May 1984. Opening it, Fowler said that he wished to listen to views expressed before reaching final conclusions on Griffiths; he hoped to publish such conclusions later in the month (*Hansard*, 4 May 1984, col. 642). But he also implied that a decision about general managers had been made, even if there was to be some flexibility about details: 'The purpose of the consultation in which we are engaged... is to seek the advice of all those with an interest in *how we can best introduce individual general managers* into the Health Service' (ibid., col. 649, emphasis added).

The Outcome

Yet it was a month later, on 4 June 1984, that Fowler announced his decision: 'The guidance I am giving health authorities today requires them to start work straightaway to establish the general management function and to identify individual general managers at authority and unit levels' (DHSS, 1984b, p. 1). As well as the usual circular (DHSS, 1984c) issued on the same day, setting out the action which health authorities were to take in creating and filling general manager posts, there was a letter from Graham to chairpersons of authorities, seeking their cooperation in putting 'all staff in the picture within ... 2–3 weeks'. To this end, the letter enclosed a video of interviews with Fowler and Bett, a list of approved speakers on the topic of Griffiths, a question-and-answer brief for other speakers, and a professionally produced 8-page, full colour printed leaflet for distribution to all staff. (The comprehensiveness of these materials, a commonplace in subsequent government marketing of its policies, would have been difficult to achieve in the month between the Commons debate and the announcement of the government's decision.) The question-and-answer brief sought to play down staff fears about general managers, stressing in particular that consultants would remain clinically autonomous and that professional disagreements would be resolved by the relevant health authority rather than by managerial fiat (DHSS, 1984d, p. 4).

The NHS was instructed that General Managers were to be appointed at all levels of organization by the end of 1985; the posts were open to persons from outside the service as well as to NHS employees of all disciplines, and were to be appointed on a fixed-term basis. Management budgeting was endorsed. The DHSS Boards were established with a slightly different membership from that proposed by Griffiths, and Griffiths himself appointed to one of them, thus setting the scene for his translation into an NHS 'insider'. Although management budgeting proceeded haltingly and although the Boards experienced various difficulties and modifications (Harrison, 1994, p. 38), general management has proved an enduring development, having subsequently penetrated the structure of NHS institutions to much lower organizational levels than actually proposed by the Griffiths team. Thus Griffiths finally had more than his way.

The length of time taken by Fowler to reach a decision has contributed towards a reputation for indecision on his part; according to one official such indecision was a 'major problem' (Davies, 1987, p. 724), a view also expressed by several respondents to the present study. On the other hand, it is likely that a reaction like that of the BMA to the general manager proposal would have given any Minister pause for thought: a powerful reaction from a powerful interest group. In the end, according to 'insiders', Fowler's hand was strengthened (or 'forced' according to some) by the Prime Minister during the late spring of 1984: 'Another of the things he's [Fowler] done right is to keep David Willett [*sic*] her social policy adviser at No. 10 informed of everything he's doing ...' (*Observer*, 5 May 1985).

Griffiths II – Community Care

Policy-makers' concerns about lack of integration, from the client/patient's point of view, of health and welfare services stretch back into the 1960s (Harrison, 1988). Indeed a major rationale for the reorganization of both health and social care services which took place in 1974 was precisely the improvement of such integration (Wistow, 1982). The immediate trigger to the commissioning of Griffiths' study of community care was a report by the Audit Commission (1986) which was strongly critical of 'slow and uneven progress' in achieving community care objectives; it identified a number of 'fundamental underlying problems' for which central government was primarily responsible. They included: organizational fragmentation and confusion; the inherent contradiction between policies requiring a shift of responsibility from hospital to local authority services, on the one hand, and the imposition of financial penalties on authorities which expanded community services on the other; and the creation of further perverse financial incentives by the availability of Social Security funds to expand residential but not community services.

This last factor, which was the most pressing politically and was central to Griffiths' terms of reference, contained two distinct, but interrelated elements. First, the Social Security budget was effectively open-ended and thus outside public expenditure cash limits. Second, it provided questionable value for money since payments were available to support high-cost institutional services but not low-cost alternatives in the community. In effect, the Social Security system was providing a virtually automatic entitlement to residential or nursing home care, whilst health and social services policies sought to enable people to remain in their own homes for as long as possible, partly on the grounds of presumed cost effectiveness.

This authoritative critique of policy disarray was a source of political embarrassment which officials in the DHSS exploited. For some time, they had been concerned both about the impact on community care of the perverse incentives created by Social Security funding and about the need for a more coherent approach to the development of community and social care more generally. A Green Paper on the latter had been promised by the Secretary of State some two years previously when he had advocated a reorientation of Social Services departments towards an 'enabling role' whereby they 'promoted and supported the fullest possible participation of ... different sources of care (as well as their own direct provision)' (Fowler, 1984). Work was undertaken on such a document but remained unpublished. Officials were similarly frustrated in their attempts to secure a ministerial response to the growth of Social Security expenditure. Indeed, there was a view in the Department that the matter did not require a 'formal external review because we sorted through the issues ourselves and had perfectly good solutions which we put up [to Ministers] to encounter this wall of silence'. At the same time, however, the notion of an independent external review provided a new opportunity for officials to overcome ministerial reluctance to confront the issues which the Audit Commission had brought into sharp relief. The Permanent Secretary was said to have suggested to Mr Fowler: 'Roy Griffiths had "pulled a rabbit out of a hat" before on the NHS. Let's see what he can do with community care.'

On 16 December 1986, Fowler announced that he had commissioned, the by then, Sir Roy Griffiths to conduct a review of community care. The choice of Griffiths had a number of clear advantages. He had worked closely with Fowler on the previous NHS review. Perhaps even more importantly, he was by then serving as the Prime Minister's personal adviser on health matters and 'the fact that he was personally known to the Prime Minister and the Prime Minister would have trusted him . . . was almost more important at that point than the Secretary of State trusting him'. The fact that he had dealt effectively with his NHS commission was seen as 'almost a guarantee that he would crack this problem for the Government'. Whilst his reputation included independence of mind and judgement, he had become to some extent an insider and a known quantity, said by one senior official to be 'regarded, so to speak, as a member of the Department'. The exercise was to be completed within twelve months and was to focus on

> the way in which public funds are used to support community care policy and to advise [the Secretary of State] on the options that would improve the use of those funds as a contribution to more effective community care. (DHSS, 1986)

In particular, Griffiths was required to compare the different arrangements which then existed for funding residential and nursing home services, with those for domiciliary care. The announcement also specified that the review should be brief and 'geared to advice on action, as was the review of management in the health service' (DHSS, 1986).

The Conduct of the Review

In the letter to the Secretary of State which prefaces his report, Griffiths noted that he had not seen his 'primary task as fact finding' (Griffiths,

1988, para. 2.8) and indeed considered that the essential facts were all contained in earlier reports from the Audit Commission (1986) and the Social Services Committee (1985). Reports from the National Audit Office (1987) and a joint Central and Local Government Working Party (DHSS, 1987) on the public funding of residential care had provided him with further material. In addition, he received large numbers of submissions some of which recommended changes in policy. However, he considered his remit as being 'essentially geared to ensuring that the machinery and resources exist to implement such policies as are determined' (Griffiths, 1988, para. 6).

Documentary evidence was supplemented by what he described as 'extensive discussions and visits' (para. 5). In all of these activities he was assisted by two groups: a small support group of relatively junior Departmental officials and an advisory group of external experts. Whereas he had some personal knowledge of the NHS through a daughter who was a junior doctor, an insider doubted 'very much if the lifestyle he had led brought him into social care and community care issues very often'. As a result he was seen as approaching his task without preconceptions, and it was through his visits to local services that Griffiths demonstrated and developed his distinctive approach to the analysis of the underlying issues. An insider recorded that:

> His focus right from start was 'I want to look at the interface between the client and the direct service which is provided. That is the focus, the rest of it is all superstructure . . . if you understand that bit, the rest falls into place . . . ' He was absolutely committed to that . . .

The same respondent emphasized that on visits Griffiths made it clear that he did not want to meet local dignitaries but to see old people's homes and day centres or go out with home care officers and the Meals on Wheels service. In all his local meetings, he was said to 'single mindedly focus attention' on the 'crucial point of contact' with the service user, concentrating on such issues as:

> Where do you get your clients from, how do you get your clients, what do you do when you get a referral, how do you make a judgement about what is needed, how do you bring into play other people who are not under your direct command, what does it feel like to be a client with all these different people . . . ?

Such an approach was novel for policy-makers and front-line service delivery staff alike. It was a perspective he was seen as having brought from 'running shops – what he did with our thing was exactly what he did in Sainsburys'. He was known for making unannounced visits to stores, either parking his car at the store as if he were an ordinary member of the public or leaving it some distance away and walking to it. A respondent reported that when he made such visits:

> From the time he approached the store, he was thinking 'if I was a customer'. I know that ... what he was looking at was how many people were standing at the checkout ... when you first walk into the store what were the first things that hit you between the eyes, did you feel this is a place that is clean and bright and tidy, do you feel comfortable in it?

In addition to this direct and experiential form of learning, he used his advisory group to test out ideas and possible approaches:

> We would all assemble and at the appointed time the door would open and in would walk Roy Griffiths with his civil servants and he would sit down and he would work through the agenda as if it was a business meeting. At the end of the meeting he would stand up and walk out ... he put the issues on the agenda, he set the agenda and he asked the advisory group to comment on these issues and he was inscrutable so you had no idea whether or not what you had said was regarded as being helpful or regarded as being totally irrelevant ... in a way that was clever ... he handled it in a way that the members of the advisory group could never think 'if I say this, this will chime in with his thinking' because you didn't know what his thinking was ...

Griffiths also maintained a continuing relationship with the Prime Minister and the new Secretary of State:

> I know that he had several meetings with Mrs Thatcher on managing the health service. I would be surprised if he didn't take the opportunity to share his early thinking with her and I have no doubt whatsoever that he got Moore's blessing for what was a critical issue about giving the lead role to local government.

Consistent with Griffiths' way of working, the report was highly ocused and wasted few words. Community care was a major area of policy failure for which central government was itself essentially responsible, and Griffiths questioned whether a policy worthy of the name existed:

> At the [political] centre community care has been talked of for thirty years and in few areas can the gap between political rhetoric and policy on the one hand, or between policy and reality in the field on the other hand, have been so great ... The absence [of financial information and accounting] processes at national level is inconsistent with any claim that there are serious national policy objectives to be achieved. (Griffiths, 1988, paras 9, 5.7)

While noting that his remit excluded consideration of the level of funding and focused on the cost effective management of existing resources, he none the less argued that it was 'self evident that resources must be consistent with the agreed responsibilities and objectives to be achieved within a given time scale'. Moreover, he hinted at his views on their adequacy by recording that 'many Social Services Departments and voluntary groups grappling with the problems at local level certainly felt that the Israelites faced with the requirements to make bricks without straw had a comparatively routine and possible task'. Griffiths also asserted that the last thing required was administrative reorganization which 'creates turmoil under a semblance of action', and concentrated on securing change in management systems and processes based on the principles of matching responsibilities with appropriate resources and ensuring accountability for performance within specified time scales. Of these he wryly observed 'nothing could be more radical in the public sector than to insist on such an approach'.

He proposed a three-tiered framework of responsibilities and accountabilities stretching from the user of services to ministers. First, at the level of individuals and their carers, he recommended the appointment of care managers to ensure that individuals' needs were holistically assessed and a comprehensive package of care arranged, paying due regard to the preferences of users and their carers. Second, he recommended that local responsibility should remain where it currently lay and that local authorities should take the lead role in community care because they were 'best placed to assess local needs, set local priorities and monitor performance' (Griffiths, 1988, para. 5.27). This vote of confidence in local government was accompanied by a major recasting of their role so that they would function as 'the designers, organisers and purchasers of non-health care services, and not primarily as direct providers, making the maximum possible use of voluntary and private sector bodies to widen consumer choice, stimulate innovation and encourage efficiency' (para. 1.3.4).

Griffiths' reasoning was as follows. First, he concluded that the division of responsibilities between local authorities and social security for the funding of domiciliary and residential care respectively, was a 'particularly pernicious split' (Griffiths, 1988, para. 4.21) which should be eliminated by the creation of a unified community care budget controlled locally rather than nationally. Second, the NHS was insufficiently local and, in any case, unable to take on new responsibilities with general management still recent and a Prime Ministerial Review (which subsequently led to the purchaser/provider split: Secretaries of State, 1989) still in progress. Third, if local responsibility was not to lie with local government but with some agency separate both from health and local authorities, a new agency would be required; at this point, he came to the conclusion, 'why invent something different when we have got something there already'. Moreover, it appears that during the course of his inquiry, if not in advance of it,

> he came to think that local government was an essential part of democracy. It was about checks and balances. It was about helping people identify with policy decisions and the allocation of resources.

Finally, Griffiths recommended the appointment at national level of a Minister of State in the DHSS who would be 'seen by the public as being clearly responsible for community care' (para. 1.2). This role would include the publication of 'a clear, short, statement of government's community care objectives and priorities' (para. 1.2.1), arranging the distribution of central funds to social services authorities (para. 6.20), and being 'responsible for ensuring that national policy objectives were consistent with the resources available to public authorities charged with meeting them and for monitoring progress towards their achievement' (para. 6.21). Community care funding for local authorities was to be through a ring-fenced specific grant, payment of which would be conditional upon the approval of local community care plans demonstrating *inter alia* that adequate planning and management systems were in place and that 'local objectives are sufficiently in line with government policy' (para. 1.5.3).

Response to the Report

The response to the Griffiths II report was in sharp contrast to the immediacy with which Ministers had embraced at least some aspects of

Griffiths I. Publication was delayed by three months and the report appeared in March 1988 the day after the Budget, when its author was recovering from major surgery and unable to make any contribution to its launch and discussion. Griffiths himself believed that this was an attempt to distract attention (Timmins, 1995, p. 473). To compound this, the report was published merely 'for consultation', accompanied by a Ministerial statement that the government would consider its contents and 'bring forward its own proposals in due course'. A further fifteen months were to elapse, during which a wide range of alternatives was explored, before the Cabinet agreed that Griffiths' proposals should be largely accepted.

The most obvious aspect of the report's unacceptability was its recommendation that local authorities should have the lead responsibility for community care and receive additional funds, transferred from the national Social Security budget, to enable it to meet those extended responsibilities, a suggestion entirely at odds with the current thrust of central policy towards local government. As a senior official noted:

> These were the very local [authorities] ministers had been castigating for years as inept, incompetent, profligate and there was good old Roy coming along and suggesting that a couple of billion quid of social security money should be made over to them. I think there was mild consternation, or rather a lot more than mild consternation in a lot of quarters about this.

Moreover, Griffiths' recommendations that central government should be more transparent in the setting of its objectives, priorities and the levels of funding that would be required to secure them were not unproblematic. The release of monies to local government would depend on the centre approving plans submitted by local authorities, thereby sharing responsibility for their feasibility and implementation. All these features implied, and were intended to imply, much more explicit accountability processes at central government level, inevitably threatening to create hostages to political fortune (Wistow and Henwood, 1988, p. 6). Moreover, in seeking to make explicit the interdependent nature of central and local government responsibilities, the Griffiths report was innocent of politics in which 'some degree of ambiguity and confusion is functional for governments of all political hues and the political barriers to introducing rationally managed systems should not be underestimated' (Wistow and Henwood, 1988, p. 7). In addition, Social Security officials were hostile to the idea of transferring resources out of their budget into local government. Griffiths himself was subsequently to go on record to the effect that

> quite a few members of the Cabinet had been blooded in the inner cities by authorities who were playing politics. There was confrontation on both sides ... [Ministers] accepted the analysis, but they didn't like the allocation of responsibilities. (May, 1993, p. 27)

Amongst these Ministers was Kenneth Clarke, who became Secretary for Health in July 1988. In the period between the receipt of Griffiths' report in February 1988 and Clarke's appointment, an interdepartmental committee had been charged with considering the report and advising on its implementation. In addition to representatives from the DHSS (which was divided into its two constituent parts in July 1988), the committee included officials from the Treasury and Department of the Environment. An insider described the committee as

> [taking the report] ... to bits and pieces and putting it together again, dreaming up options and alternatives for our masters and mistresses ... [it] ... looked at what other options that a mortal mind can fantasise about and they actually didn't look as good as Griffiths'. We thought about a new community care authority ... the integration of primary health care services with the adult services of local authorities ... We looked at giving it to the health service ... we put that right of court. They had enough troubles of their own without landing this burden on them. We thought about splitting Social Services responsibilities – the adults floating off into a new community care agency and the children going to education departments ... We inevitably came back to the Griffiths solution as being the best option.

Though Griffiths' proposals were not entirely without their supporters at Ministerial level, Clarke remained an implacable obstacle: he

> hated local government and the last thing he was going to advocate was handing [community care] over to it.

He would have preferred the NHS to take the lead in purchasing community care but became convinced that it was impractical to add such responsibilities to the huge change agenda resulting from the Prime Ministerial NHS Review. According to Timmins (1995, p. 474), Clarke and John Major (then Chancellor of the Exchequer) attempted what Clarke later admitted to be a 'dingbat solution' under which applicants for social security payments would be subject to a medical and social work test of their needs. In these circumstances, officials were understandably pessimistic about the possibility of Griffiths' recommendations ever being accepted; one noted that he 'couldn't conceive the Griffiths recommendations being carried when the Secretary of State who had got to carry them was deeply opposed'.

It was at this point that Griffiths himself appears to have made a decisive contribution to the outcome through his access to the Prime Minister. He had been in the Department and Downing Street contributing to the NHS review and '[used his NHS experience]... to talk to her about community care. My guess is that he focussed very much on Mrs Thatcher.' According to Timmins (1995, p. 476), by the summer of 1989 Clarke had persuaded the Prime Minister that she should tell Griffiths his solution was being rejected. However,

> at virtually the same moment, Griffiths on his own initiative, had put in a paper arguing that the Clarke/Major plan would not work. It did not address a problem that went far wider than the Social Security budget... and it underestimated the seriousness of the crisis affecting the mentally ill, the elderly and the handicapped.

Timmins recalls that, when Griffiths was invited to meet Mrs Thatcher, his half an hour with her became an hour and a quarter as 'he went through all the arguments again' (Timmins, 1985, pp. 476–7). An insider suggested that the idea that he had advanced to the Prime Minister was that

> you think there are problems in the health service on Minister's desks... you don't realise what a safe harbour I am offering you by giving you the defence of... failures in local government and not central government.

The same informant also said that Griffiths had seen the growth of social security spending as

> an important safety valve in the system and, I think, that he must have said to her 'you block off the safety valve and pressure will build and I can't tell you [to what degree]... but it will certainly build and I think you ought to seriously distance yourself and distance the

government from all of this'... and my view is, and this is only a guess, that he worked on her and she became convinced... not that she liked local government but because she thought in the interest of the government it was a sensible conclusion.

After this meeting, the Prime Minister reviewed the documents again, waved the report at a Cabinet committee and asked if there were good reasons not to implement it. They all stared back at her; 'most of them thought *she* was the good reason' (May, 1993, p. 27; Timmins, 1995, p. 477).

The Outcome

The Secretary of State announced in Parliament on 12 July acceptance of the broad thrust of Griffiths' recommendations (Clarke, 1989). A White Paper *Caring for People* (Secretaries of State, 1989) was published in November and the necessary legislative changes secured through the passage of the NHS and Community Care Act in June 1990. Yet implementation of Griffiths' proposals proved far from secure; within a month full operation of the Act had been put back from April 1991 to April 1993 and subjected to a further prime ministerial review in the summer of 1992 (Brown, 1992), As a senior civil servant was subsequently to acknowledge, the underlying 'policy was not secure until it was implemented'.

Griffiths described the government's proposals as a 'three wheel' version of the 'four wheel vehicle' he had proposed (Griffiths, 1989). The missing 'wheel' was finance and the role of central government. In particular, the link between the approval of local community care plans and the allocation of resources was not accepted. Consequently, resources were to be allocated through the general revenue support grant rather than through a ring-fenced, specific grant (Wistow and Henwood, 1991, p. 81). The result was to distance central government from local outcomes since it would be no longer possible to argue that it had endorsed local plans in authorities where implementation proved to be problematic, an important safeguard for those ministers who were still concerned about the minority of left-wing authorities. In addition, by transferring resources into the general pool of local authority resources, the volume of community care funding would be less transparent and it would be possible for Ministers to argue, as they had habitually done, that resource inadequacies were due to local authorities misallocating funds rather than because the volume of money available to them was insufficient.

The form in which the policy was ultimately implemented was closer to the four wheel vehicle which Griffiths had designed. The resources transferred from Social Security were in the form of a specific grant for a single year, before being absorbed into the general revenue support grant. Although the linkage between the approval of community care plans and resource allocation was not reinstated, eligibility for receipt of the transferred Social Security resources depended upon local authorities formally certifying that they had acceptable joint plans with their relevant health authorities for hospital discharge and the purchase of nursing home places. Despite the anticipation of serious difficulties in implementing the government's final proposals, they have been successfully put into effect (Audit Commission, 1994; 1995).

Conclusions

It is clear that Griffiths made a substantial individual contribution to the formulation and implementation of health and community care policy. In terms of the appropriate counterfactuals, it is unlikely that without Griffiths' personal contribution the outcomes which we have described would have occurred. Had he not insisted on modified terms of reference for Griffiths I, a more narrowly focused 'manpower' inquiry would have resulted. In respect of both reports, it seems likely that most sophisticated potential leaders of government inquiries would have recognized the political implications of, and steered well away from the radical solutions which Griffiths actually proposed. The recommendations of both reports were eventually implemented despite considerable opposition from a range of quarters. Moreover, both reports had a long-lasting impact, with the second also serving to shape the subsequent 'purchaser/provider' split in health care. Griffiths' success accords well with the literature on policy entrepreneurship summarized above.

One obvious characteristic of Griffiths' approach was a political naiveté which most of our respondents felt was genuine rather than cultivated. Both Timmins (1996, p. 408) and our respondents referred to a genuine commitment to the NHS, born of his social origins, and a belief that an NHS which could show itself to be efficient could legitimately claim additional government resources. In terms of the literature, this is 'uncommon rationality'. A senior official suggested that someone who had run 'an enormous business' was bound to experience 'an element of incredulity' about political processes:

[Griffiths] would harbour within himself the conviction that... there was a rational, planned, logical approach to the problems... he believed that inside himself. If he hadn't believed it, he wouldn't have done what he did.

Moreover, Griffiths had a *Weltanshauung*: strong *a priori* views that organizations ought to be managed from the perspective of the client or customer, coupled with self-confidence and optimism (Smith and Young, 1996, p. 134), other characteristics cited in the literature. Thus he had to work hard to have his rationality accepted; an official noted:

I think with rational people he was pretty successful, but with those who had got ideological convictions that cut across that or blind spots or levels of ignorance or incompetence, it wasn't going to work.

Given the background of antipathy to local government, particularly pronounced on the part of Kenneth Clarke as the relevant Secretary of State, it is improbable that the same set of proposals would have been made by anyone who did not have Griffiths' independence of view and confidence in his own judgement. Equally, it seems no less improbable that anyone else on the 'inside track' could have persuaded the Prime Minister and her colleagues to accept proposals which were apparently contrary to the broad thrust of everything they had attempted in the field of local government. Yet this fairly simple-minded rationality (perhaps the product of legal training) is both a strength and a weakness; in Griffiths II, logic rightly questioned the need to create a new social services agency when local authorities already existed, but in Griffiths I it can be seen as having led to a questionable assumption that the absence of a chief executive was a cause rather than a consequence of the relative power of the professions (Harrison and Pollitt, 1994, p. 43).

Though he could employ coyness about his thoughts and plans, Griffiths had a capacity to inspire individuals and can fairly be seen as the mobilizer or catalyst described in the literature. Though an indifferent public speaker, and capable of devastatingly critical written prose (the 'Florence Nightingale' and 'Israelites' remarks quoted above from Griffiths I and II respectively are classic examples), he was able to convince those with whom he spent time face-to-face (ranging from Mrs Thatcher to the consultants encountered during hospital visits) of his essential wisdom. Of course, as the reaction of the BMA to Griffiths I showed, convincing individuals did not necessarily change the stance of an institution.

Griffiths' own status was different in the two inquiries; in the first, he was an unknown quantity in Whitehall, giving rise to a certain degree of apprehension about what he might conclude, whilst in the second he was an insider. Yet there was no obvious process of learning by Griffiths over the period that we have examined. His personal assumptions and his basic method of work remained unchanged: field visits to form an impression of the problem and consultation without revealing his own thoughts. Intellectually, he perhaps remained an outsider, though throughout his Whitehall career he retained and skilfully employed the crucial patronage of the Prime Minister.

Griffiths' achievements cannot be seen apart from their political, economic and social context. General management for the NHS was not a new idea, nor was the idea that some form of enhanced organizational coordination was necessary to prevent patients/clients falling, as it were, into the gaps between organizations and services; thus there is a question about how these old ideas achieved, apparently at Griffiths' hand, the status of ones whose time had come. Although the literature characterizes policy entrepreneurs as opportunist, and although policy vacuums existed, the two Griffiths Reports may represent different scales of achievement. Griffiths I, for all it conflicted with the interests of key actors, went with the political grain; Kingdon's (1984) model, which explains political agendas in terms of the joining of otherwise independent 'streams' of general political ideology, particular problems perceived as pressing by policy-makers, and potential policies, often being developed in academic or other locations outside government, seems an adequate explanation for Griffiths I (Harrison, 1994, pp. 133–7). There was a financial crisis to which policies aimed at improving the efficiency of public services were a logical alternative once more radical alternatives had been abandoned, and notions of having one person 'in charge' clearly accorded with the ideological cast of the Thatcher governments. This is clearly, however, not so of Griffiths II; though there was certainly some pragmatic appeal, on grounds of what Klein (1983, p. 140) calls blame diffusion, in handing much of the task of community care to local authorities, such a solution was well outside the government's ideological predilections, an observation which underlines the importance of Griffiths' own contribution.

In the management literature which has flowed from James Mac-Gregor Burns' Pulitzer prize-winning categorization of 'transforming' and 'transactional' leadership (Burns, 1978), there is some consonance between the characteristics attributed to transforming leadership and those associated with successful policy entrepreneurship. This is clearest in respect of the behaviours employed to mobilize others and in the perception by the leader/entrepreneur of a desired future state which goes beyond what is conventionally deemed to be pragmatically possible. According to one review of leadership in relation to organizational effectiveness (Bass and Avolio, 1994, p. 3), what has been renamed 'transformational' leadership is characterized by, *inter alia*, 'inspirational motivation' (team spirit aroused by the leader's provision of both challenge, and meaning to followers' work in the form of desirable future states) and 'intellectual stimulation' (including the questioning of assumptions).

Yet successful policy entrepreneurship does not simply *equate* to transformational leadership. In part, this is because the basis of the latter literature is in *continuing* relationships between leader and followers, whereas Griffiths never occupied an executive role in the NHS and his remit was limited to the topics on which he was asked to report. But it is also because these topics concerned processes rather than outcomes. That Griffiths may well have had aspirations to transform is shown by his concern with patients' and clients' perspectives and his belief in politics as a worthwhile endeavour, but it can hardly be argued that the outcomes of his policy entrepreneurship meet Burns' formulation for transforming leadership, which is 'concerned with end values such as liberty, justice [and] equality' (1978, p. 426) and occurs where 'persons engage with others in such a way that leaders and followers raise one another to higher levels of motivation and morality' (p. 20).

References

Audit Commission (1986) *Making a Reality of Community Care* (London: HMSO).
Audit Commission (1994) *Taking Stock: Progress with Community Care*, Community Care Bulletin no. 2 (London: HMSO).
Audit Commission (1995) *Balancing the Care Equation*, Community Care Bulletin no. 3 (London: HMSO).
Bardach, E. (1972) *The Skill Factor in Politics* (Berkeley: University of California Press).
Barton, K. (1984) 'Will the 85 percent principle work?', *Health and Social Service Journal*, 12 Jan., pp. 41–2.
Bass, B. M. and Avolio, B. J. (eds) (1994) *Improving Organisational Effectiveness Though Transformational Leadership* (London: Sage).
Blackstone, T. and Plowden, W. (1988) *Inside the Think Tank: Advising the Cabinet 1971–1983* (London: Heinemann).

Brown, C. (1992) 'Major Demands Review of Care in the Community', *The Independent*, 23 June, p. 7.

Burns, J. M. (1978) *Leadership* (New York: Harper and Row).

Davies, P. (1987) 'Norman Fowler: a failure of vision', *Health Service Journal*, 25 June, pp. 724–5.

Department of Health and Social Security (1983) 'NHS Management Inquiry'; Press release no. 83/30, 3 Feb.

Department of Health and Social Security (1984a) 'Social Services Committee Report on Griffiths Welcomed by Norman Fowler', Press Release no. 84/72, 15 March.

Department of Health and Social Security (1984b) 'Griffiths Report – Health Authorities to Identify General Managers', Press Release 84/173, 4 June.

Department of Health and Social Security (1984c) *Health Services Management: Implementation of the NHS Management Inquiry Report*, circular HC(84)13.

Department of Health and Social Security (1984d) 'Implementing the Management Inquiry Report – Informing Members and Staff', letter to Health Authority Chairmen, 4 June.

Department of Health and Social Security (1986) *Sir Roy Griffiths to Review Community Care*, Press Release 86/410, 16 Dec.

Department of Health and Social Security (1987) *Public Support for Residential Care*, Report of Joint Central and Local Government Working Party, London.

Department of Health and Social Security and Welsh Office (1979) *Patients First: Consultative Paper on the Structure and Management of the National Health Service of England and Wales* (London: HMSO).

Doig, J. W. and Hargrove, E. C. (eds) (1987) *Leadership and Innovation: a Biographical Perspective on Entrepreneurs in Government* (Baltimore: Johns Hopkins University Press).

Fowler, N. (1982) *Speech to Conservative Party Conference*, 6 Oct. Issued in Conservative Party News Service Release no. 640/82.

Fowler, N. (1983a) *Statement on National Health Service Management Inquiry*, Distributed with circular no. DA (83)38, 25 Oct.

Fowler, N. (1983b) *NHS Management Inquiry*, letter to Chairmen of Regional Health Authorities, District Health Authorities, Special Health Authorities and Boards of Governors, 18 Nov.

Fowler, N. (1984) Speech to Joint Social Services Annual Conference, 27 Sep., Buxton.

Griffiths, R. (1988) *Community Care: Agenda for Action* (London: HMSO).

Halpern, S. (1983) 'The quality quiz', *Health and Social Service Journal*, 14 July.

Harrison, S. (1982) 'Consensus decisionmaking in the National Health Service: a Review', *Journal of Management Studies* 19(2), 377–94.

Harrison, S. (1988) *Managing the National Health Service: Shifting the Frontier?* (London: Chapman and Hall).

Harrison, S. (1994) *National Health Service Management in the 1980s: Policymaking on the Hoof?* (Aldershot: Avebury).

Harrison, S. and Pollitt, C. (1994) *Controlling Health Professionals* (Buckingham: Open University Press).

Ioannou, A. (1992) *Public Sector Entrepreneurship: Policy and Process Innovators in the UK*, Ph.D. thesis, University of London.

Kingdon, J. (1984) *Agendas, Alternatives and Public Policies* (Boston: Little, Brown).

Klein, R. E. (1983) *The Politics of the National Health Service* (London: Longman).

Lewis, E. (1980) *Public Entrepreneurship* (Bloomington: Indiana University Press).

Management Advisory Service (1983) Report to NHS Management Inquiry, 2 Sept.

Marmor, T. R. and Fellman, P. (1986) 'Policy entrepreneurship in government: an American study', *Journal of Public Policy* 6(3), 225–53.

May, A. (1993) 'Full circle', *Health Service Journal*, 7 Oct., 24–7.

National Audit Office (1987) *Community Care Developments. Report by the Comptroller and Auditor General*, HC108 (London: HMSO).

National Health Service Management Inquiry (1983) *Report* (London: Dept of Health and Social Security).

Oliver, T. R. and Paul-Shaheen, P. (1997) 'Translating ideas into actions: entrepreneurial leadership in state health care reforms', *Journal of Health Politics, Policy and Law* 22(3), 722–83.

Polsby, N. W. (1984) *Political Innovation in America: the Politics of Policy Initiation* (New Haven: Yale University Press).

Secretaries of State for Health, Wales and Scotland (1989) *Working for Patients*, Cm 555 (London: HMSO).

Secretaries of State for Health and Wales (1989) *Caring for People: Community Care in the Next Decade and Beyond*, Cm 849 (London: HMSO).

Sherman, J. (1982) 'Oxford RHA goes off the deep end', *Health and Social Services Journal*, 14 Oct., 1210.

Smith, T. and Young, A. (1996) *The Fixers: Crisis Management in British Politics* (Aldershot: Dartmouth Press).

Social Services Committee (1984) *First Report, Session 1983–4: Griffiths NHS Management Inquiry Report*, HC209 (London: HMSO).

Social Services Committee (1985) *Second report, Session 1984–5: Community Care*, HC13 (London: HMSO).

Timmins, N. (1995) *The Five Giants: a Biography of the Welfare State* (London: HarperCollins).

Wickings, I. (1983) 'Consultants face the figures', *Health and Social Service Journal*, 8 Dec., 1466–8.

Wistow, G. (1982) 'Collaboration between health and local authorities: Why is it necessary?', *Social Policy and Administration* 16, 44–62.

Wistow, G. and Harrison, S. (forthcoming) 'Rationality and rhetoric: the contribution to social care policymaking of Sir Roy Griffiths 1986–1991', *Public Administration*.

Wistow, G. and Henwood, M. (1988) 'Intoduction: a framework for action', in A. Harrison and J. Gretton (eds), *Healthcare UK 1988* (Hermitage: Policy Journals).

Wistow, G. and Henwood, M. (1991) 'Caring for people: elegant model or flawed design?', in N. Manning (ed.), *Social Policy Review 1990–91* (Harlow: Longman).

9
Executive Agency Chief Executives: Their Leadership Values

Elizabeth Mellon

Introduction

A great deal has been written about the potential impact of New Public Management (NPM) on the values and mores of the public sector. A century ago, proponents of the 'science of administration' believed that a well-structured hierarchy would ensure efficiency (Wilson, 1887). In contrast, the essence of the NPM reforms of the 1980s and 1990s has been that increased efficiency and control in a public bureaucracy can be achieved with similar methods to those adopted by the private sector. (Ironically, over the same period, research in the private sector has placed greater emphasis on cooperation and teamwork as sources of effective organizational cultures.) Culture change programmes in UK government organizations have tried to encourage more emphasis on productivity, measurable outputs, individual responsibility and rewards for performance.

In addition to culture change in the UK public sector, there has been structural change. One significant NPM reform has been to establish executive agencies. These agencies are separately identified units, headed by civil servants who are publicly and directly accountable for the results achieved by the agency they lead. In this way, an agency chief executive (ACE) is comparable with a general manager of a wholly owned subsidiary of a publicly listed company. By October 1997, there were 138 executive agencies, with nearly 384,000 civil servants working in them, or in similarly organized units (e.g. the Inland Revenue), that is, over 75 per cent of the total UK civil service workforce. Of the 138 ACEs, 93 were recruited by open competition and 34 from outside the civil service. There had been 78 internal, 34 external and 24 Armed

Forces appointments; but only 6 were women (Next Steps Briefing Note, Oct. 1997).

However, despite significant structural and cultural change, the view of politicians and of the top management of the UK civil service has been that the values of civil servants should remain unchanged. At the same time as articulating more 'commercial' values, normative statements have been made requiring public servants to retain traditional public service values of integrity, impartiality, objectivity and accountability. This juxtaposition of commercial and traditional civil service values has provoked much debate. Some commentators have argued that the traditional civil service values never existed and that the 'ideal administrator' was only a theoretical concept. Further, the normative values of 'integrity' and 'impartiality' bring with them a heavy cost, in terms of an anti-intellectual and passive approach to public business (Fry, 1969). Hood (1991) contended that only one value set (commercial *or* public service) could be preserved at the cost of the other. Generally, NPM reforms assumed a public service culture of honesty; therefore, it was felt acceptable to remove some of the devices designed to ensure honesty and neutrality in the public service. Yet civil service values cannot be assumed necessarily to be a function of a different, more honest type of personality being recruited into the public sector.

> We have evolved rules for the appointment and promotion of staff, for the control of public money, and for other formal accountabilities, such that even the *temptation* to use public power for private ends has, in these areas, been very largely eliminated. (Derek Morrell, former senior civil servant, quoted in Hennessy, 1989, p. 163)

Despite these concerns, no empirical evidence had been gathered to explore whether civil servants really do espouse a different set of values from private sector employees, or the extent to which any such different values might be eroded by NPM reforms. Therefore, the author designed questionnaires to elicit managerial values and administered them to 450 managers, over half of them public sector managers, in two phases, from 1995 to 1997. This research demonstrated that civil servants do hold different values from private sector managers. In the second phase, the revised questionnaires were administered also to ACEs and were supplemented with interview data. These data showed that ACEs, on average, hold different values from both civil servants and from private sector managers. Therefore, ACEs may provide a significant source of culture change in the UK civil service. This is not to suggest that such a process of change would be straightforward. The concept of a clear demarcation between 'politics' and 'administration', designed to protect public officials from the irrationalities of political interference (Pollitt, 1990), has proven difficult to enact, particularly in politically sensitive areas of public sector activity, such as the prison service (Lewis, 1997). Moreover, ACEs recruited from the private sector may find this (occasionally fluid) distinction between policy and administration especially difficult to understand, as they have had no training in this aspect of public sector employment (Mellon, 1993).

Turning again to the empirical research underpinning this chapter, it has been difficult always to assess whether any research has been truly successful in accessing deeply-held, fundamental human values. This is because the most popular research instrument has been a questionnaire (Rokeach, 1973; Ravlin and Meglino, 1987). While questionnaires have been successful in eliciting individuals' preferences for words such as 'integrity', which purport to represent values, there has been only limited research investigating the link between such words and repetitive patterns of behaviour over time. It will be seen, from the definition given to 'values' below, that one distinctive attribute of values is their impact on behaviour and decision-making. In an attempt to address the question of whether the author's research had been successful in accessing what could be termed 'real', or fundamental, values, ten ACEs were interviewed also as part of the research effort. In addition, this chapter presents a case study of one former ACE, Derek Lewis, Director Gereneral of Her Majesty's Prison Service from 1992 to 1995. Core values are held to result from processes of socialization acting upon innate desires. Therefore, formative experiences can help to explain values held by adults. Derek Lewis's life story, based on two three-hour interviews with him, is used to illustrate the extent to which conclusions drawn from the author's empirical research about ACEs' values can be explained further by the formative experiences of one of their number. The author's empirical research data on civil service, private sector managers' and ACEs' values are summarized and presented briefly, to provide context.

This chapter does not repeat the story of Derek Lewis's dismissal from the Prison Service; this is explained amply in his own book, *Hidden Agendas: Politics, Law and Disorder*, published in 1997. The intention is to examine the proposition that, on average, ACEs espouse values that are different from the values espoused by both public and private sector managers. If this is so, the author's research suggests that ACEs may, by acting in accordance with their values, safeguard yet the best of the UK civil service tradition of 'fair play', while ensuring a proactive approach towards modernization. It should be emphasized that the opinions and analysis presented in this chapter are the author's own. Derek Lewis's actual words are used also for purposes of illustration.

What is a Value?

'Values' is a term used loosely. It is used interchangeably to describe organizational cultures, attitudes, beliefs, motivation and commitment. In fact, the definition provided by the research literature is clear. Values are core beliefs held by individuals concerning how they should or ought to behave in broad ranges of situations. They are beliefs about the desirable, but values with feeling and beliefs are held to be affectively neutral (Rokeach, 1973). Values form a primary component of the self-schema. A value 'is a standard that guides and determines action, attitudes towards objects and situations, ideology, presentations of self to others, evaluations, judgements, justifications, comparisons of self with others, and attempts to influence others' (Rokeach, 1973, p. 25). Because beliefs about the self tend to be the most deeply held and influential of cognitions, 'values are stable and central and are pervasive in their influence on other cognitions, perception and behavior' (Ravlin, 1994, p. 599).

Values have cognitive, affective and behavioural components and are different from attitudes, social norms, needs, traits, interests and beliefs (Feather, 1975). Values are often confused with attitudes, but an attitude can be defined as an organization of beliefs focused on a single object or situation. An individual may hold thousands of beliefs, which cluster into attitudes, whereas the individual will only espouse a small number of values, perhaps as few as forty (Feather, 1975). They are arranged in a hierarchy and only the relevant part of a value system will be activated for particular decisions (Rokeach, 1973; Ravlin and Meglino, 1987). They differ also from needs in that, while they can be described as cognitive representations of psychological needs, they are expressed in socially desirable terms (Rokeach, 1973).

Therefore values influence our attitudes, provide standards for how we present ourselves to others (Goffman, 1959) and provide a basis for judging our own and others' conduct. They serve as standards in the persuasion process and in social influence, in terms of what is worth arguing about and whether it is worth trying to influence others. Values provide a basis for rationalizing thought, undertaking action, making general plans for resolving conflict and taking decisions. They are fundamental to the human psyche and consequently difficult to access and measure. Yet, because values determine patterns of behaviour and decision-making over time, choosing different individuals with different values, especially in leadership positions, can have a significant impact on the employing organizations.

Empirical Evidence of Civil Service, Private Sector and ACE Values

The empirical research upon which this chapter is based took place in two phases. The first phase administered two questionnaires about values to 172 civil servants and private sector managers. Statistical data analysis, academic peer review and comments from questionnaire respondents led to numerous changes in item wording and format. In the second phase of the research, the revised questionnaires were administered to 281 civil servants, private sector managers and ACEs. Subsequently, 10 ACEs, of the 44 surveyed, were interviewed. The purpose of the interview schedule was to test the proposition that the questionnaire data had succeeded in accessing and codifying core values. This proposition was supported by the interview data. Therefore, the results summarized in Table 9.1 represent average differences in meaningful values espoused by the three groups.

In the author's research, the value of *change* represents a willingness to discard current working practices in favour of new ways of working. The value of *principle* represents a willingness to consider the moral implications of decisions and to speak out against, or even to resign, rather than condone behaviour that contravenes an individual's principles. The value of *control* represents the desire to anticipate and control change and to shape the future by using initiative. The value of *hard work* represents the importance of hard work and achievement. The value of *pragmatism* represents a willingness to bend the rules to achieve results.

Some of these results might have been expected from general readings about the UK civil service (Hennessy, 1989): for example, that civil servants appear to possess an exaggerated sense of *principle*. Others were more surprising: for example, that civil servants appear to be as willing as private sector managers to bend the rules to achieve results. This implies that the carefully honed rules and practices advocated by Derek Morrell, in the quotation above, are necessary to ensure public service accountability.

However, focusing particularly on the average values of the ACE sample, it appears that this group is as *change*-oriented as private sector managers,

Table 9.1 Interpretation and explanation of statistically significant differences between the average value scores for civil servants, private sector managers and ACEs (N = 281)

Value	Significant difference between civil servants and private sector managers	Significant difference between civil servants and ACEs	Significant difference between private sector managers and ACEs	Explanation
Change (favour new ways of working)	yes	yes	no	Private sector managers and ACEs stronger agreement
Principle (question managers behaviour that contrvenes principles)	yes	no	yes	Public sector and ACES stronger agreement
Control (shape the future)	no	yes	yes	ACEs stronger agreement
Hard work (hard work and achievement)	no	no	no	No difference between the three samples
Pragmatism (bend the rules to achieve results)	no	yes	yes	ACEs stronger disagreement

while being as *principled* as public sector managers. ACEs also value more strongly being in *control* and are less willing to bend the rules (non-*pragmatism*) than either civil servants or private sector managers. Derek Lewis's life story is explored to understand the extent to which these four value propositions about ACEs may be supported and from which formative experiences, for this particular ACE, these values may have resulted.

Derek Lewis as a Child and Young Adult

Derek Lewis was born on 9 July 1946: his mother was 37 years old and his father 39. He is one of three children, the only boy and the youngest. His sister Barbara was 8 years old, and his sister Janet, 4, when he was born. Both his parents were Oxbridge educated teachers. His mother is a gifted mathematician, who also played tennis for her university, Oxford. As was expected of a woman of her background, she gave up her teaching job on marriage, to concentrate on the job of raising a family. She is a highly disciplined woman and has never complained about any frustration involved in giving up her career. She is riding horses still, at the age of 88. Derek's father was a fencing blue at Cambridge University and a geography teacher. He taught in private prep schools, but, by the time Derek was born, he was Headmaster of a prep school, Ryedale, in Wales. This, then, was the background for Derek's development from the age of six months until he graduated from university.

The family atmosphere created by his parents was one of endeavour and serious pursuits. Holidays tended to be spent in Devon or Scotland on healthy, outdoor activities. The children were encouraged to enjoy music and there was not a great deal of frivolity at home. 'We were not a close family in the sense of being warmly close. The family worked to well-understood rules. You were expected to behave in a way that was considerate to others. I remember an occasion when the older of my two sisters stepped out of line and rebelled, having a tantrum and missing her lift to school. This behaviour was unacceptable, because it created difficulties and embarrassment for others. There were things that were right, and there were things that were wrong, but there was never a need to exercise any very strong discipline, because the general ethos made it unnecessary. Stepping out of line brought very strong disapproval very quickly and although there was very rarely any punishment in the family, the weight of disapproval was quite intimidating. And it was not only about what you were allowed to do, but also about what you were allowed to believe' (interview with Derek Lewis).

Derek's father was reasonably well paid, but there was not a great deal of spare money. The family had an abhorrence of borrowing; expenditure was prioritized and large purchases, such as a car, calculated carefully to ensure that they could be covered by income. Money was not regarded as a worthy objective. This tendency towards frugality was to stand Derek in good stead when he took the large pay cut necessitated by moving from the private sector to become Director General of the Prison Service. Implicit academic expectations of all three children were high and possibly exacerbated by living in a flat within the school premises. Derek's parents had done well, both academically and at sport, and they established a demanding environment for their children. Derek's oldest sister went on to qualify as a doctor and his second sister as a pharmacological researcher. 'I went initially to a small, private, primary school, in fact, there was anxiety at the time that I was not applying myself as earnestly as I should do. There were apparently consultations about what should be done with this idle youngster' (interview). After primary school, Derek attended his father's prep school and then went on to Wrekin College public school in Shropshire, a single-sex boarding school. He sat for, and gained, a BICC scholarship to Wrekin. His sisters also went to boarding school. 'I never stayed away from school during term at all. My parents visited for half term, which was a couple of consecutive days over a weekend. It was relatively difficult for my parents to get away, as they were running a boarding school, so their visits were not frequent, or long. As children, we were not expected to commit to anything that involved either of our parents in having to go out of their way, or to forgo something that had already been planned' (interview).

There was a very strong work ethic in the family, from both parents. Derek's mother undertook voluntary work and gave talks at the school, in addition to caring for the three children. 'My father worked particularly hard. There was not a lot of support given to running the prep school, because most resources were directed towards the senior school, so he had to undertake a range of functions. In addition, my father naturally tended to adopt the philosophy that something could always be done better and that, unless he had used all the hours available to improve something, then he would not have done as much as he could. I started my working career being very earnest indeed and having quite a reputation for being a very cold fish and a total workaholic' (interview).

The prep school, of which his father was Headmaster, was a Methodist school, but most of the pupils, including Derek, came from Anglican families. 'I probably thought that there was some influence of that in my life, which was a bit more Calvinist than might otherwise have been the case. Then I went off to the straightforwardly Anglican public school [Wrekin College]. It was one of those public schools that are typical of the middle-of-the-road British public schools, not particularly distinguished, but quite solidly good throughout. It was quite strong in encouraging people to indulge [*sic*] in non-academic activities, whether it be sport, or other things, and I developed a very strong interest in cabinet-making while I was there. I was really introduced to music there and one of the legacies I have from it is an undying interest in playing the violin. And in the sporting world, I was an indifferent rugby and cricket player, but I did acquire a very strong love of squash.'

Wrekin College had high expectations of Derek. 'I think I was kind of regarded as one of two or three in the school who had the potential to do well and were Oxbridge scholarship candidates. As a result, the school put a fair bit of effort into me and I came out with the maximum grades in two A levels and close to maximum in the other A level I did. [*Author's note*: Derek Lewis gained four A levels: A1 in Physics and in Chemistry, A2 in Mathematics for Science and B in the General Paper.] Prior to A level, there was some discussion about what I was going to do about university. My father and both his brothers had been at Queens' College Cambridge and that was the sort of natural place to start. So I applied for a place there. I was interviewed pre-A level. Science was my first choice, as I was in the science stream at school, but they did not consider my science was quite strong enough and recommended Economics instead. Then I got my A level results and went on to do the scholarship exam and got a scholarship in Natural Sciences. This pleased me enormously, having been told that I was not strong enough.'

While Derek's family was Anglican, it was not a strongly religious family and none of his immediate family were clerics. 'There was never any pressure put on us, nor even any very great attempt to encourage us into particular beliefs, that was very much delegated to school.' None the less, Wrekin College reinforced Derek's interest in the church and he was confirmed into the Anglican Church there. He had a number of friends who were very strong Christian believers, one of whom was the son of an Anglican clergyman who was planning to go into the church himself. Therefore, Derek decided to take Part 1 in Natural Sciences and Part 2 in Theology at Cambridge and then to be ordained into the Anglican Church. 'I'm not sure that I ever thought very much about what I personally had to offer, or indeed whether I was suited to it. I don't really use the expression "having the calling" to do so, it was more a belief that it was the right thing for me to do. I went to Germany for the intervening period between A levels and Cambridge and was employed by the YMCA in one of its clubs for servicemen with the British Army on the Rhine.' He was involved with the Christian activities of the YMCA and the local garrison church during his time on the Rhine and with Christian societies and activities during his first year at Cambridge. 'I think I was driven more by a kind of belief in theology. I thought that theological reading and debating was important and I had a desire to disseminate those values: the basic characteristics of integrity and honesty, care for others.'

Derek's time at Cambridge brought a change in his aspirations. From a fairly insulated, well-regulated home life in Wales and the cloistered, structured atmosphere of a public school, he was propelled into a university life of choice and freedom. 'I have to say that I spent two years doing my Part 1 in Natural Sciences probably learning, in large measure, to live with that freedom. I was involved in sports and other interests and not doing that much work. I suppose I had been driven and drawn on at school by the expectations of the school and those around me. At university, I found that those expectations did not exist any more and that I was very much on my own. I actually chose to devote a lot of my time to other things, particularly the opportunity to get involved in other subjects. I spent quite a lot of time on the philosophy of science. I enjoyed mathematics a lot more than chemistry and physics. The fact that I could get by without doing a great deal of work, and was not very strongly motivated, meant that I came out of the second year with a 2:2. My parents were quite disappointed really.'

His original commitment to becoming ordained started to diminish during his second year at university, as he explored more closely both the academic subjects and the potential careers in which he was really interested. The business world started to sound attractive to Derek. He had attended an industry-sponsored weekend in London while at Wrekin College, looking, among other activities, at Millbank Tower being built. In addition, two of his friends from home were the children of entrepreneurs. Completing Part 1 of his degree meant that all he needed to qualify was a third-year certificate of diligent studies; he did not need to take a Part 2 in Natural Sciences. He had heard that the newly formed London Business School, which was just starting its two-year M.Sc. programme in Business Studies, would admit straight into the second year students who had taken the one-year programme in industrial management run by the engineering department at Cambridge University. 'So, I opted to do the one-year industrial management course, which was quite fun, because it was Economics, Social Psychology and a whole bunch of subjects. I always found new things very stimulating and part of the problem with my natural sciences was that I was getting bored with it, because I had been doing it for too long.'

This seems an appropriate moment to step out of the story and reflect upon what we have heard. Derek Lewis's main formative experiences are behind him, so before the story continues with his graduation from London Business School and his first job with Ford, let us consider what we know about him. He comes from an intellectual, controlled family environment, where unwritten rules are understood and obeyed. Expectations, of him and of his sisters are high, both in terms of their academic achievement and their standards of behaviour. A serious work ethic has been inculcated in him. His Christian beliefs reinforce a serious and responsible attitude towards life and personal endeavour and he describes the important values he wishes to disseminate as those of honesty, integrity and care for others. Derek notes, and remembers, times in his life when he failed to meet the high expectations held for him, even as young as when he attended primary school. He describes himself at work in his early career: 'a very cold fish and a total workaholic'. Even his descriptions, and the language he uses, seem to represent the way he has been brought up to see life, in black and white: things are either right or wrong.

The empirical research into values underpinning this chapter does not purport to locate or explain all forty values that individuals are held to espouse (Feather, 1975). The research design looked for differences in values between the three managerial groups studied and values held in common were eliminated as part of the early design process. Yet it is noticeable that the value differences established through a quantitative research methodology appear to be discernible also from the qualitative data gained through interviews. The interview data are not used selectively; indeed, large *verbatim* extracts are reported. Turning to consider Derek compared with the average ACE values, we can see how important are rules and keeping to the rules for Derek (non-*pragmatism*). The weight of displeasure to be borne at home, should the rules be transgressed, was palpable. The ethic of *hard work* is established from an early age, both from observing his parents and from the high expectations held for him. *Principle* and the purpose of strong values are clearly established through his Christian beliefs. There is also evidence of a desire for *change* in his preference for variety and his tendency to become bored if required, for example, to study the same subjects for too long. The desire for *control* appears less well-established at this point. However, it could be argued that Derek's parents always set the tone, but left the choice of direction to the children. For example, Derek's decision to be confirmed while at Wrekin College did not provoke a strong parental reaction. 'When I announced I was going to do so, it was met with mild approval, but not strong encouragement, it was very much left to me to make up my own mind.' Changing the direction of his university education is one piece of evidence of Derek's desire to shape his own destiny. It may be recalled also how pleased Derek was when he gained a scholarship in Natural Sciences, his first choice of study, after having been advised that his scientific skills might not be strong enough.

Derek Lewis also allowed the author access to psychometric assessments, carried out on him as part of the recruitment process to various senior positions. He is described as intellectually very able (in the top 10 per cent of all senior managers surveyed), highly competitive and dominant (*control*). He is at his most comfortable operating in an established organization with a clearly defined structure, where standards of work practice and behaviour are established, and to be more conventional than 'commercially expedient' (non-*pragmatism*). He has a great deal of integrity (*principle*) and can be expected to be compulsive in his desire to get things right. He is highly self-disciplined and thorough in following tasks through to completion (*hard work*). Finally, he is described as capable of reaching innovative and unconventional solutions for established problems (*change*), although he is less prepared to accept change (rather than impose it) and generally adopts a low-risk, cautious approach, because of his desire to get things right.

The proposition that the author's quantitative research into values has succeeded in accessing fundamental, or core, human values is supported by the Derek Lewis interview data. Further, it is possible to trace the formation of these core values to his early experiences before adulthood. We now turn to consider his working life as an adult, to consider the extent to which his values might have been reinforced, or contradicted, by later experiences. Research suggests (England, 1967; Meglino *et al.*, 1989; Chatman, 1991) that individuals choose, as employing organizations, those which have values congruent with their own. This can lead to enhanced commitment and satisfaction with both a job and with a supervisor or leader.

Derek Lewis at Work

Before leaving Cambridge, Derek was offered a job with Ford Motor Company. 'Ford was at the top of my list because the company was at that time regarded as pre-eminent among the prime employers in providing financial training and background. During that third year at university, a combination of my quantitative mathematical background and the belief that finance was the glue that held a lot of these companies together in the late 1960s, meant that I was interested in joining the finance function at work' (interview). In addition, he was impressed by the way Ford had professionalized the recruitment process. They offered an initial round of selection interviews at Cambridge, followed by a further day of interviews, for the successful candidates, at the company headquarters in Essex. At the end of the day in Essex, the candidates were assembled into two groups; one group was offered jobs and the other was not. Derek, for whom high standards were important, was impressed and accepted a job. However, 48 hours later he was also offered a place on the second year of the M.Sc. programme at London

Business School. Luckily, this dilemma was resolved when Ford acquiesced in Derek's suggestion that they sponsor him at business school.

He also became engaged at this time. His wife, Louise, is the youngest of three sisters and the daughter of the senior partner of the General Practice that cared for the pupils of Ryedale School. Louise's early life had paralleled Derek's in many ways. Both were the youngest of three children, with two older sisters. Both of their mothers had given up their career prospects on marriage, to raise the family and to undertake voluntary work. Louise had been intending to qualify as a speech therapist, but, in keeping with the expectations against which both she and Derek had been raised, she abandoned those plans when she became engaged to Derek at the age of 18. When Derek was chosen to work in corporate headquarters in Detroit, after four years with Ford, Louise gave up her job as a secretary and did voluntary work in the USA. When he was posted subsequently to Germany, she invested time in learning German. Their two children, Annabel and Julia, were born in the 1980s, Annabel when Derek was 36 and Louise 34, Julia, prematurely, fourteen months later. It will be remembered that Derek's parents also had their children in their thirties. 'We got married earlier and had children later, so we had a very long period of marriage, thirteen years, without children. During that time my life was very heavily dedicated to my career. Louise played a vital support and partnership role to my career, because I could not cope with that sort of career without her, simple story.'

A shy person, he was quite nervous at being propelled into the large organization called 'Ford of Europe'. However, he found that his chosen function of finance played a central role in transforming this 10 billion dollar per annum business from a national to a functional operating base. 'When things did not work, the finance people were called upon to find out what was going wrong. We were the people who controlled such information as there was. The critical role that finance played in Ford throughout the world was even stronger in Europe at that time, when the organization was struggling to make this thing work. There were few, if any, companies of that size operating on a pan-European basis, so I found myself in this world of very bright, very able, people, who had this common approach of rigorous analysis.'

Research, rigorous analysis and presentation were the skills that Ford honed in Derek. 'People were merciless in tearing apart your analysis. Everyone worked long hours to make sure that they were impregnable and a lot depended on how you appeared in the meetings where you presented your conclusions. If you didn't have all the answers, then you were regarded as being ineffective. It was not acceptable to say that you did not know and that you would report back. A lot of effort went into preparing back-up material for meetings, a thick book of questions and answers. Eventually, it was elevated into an art form on the one hand and a game on the other. You never surprised anyone in a meeting, least of all your boss. There were even rules about how the question and answer book should be prepared for the Chief Financial Officer in the US, down to what language should be used and how the tabs and cross-references should be set out. Every question the CFO asked in a meeting had been communicated before the meeting and both the question and the expected answer incorporated in his book. The CFO would be satisfied that a meeting had gone well if all the expected questions had been asked and had received their expected answers. The day that one rebellious Division Head responded to a question from the CFO by saying "you've got the answer in your book" was a great shock all round.'

It can be seen that the value Derek placed on rules would have been reinforced during this period. He was given also considerable responsibility and thus became used to exercising authority. Hard work was expected of him also. 'Ford was one of the first companies to go to the Price Commission and we worked day and night, all the hours God gave, to build an impregnable case.' Other aspects of his upbringing did not serve Derek quite so well at Ford. It became apparent to him that getting to the top in a large organization required more than ability, it required also an understanding of, and a willingness to play, political games. 'I was very idealistic in those days and I found that a very hard thing to stomach. I don't think I was ever significantly political at Ford.' The variety and challenge of the various assignments offered to him encouraged Derek to stay with Ford for fifteen years, much longer than the three or four years he had envisaged on first joining them. This length of employment can be taken as an indication that Derek had found, in Ford, a company where the prevailing values were in sympathy with his own. However, in the early 1980s, he foresaw a period of cost-cutting and survival tactics at Ford, following the second world oil crisis, and, therefore, decided to move to the Imperial Group plc in 1982.

He found quite a different organizational culture at the tobacco giant. The company had diversified into different businesses, without much strategic focus. So much of the price of cigarettes reflected tax and duty that inefficiency in the group was masked. The corporate day revolved around senior management privileges. There were four different grades of dining room at headquarters, there were different entrances for different classes of employee and the most senior managers had their names on their own towels in the toilets. Derek set about rationalizing the group's portfolio and introducing financial disciplines, not easy in 'an incredibly civilized company on the surface, with a fearful amount of back-stabbing behind the scenes'. Derek left the group just under two years after he arrived. The reasons he gave to the author were the high level of inertia in the company and the growing inevitability of the eventual takeover (after Derek had left) by Hanson. However, it is clear also that this would not be a corporate culture that would sit happily with Derek's values. The Imperial Group felt, to him, inefficient, with senior managers indulging in sponsoring their hobbies (e.g. Formula One motor racing), exercising privilege and undertaking political manoeuvring. Derek was head-hunted to the Granada Group plc as Group Finance Director in 1984.

This was his first chance to be in charge of the finance function in a public company. Granada was an entrepreneurial group, driven by its founder, Sidney Bernstein, and his cousin, Cecil, with an opportunistic portfolio of companies. Sidney Bernstein was a strong character, who had handed over the day-to-day running of the company to his nephew, Alex, but retained a paternalistic hold on affairs by becoming life President and attending board meetings. Derek set about rationaliz-ing the portfolio of companies, selling unrelated activities like music publishing and insurance, while diversifying into related businesses, in order to spread the risk from the core business of television rental, which was in decline. Under his guidance, the company undertook its first systematic review of strategy and introduced more rigorous target-setting and performance reviews. It was during this period that he acknowledged the need to address issues of organizational politics in order to get things done. 'I really acted in a more political or manipulat-ive way, not in a subversive or self-protective way, but in terms of actually getting the things I wanted, done. Once I accepted this as a necessity, I was able to derive as much satisfaction from achieving something by having to jump over these hurdles, as from the basic quality of whatever it was that I was trying to do.' There is a strong sense that the ultimate aim for Derek Lewis was task achievement, not personal gain.

In recognition of his ability, Derek was given more responsibility rapidly at Granada. First, he combined the position of Finance Director with running the Business Services Division, then moved on to become Managing Director and ultimately Chief Executive of the group, in 1990, under Alex Bernstein as Executive Chairman. This one-on-one relationship at the top of the organization brought some confusion over roles and reporting lines. 'It was an extremely amicable relationship, but it didn't necessarily work very well. Everyone was reporting in to me, but Alex did not feel that his role was necessarily to be the principal initiator and driver of strategy. There was some confusion at this double layer of management and about who was actually the operational leader of the Group.'

Derek learnt here the lesson that he was to try to apply later in the prison service under Michael Howard: the need for a clear separation between strategy and operations, in order to avoid blurred lines of accountability. Again, this accords well with the value Derek places upon the need for well-understood rules and clear structures. The overlap between his and Alex Bernstein's role in the Group confused the City, as well as internal company reporting lines. This confusion was magnified by the differences in personality between the two individuals. Derek had been schooled in the need to prepare a strong, factual case for business decisions and to argue hard for it. Alex Bernstein was a gentle character, overshadowed throughout his life by his uncle, Sidney. He had a strong, intuitive understanding of the business, which he did not feel capable always of expressing in the face of strong, contrary opinion. Things were brought to a head by the Group's heavy investment in the then brand new satellite industry. Spending on BSkyB stretched the Group's balance sheet and the City was nervous about this little-understood industry. A rights issue was approved only in exchange for new management at the top of the Group, with industrial shareholders, such as Scottish Widows, outraged at the extent of investment being poured into 'that black hole called BSkyB'. It was unthinkable that the Bernstein family name should quit the company in a time of crisis and so Derek was the one to leave.

'This was an interesting example to me of really quite how difficult the City finds it to get its mind around potential businesses. I'm sure my effectiveness was limited by my rapid rise within Granada. I never had the opportunity to run an individual business, to learn to get its performance and strategy right. My skills of leadership and communication were underdeveloped. I was very busy getting the portfolio right, which meant disposals and acquisitions, but I was very inexperienced personally in understanding what could go wrong with acquisitions and their subsequent management. None the less, the mistakes we made were more of timing than anything else; BSkyB actually turned out to be a very popular investment, despite the high cost of its launch' (interview).

Derek handled his departure from Granada in 1991 in a manner entirely consistent with his character. While Alex Bernstein had the backing of the non-executive directors, the executive directors were loyal to Derek. It is feasible that he could have mounted a political campaign to stay and have ousted Alex. Instead, he handled the press conference, presenting the analysis both of the need for the Group's rights issue and details of the reshuffle of senior management. Today, with the resilience that typifies leadership, he emphasizes what he learnt from that period of his career. 'I learnt about the importance of the theatre side of leadership, of selling ideas and taking stakeholders along with you. I also learnt that the theory of what sits where in the business plan can be confounded by human intervention, either by conscious opposition and subversion, or simply by not having the ability or the understanding of the need to do it. At that time, I needed someone who would play a strong role with me and Alex played a very retiring role, more like a non-Executive Chairman. I had learnt at Ford how to push my proposals through and that style can be quite intimidating. Alex told me later that his instinct told him that some of our business decisions were wrong, but that he had not had the confidence to argue with me. Today, I value much more the role of intuition in business decisions and have tried to develop that in myself.'

This period of employment at Granada, from 1984 to 1991, can be seen as reinforcing Derek's values, while at the same time leading him to question some of his fundamental approaches to business. He has worked hard, won rapid promotion and been faced with variety and challenge. He has sought, without success, clarity in the working relationship with his immediate boss, Alex. He has recognized also that politics can be used to achieve organizational results, but that human beings can use these, and other, tactics to undermine the best-laid plans. Finally, he begins to value the roles of theatre and intuition in leadership.

After a short, but interesting, interlude with Maxwell Communications in the confusion immediately following Robert Maxwell's death, and spending more time on his existing non-Executive Directorship of Courtaulds Textiles plc, Derek moved on to head up and later become Chairman of UK Gold Television in 1992. 'I was asked by the BBC and Thames TV if I would take what was at that time just a single sheet of paper concept for a new television channel, which would run library material from the BBC and Sky, and turn it into a real, live, on-air business. I thought that might be quite fun, actually. This television channel was really the first time I had to create something from scratch, with the ability to shape it as I wanted to. Before, I had been playing always with someone else's train set. I arrived with just me and a desk and nothing else. I put a business plan together and then I had to go out and raise the £35 million that it would take to finance the losses in the early years. I negotiated a company "asset", a 10-year licence agreement with the BBC and Thames TV. We had to organize the ground facilities to support satellite access and recruit a team of people to run it and so on. It was invaluable experience for me, because having gone up the finance function and moved across into general management, this was my first opportunity to get to grips with the real nuts and bolts of how a business works and assemble it.' Derek took some risks, in addition to the obvious one of taking on the start-up in the first place. For example, he sacked the merchant bank charged with raising the finance, because he thought that their fees for doing so were outrageous. This meant that he had to raise the finance himself. The service was launched successfully after six months. Derek's face lit up, during the interview, as he described the success of his achievement. 'It was a tremendous first night and our audience share was 30 per cent higher than we'd expected. It was the first time I'd really sensed the elation of feeling one had created something.'

Derek was approached about the job of Director General of HM Prison Service while in the middle of fundraising for UK Gold. 'I had never expected UK Gold to be long-term employment. Getting it on the air was the task; after that, it would actually become a less interesting task, because the most difficult thing would by then have been done. I was very interested in the prisons job and found exposure to it, through the head-hunters and others, totally absorbing. But as the final decision came closer, I really began to worry about the risks involved and some of the stresses from the nature of the job. The organization clearly needed major surgery and change. I understood that, even if there were no serious problems, relations with politicians could be quite difficult in that job. But I took the view, at that time, that it was sufficiently attractive, stimulating and seemed worthwhile enough to make those risks worth taking. I don't think Louise or I were quite prepared for it being as totally absorbing as it turned out to be. She'd been used to work being a dominant part of my life, but not dominant to the extent that it became almost exclusive. Yet this is what it became in the prison service.'

The Home Office must have considered Derek Lewis to be an ideal candidate. Extremely hard-working, principled, bright and Oxbridge-educated, comfortable with structure and more interested in getting things done than in political manoeuvring. He was keen to improve and change things, but at the same time anxious to get it right, so that he was not overly risk-taking in his approach and he had experience of being given an area of responsibility and getting on with it. Even the low salary, in comparison with the private sector standard for jobs of similar responsibility, was not a problem. 'We'd never been lavish livers or spenders. Although I took over a 50 per cent cut in pay, it didn't feel like that, because I spent only about 50 per cent of my salary anyway.'

The sad ending to this potentially successful transition into the public sector has been well documented. Press coverage of his departure in 1995 was extensive. Derek's own book, *Hidden Agendas* (Lewis, 1997) tells the story of his dismissal by the Home Secretary, Michael Howard, from his own viewpoint. Later, Ann Widdecombe, Minister for Prisons under Michael Howard, added her own explosive comments in a lengthy statement to the Commons in May 1997. The following *verbatim* extracts give her view of the saga.

Honourable treatment means that we treat those in our power justly. I profoundly regret that, in the previous Parliament, Ministers were criticised in independent reports and did not resign. Regularly to protect and excuse ourselves while visiting serious vengeance on others corrupts justice and demeans office. Mr Lewis was an outstanding director general. He inherited an appalling and troubled service. The agency met all targets set by Ministers and new initiatives were successfully implemented. All that was managed in the space of two and a half years. Ministers, very senior civil servants, the Prisons Board and its non-executives urgently advised the then Home Secretary that he should not dismiss Mr Lewis. It was for those reasons that two of the four non-executive directors resigned in protest and that others chose other forms of making their views known. It was for those reasons that I nearly resigned and now regret not doing so. If Mr Lewis had been an indifferent director general, there would have been less achievement and certainly less support. My right hon. and learned Friend [Michael Howard] is very skilled forensically and I cannot believe that he was taken in by the superficiality of some of the [Learmont] report. It is hard to conclude other than that the report was his pretext rather than his reason. There is evidence within the Home Office that he had wanted for a long time before that report was produced to remove Mr Lewis from his post.

What did we actually achieve by the dismissal of Mr Lewis? We had to pay him £220,000 in compensation. We had to pay his costs, in the sum of £41,000. We had to pay our own costs, in the sum of some £16,000. A most unnecessary bill of more than a quarter of a million pounds was the cost to the general public. We severely damaged relations with the private sector, as we found out when we considered the possibility of running an open competition for Mr Lewis's job – a possibility from which we quickly retreated. We left the Prison Service without a confirmed leader for five months and we shattered its morale.

Quite apart from the merits of the case, the handling was deplorable – and personally witnessed by me – and was the cause of the distress that has now become public knowledge. The former director general was refused point blank on two occasions the opportunity to discuss the basis on which he was being dismissed. We demean our high office if we mistreat our public servants. My decision to do what I have done today was extremely difficult to reach. I reached my decision in the interests of giving very belated justice to Mr Lewis, of giving some comfort to his wife Louise – who supported him faithfully while he gave us seven days a week looking after the Prison Service – partly of clearing my own conscience, because I should have resigned at the time and did not.

Derek Lewis moved on successfully, in 1996, to another start-up, as Director of a project called New Horizons, on behalf of major cable TV companies. It may be recalled that, after he left Granada, he was candid in his comments to the author about his own failings, particularly in his relationship with Alex Bernstein. Could he have acted differently, in his relationship with Michael Howard, in order to have avoided his own dismissal? Derek's view is that third parties might have been able to change the situation. 'The Prime Minister certainly had it within his power to say "no", but chose not to. Had Ann Widdecombe chosen to resign, or to make the threat of doing so, I don't think Michael Howard would have done what he did and survived. The role of Richard Wilson, the permanent secretary at that time, was interesting. He made an effort and pushed the issues as far as he could. Apparently, Richard Wilson was instructed to fire me, but at first refused to write the letter. However, in the end, it was the good civil servant obeying orders that came through. But, actually, had Richard Wilson said I'm not going to do it, then that probably would have stopped Michael Howard from doing what he did. When I refused to sack John Marriott [a prison governor, for whom Derek insisted on following disciplinary procedures, rather than sacking him outright] the Home Secretary had to acquiesce.'

This is not to say that Derek did not learn from his experiences in the prison service. As the author had by now learnt to expect from him, he was keen to explain what lessons he had taken from his time as Director General of HM Prison Service. 'I am glad I took the risk because it has changed me in a whole variety of ways. It has given me experience and skill in managing change that I never had before. It has made me a much broader person. I had a very narrow, focused, business-based view of the world. The prison service confronted me with a whole lot of social, ethical, political and justice decisions and I'm a better balanced person as a result of that. I question whether I could have moved change faster, but equally, it might have been set back in bouts of recrimination and subversive actions. The freedom to change senior civil servants on my team was confirmed in my letter of acceptance but, because I moved the finance director, everyone regrouped to make sure I didn't do something similar again. There is a very strong sense of camaraderie among "prison professionals" and I wanted them on my side. So I moved at the rate necessary to take them with me. I can look back on my time in the prison service and derive a lot of satisfaction from the changes that we were able to make. People changed and started to think in terms of commitment and personal responsibility for results. They started to understand that you could combine the disciplines of financial performance with the softer values of care and rehabilitation. So I don't have any regrets at all.'

Conclusion

It is unfortunate that Derek Lewis's time at the Prison Service was cut short. However, the story of his life, rather than of that one period, supports the proposition derived from the author's quantitative research, that ACEs, on average, espouse a different set of core values than those espoused by either private or public sector managers. Derek Lewis's life story demonstrates, for this particular ACE, how these values were formed and reinforced over time. Such values, if given free rein, may bring about culture change in the UK civil service. ACEs appear to espouse the normative civil service value of integrity, alongside the more proactive, private sector approach to change. This is true, again on average, of ACEs promoted from within the civil service, as well as ACEs recruited from the private sector.

It is probably appropriate to give the last word to Derek Lewis, recording his response, at the end of the final interview, to a direct question about his values: 'A determination to achieve high quality, perfectionism, if you wish. Integrity, a high degree of commitment to an organization and its goals; no manipulation for personal gain. I need to believe that what I do is worthwhile. Creation, doing what is new, or change; not just solving yesterday's problems. Treating people fairly and decently. Integrity and honesty, care for others, tend to be the values that come from a public service or civil service background to some extent. People who choose to come in from the private sector tend to self-select, because one of the appeals of a public service job is the opportunity to live to these values to a greater extent than is the case in the private sector.'

References

Chatman, J. A. (1991). Matching people and organizations: Selection and socialization in public accounting firms. *Administrative Science Quarterly*, 36, Sept.: 459–84.

England, G. W. (1967). Personal value systems of American managers. *Academy of Management Review*, 10 (1): 53–68.

Feather, N. T. (1975). *Values in Education and Society* (New York: The Free Press).

Fry, G. K. (1969). *Statesmen in Disguise: the Changing Role of the Administrative Class of the British Home Civil Service, 1853–1966* (London: Macmillan).

Goffman, E. (1959). *The Presentation of Self in Everyday Life* (Garden City, NY: Doubleday).

Hennessy, P. (1989). *Whitehall* (London: Secker & Warburg).

Hood, C. (1991). A public management for all seasons? In Rhodes, R. A. W. (ed.), *The New Public Management. Public Administration*, 69 (1): 3–19.

Lewis, D. (1997). *Hidden Agendas: Politics, Law and Disorder* (London: Hamish Hamilton).

Meglino, B. M., Ravlin, E. C. and Adkins, C. L. (1989). A work values approach to corporate culture: A field test of the value congruence process and its relationship to individual outcomes. *Journal of Applied Psychology*, 74 (3): 424–32.

Mellon, E. O. (1993). Executive agencies: Leading change from the outside in. *Public Money and Management*, 13 (2): 25–31.

Pollitt, C. (1990). *Managerialism and the Public Services: the Anglo-American Experience* (Oxford: Blackwell).

Ravlin, E. C. (1994). Values. In Nicholson, N. (ed.) *Encyclopedic Dictionary of Organizational Behaviour* (Oxford: Blackwell).

Ravlin, E. C. and Meglino, B. M. (1987). Effect of values on perception and decision making: A study of alternative work values measures. *Journal of Applied Psychology*, 72 (4): 666–73.

Rokeach, M. (1973). *The Nature of Human Values* (New York: the Free Press).

Wilson, W. (1887). The study of administration. *Political Science Quarterly*, 2 (2): 197–220.

Index